ALTERNATE LYRICISM

Presented by

The Guild
Art Gallery

28A, 1st Floor, Prince Chambers,179 Colaba
Mumbai - 400 005

gallery "espace"

16, Community Centre, New Friends Colony
New Delhi - 110 065

ALTERNATE LYRICISM

JEHANGIR JANI

Edited by
Ratnottama Sengupta

Mapin Publishing

First published in India in 2006 by
Mapin Publishing Pvt. Ltd.

Simultaneously published in the
United States of America in 2006 by
Grantha Corporation
77 Daniele Drive, Hidden Meadows
Ocean Township, NJ 07712
E: mapinpub@aol.com

Distributed in North America by
Antique Collectors' Club
East Works, 116 Pleasant Street, Suite 60B
Easthampton, MA 01027
T: 1 800 252 5231 • F: 413 529 0862
E: info@antiquecc.com • www.antiquecollectorsclub.com

Distributed in the United Kingdom, Europe and the Middle East by
Art Books International Ltd.
Unit 200 (a), The Blackfriars Foundry, 156 Blackfriars Road
London, SE1 8EN UK
T: 44 207 953 7271 • F: 207 953 8547
E: sales@art-bks.com

Distributed in Southeast Asia by
Paragon Asia Co. Ltd.
687 Taksin Road, Bukkalo, Thonburi
Bangkok 10600 Thailand
T: 66 2877 7755 • F: 2468 9636
email: rapeepan@paragonasia.com

Distributed in the rest of the world by
Mapin Publishing Pvt. Ltd.
31 Somnath Road, Usmanpura
Ahmedabad 380013 India
T: 91 79 2755 1833 / 2755 1793 • F: 2755 0955
E: mapin@mapinpub.com • www.mapinpub.com

ISBN: 81-88204-65-X (Mapin)
ISBN: 1-890206-41-5 (Grantha)
LC: 2005937096

Designed by Vishal Rawlley / Mapin Design Studio
Edited by Ratnottama Sengupta
Processed by Reproscan, Mumbai
Printed in Malaysia

CONTENTS

INTRODUCTION

CRITICAL INTERFACES IN JEHANGIR JANI'S ARTISTIC EXPLORATIONS

Shivaji K Panikkar

Jehangir Jani vehemently casts the male nude into the visual field, displacing the habitual and the mainstream expectations about human figuration: a tortured and oddly placed image, reclaimed from a humiliated hinterland's margins, and largely speaking from oral histories. JJ is indeed an artist and an activist. He engages with multilayered discourses around phenomenological experiences on the one hand and on the other with the systemic socio-political structures that undergrid and discriminate the lives of sexual and communitarian minorities. Despite the fact that today the concerns of art and activism may seem relatively unproblematic within the operative field of 'high' art, these issues cannot be serialized or prioritized as to which comes first – or, which is more important. This is still a problem, and the issues can neither be reduced to an unproblematic conflation of art and activism, nor can these categories be discussed in terms of irreconcilability. The questions that emerge from his art certainly relate to lived interfaces between art and activism, of living life within institutional and non-institutional structures and outside a subculture, or subcultures; doing art within available systems and the broad differences that divide them, as well as the connections that exist in between.

This is because JJ's art uninhibitedly represents experiential realms of sexual and communitarian subcultures as he speaks his political dissent from within these experiences. Particularly significant is that minority sexual identities and their subterranean cultures have yet to be seriously registered in popular and public view as significant positions of difference, which make valid claims for equality and dignity. Apart from possibly venting these private and/or public experiences, JJ's decision to engage with minoritarian struggles for empowerment has taken him far in his chosen vocation.

JJ's art uninhibitedly represents experiential realms of sexual and communitarian subcultures as he speaks his political dissent from within these experiences.

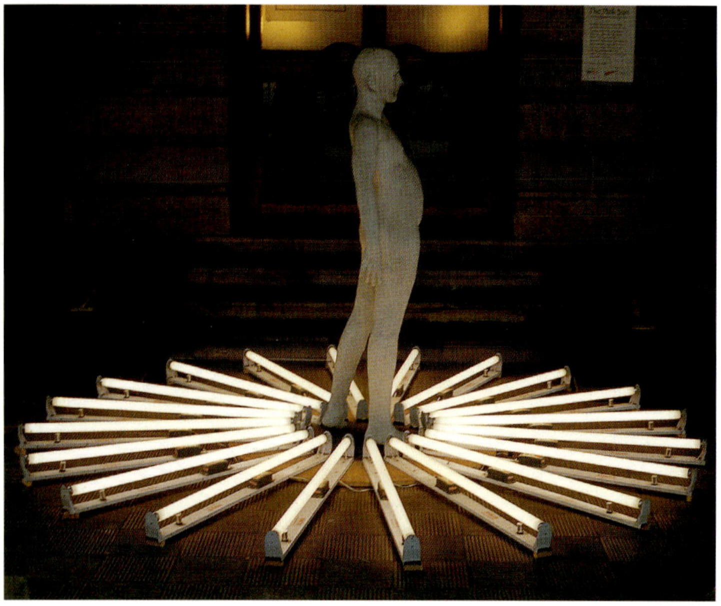

Pink Sun
183 x 305 cm. Plaster of Paris and neon lights.
2000

Through his sculpture, JJ persistently puts forward certain thematic concerns. These include irrepressible 'deviant' sexual desire, and its innumerable silencing and humiliations, painful tortures, and above all, the insuppressible assertion of the will to survive with dignity.

JJ started his art career with concerns about women's identity in the minority community and represented his ideas using the medium of oil painting on canvas. Perhaps this concern with women was a deflected, yet nascent, engagement with the question of sexual identity. As his concerns evolved, he withdrew from painting and turned to making sculpture in round, and today this has become JJ's forte. It is a deliberate choice and it is perhaps also not farfetched to suggest that making figural sculptures is a protest against and subversion of the institutionalized religious premises of Islam and the expectations with which he has been raised.

Through his sculpture, JJ persistently puts forward certain thematic concerns. These include irrepressible 'deviant' sexual desire, and its innumerable silencing and humiliations, painful tortures, and above all, the insuppressible assertion of the will to survive with dignity. The symbolic, the metaphoric, and the allegorical in the visual image enable JJ to achieve conceptual complexity. Among his many sculptures of the past decade, there are hardly two full figures. *Pink Sun* (2000) is one such, and it displays a naturalism that poignantly describes the queer languidness of the effeminate male.[1] In this work, the conventional sense of beauty becomes jeopardized. More than that, the figure's presence curiously unsettles macho and patriarchal expectations. By evoking metropolitan spaces in which the evening darkness is illuminated by creepy neon lights and in which men hang out, the sculpture's nudity becomes a vital and public assertion of this yet-to-be-respected identity. On the other end of the spectrum is another work, titled *Survival (a continuum)* (2000), in which a complete figure sits upright like a deity, reclaiming its dignity, while asserting the right to a person's own 'deviant' desire.

In most of his other works, JJ deliberately fragments figures so that they have a propensity to become fetishes. Manipulated to assert the frontal, iconic presence, JJ's sculptures ironically objectify themselves through their odd and seemingly inevitable bodily shifts and inflections. Characteristic traits of the effeminate body in movement are transcribed onto their masculinity and spread over un-idealized or even unattractive flesh. The face, the human body part that gains the most focus, is often repeated like a chant across his works. This face beams and smirks. When a work such as *CHakka, CHakka, CHakka, CHakka, CHakka, CHakka* (1998) is viewed, while reading the title, the affirmative smile and wide open eyes appear to objectify the internalization of the abuse and, subversively, turn it back on the abuser in a spirit of self-assertion. Such confrontational, yet calm, auto-

[1] Termed as *kothi* in "gay" parlance, an effeminate gay male's identity is abusively referred to by various names such as *chhakka*, fairy, sissy, queen, pansy etc.

referential faces smile away inwardly in the spirit of a self-mocking saint who also scorns the world with a smile and in total self-abandon. However, there are also instances when the wide open and anxiety-ridden eyes face the world with contradictory expressions of guilt, even as they hesitate to hide his self (*Nu's Boat,* 1998).

In accordance with the thematic concerns, JJ's use of various materials also creates uncanny juxtapositions and contradictory possibilities. He makes this possible by allowing the materials to embody their intrinsic qualities and meanings, but in odd ways. The fragility of ceramics is juxtaposed to the hard, cold sheet metal; through such a combination, JJ speaks of the inequality of power in confrontations between minorities and majorities. Or, when the artist covers a figure in gold and silver, as in *Survival (a continuum)*, preciousness and godly dignity become qualities of the rejected and the humiliated.

De-familiarizing familiar objects is a surrealist strategy to which JJ often resorts. Images of a flower, chili, box, dagger and boat constantly deflect and speak more than their familiar functions, as he symbolically encapsulates historical discourses of stigma around the alternative and minoritarian sexual disposition.

In more recent sculptures, mutilation as a sign attempts to reclaim losses. The partially concealed figures speak of the closeted identity under duress, where the fragmented visibility of a figure or a persona, hidden and dwarfed by authoritarian structures like a wall or a gateway, begin to speak through the challenging acts of silencing and coercion. The exuberant, exhibitionistic, phallic protrusions are counterpoints that reveal the irresistible secret desires, as they farcically celebrate male, homosexual bodies as glimmering flowers which desire eternally and vacantly, if not tragically.

Although painting, installation, and multimedia works by JJ may be primarily viewed as extensions of his sculptural assemblages, he has seen linear continuity and fidelity to a particular medium, a method, or a language as a constraint. Hence, JJ explored various avenues simultaneously. It is with *Faerie Tales…A Re-Look* (1998), works in ceramic and sheet metal, that JJ asserted his artistic credentials. This was followed by the show titled *Stories* (2000), with works done in fibreglass, metal and gold, and silver leaf. Plucking out a myth of moral dilemma to form a subtext, the next show, titled *The Patience of Job* (2002), brought painting and

The fragility of ceramics is juxtaposed to the hard, cold sheet metal; through such a combination, JJ speaks of the inequality of power in confrontations between minorities and majorities.

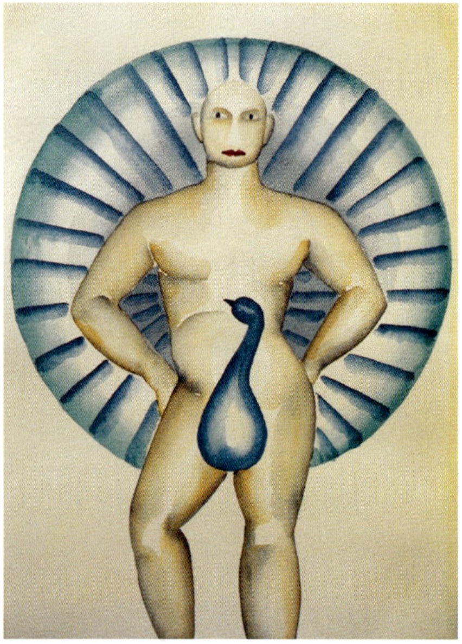

Untitled
50 x 40 cm. Watercolour on paper.
2001

Often pictured as seated on animal vehicles like great Hindu gods, the humorousness of their presence is heightened by the effeminacy of their large, monumental bodies. They become doubly comical as they sport their over-blown phallic similes rendered through the seemingly innocuous sword, flower, animal or bird's neck and head.

sculpture face to face, lending both a space for dialogue. Conceived primarily as relief sculptures, the diminutive ceramic faces set against a textured, painted background, endowed the smiling androgynous faces with a mysterious spiritual aura and a precarious preciousness.

The narrative pictorial logic of his early 1990s oil on canvas works was already reversed through the emblematic iconicity of the figural forms of his 2000–05 watercolours, a positive spillover from his sculptural activities. Used like the Kalighat painter's technique of shading darkly with garish colours on both sides of the forms, while leaving the larger parts of the contours with sumptuous light pink washes, JJ foregrounded an iconography in which male figures are endowed with the demigod-like appearance of the pre-modern popular. This re-take on 19th century Bengali popular naturalism has very well suited JJ's purpose by joining the fluffy, non-muscular, and effeminately flexed male body with an ordinariness of the quotidian. Often pictured as seated on animal vehicles like great Hindu gods, the humourousness of their presence is heightened by the effeminacy of their large, monumental bodies. They become doubly comical as they sport their over-blown phallic similes rendered through the seemingly innocuous sword, flower, animal, or bird's neck and head. However, recent works in the same direction assume a grave sense of psychological depth, as the linear and tonal rendering have become gentler, where partially rendered bodies are overlaid with various darker and colourful phallic bird-animal metaphors of desire.

JJ's show *Portraits* (2004) is a return to working exclusively on canvas. He used an entirely different approach to form-making and the rendition of meanings. Developing his earlier sculptural work with gold and silver, these oil and acrylic frontal torsos and heads in golden ochre and brown are laid out over evenly painted pitch-black canvases. They are strikingly stark, like actors under the spotlight on a stage. Silent and inward looking, these figures have an intensity of expression. JJ's calculated strokes of impasto made with a palette knife are subtly smudged, and the blurred edges of the silhouettes are delicately still, even as they heave and quiver. Reclaiming and asserting the magnificence of the protagonist, there is a stoic resilience in these figures.

An artist such as JJ finds immense possibilities for further explorations through multimedia installations and other diversifications. Such experiments lend him an unprecedented freedom to express the concerns that are, until then, not fully recognized. Particularly noteworthy are his installation shows *Lazarus & Anarkali* (2002–03) and the *Untitled* (2004) installation in the group exhibition *Iconography in Transient Times*. Through these works, he negotiates the over-disputed terrain of religious faith. JJ speaks of the healing power of faith by threading together fragments of Koranic verses, a rosary, blood, and surgical gauze. His conflicted relation with the religion into which he was born is resolved in several different ways, as is the threat that is inherent in the politicization of religions, and the experience of violence at home and elsewhere. Through art-making, JJ plays out a role similar to a Sufi by transgressing dogma as he lifts himself out of a burdensome authoritarian rule. The unconventional medium allows him to be experimental, dramatize, and at the same time remain impersonal, as he links various disparate references. A work such as *Lazarus & Anarkali* has allowed him to engage with various stigmas and oppressive social hierarchies, while permitting him to yearn and speak in a universal language about wide ranging concerns such as love, death, renewal, and resurrection, from his own specific, local realities. The installation re-created a total sensorial environment with sounds and sights and the presence of body allusions – body casts, cast body parts, a cloth-covered corpse, pink lamps flickering through simulated TV screens, sounds of ritual breast-beating, and invocations written to God. These became signs of desire, betrayal, death, and the hope of resurrection, all weaved together with the shade of gay-ish pink, an ironical marker of the maker's sexual identity.

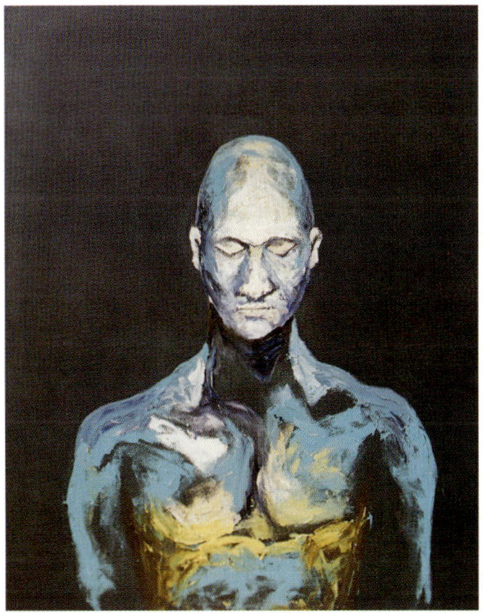

Untitled
153 x 122 cm. Oil and acrylic on canvas.
2005

...these oil and acrylic frontal torsos and heads in golden ochre and brown are laid out over evenly painted pitch-black canvases. They are strikingly stark, like actors under spotlight on a stage. Silent and inward looking, these figures have an intensity of expression.

Can Activism Undermine Art?

For anyone who is self-consciously practising an alternative sexual life, the nation state fails to create a crucial support for the self. The obsolete Penal Code 377 considers such alternative sexual practices unnatural, and the nation thus weighs heavily on people who do not live heterosexuality. Sexual minorities question religions, communities, and systems and ask if there is any accommodative place within, for them. To 'normal' families, they ask: "Will you consider ours as equal to yours?" To parents, young people of such identity plead to be exempted from conventional expectations. To history, they ask where, when, and how have we been, and to what kinds of acceptance, discriminations, hostilities, annihilations, and erasures have we been subjected?

The significant act of coming together of those who practise alternative sexual life choices in our country was signaled in Bombay in the years 1989–90 with the publication of the quarterly newsletter *Bombay Dost*. JJ's art career coincides with the rise of such activism: while he seriously engaged in art-making, he also remained an active member participant of the Hamsafar Trust, a Mumbai-based community organization. Despite this, JJ finds himself at crossroads today, between his concerns with meanings, materials, forms, and aesthetics on one hand, and his minoritarian political identity, on the other. Though his sexuality is undoubtedly central to his work, JJ understandably rejects a reductive reading of his art. He is wondering legitimately if his works will speak of anything when the issues of identity politics become no longer relevant.

This is a quintessential problem of working upon specific identity issues and having to deal and exist within the mainstream/heterosexual world of art. At the extreme end of its spectrum is the argument that art should be art, and should not be mixed with what it wants to say or communicate through subject matter. Is it possible to talk about art as art, separate from what it represents? I read such polarizations as one among the many ways in which elite art imposes its credo upon practitioners. It is crucial to see the tensions and negotiations between such positions in an artist like Jehangir Jani.

Baroda, September 2005

SCULPTURE

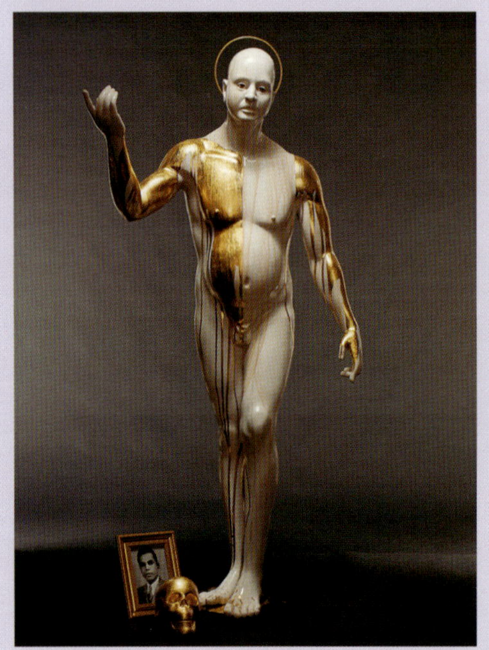

Untitled
Lifesize. Fibreglass, resin, goldleaf, mild steel and photograph.
2005

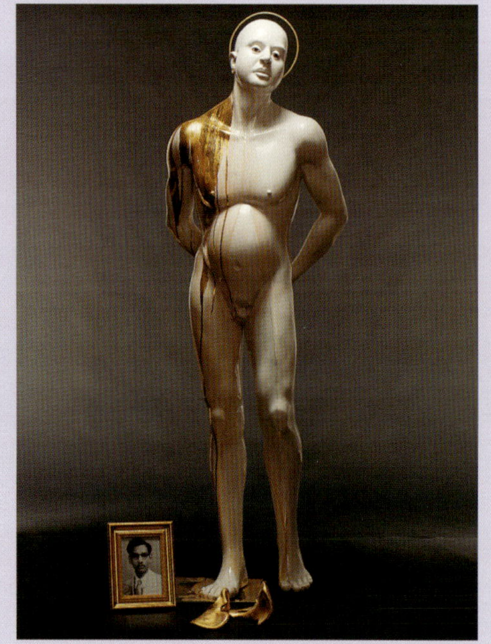

Untitled
Lifesize. Fibreglass, resin, goldleaf, mild steel and photograph.
2005

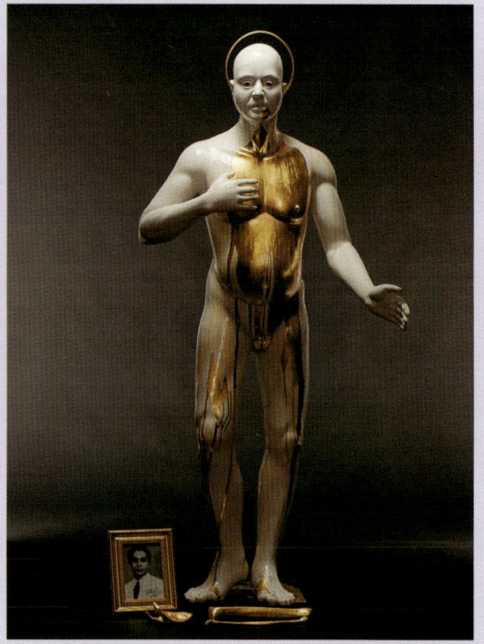

Untitled
Lifesize. Fibreglass, resin, goldleaf, mild steel and photograph.
2005

Jehangir Jani, The Making of 'Peers'

Mortimer Chatterjee

Enter the makeshift studio of Jehangir Jani, in central Mumbai, in early August 2005. Here is El Greco's *Christ from the Spoliation,* a hand held to his chest and an arm swept outward. Next to him is Masaccio's distraught Adam, hands clasped to face, a soul in anguish. Lastly, Titian's St. Sebastian lies prone on the floor, waiting for martyrdom. Faithful representations of the originals, save two elements: each has developed a paunch, and none have faces that bear any similarity to their originals, but, instead, have been tweaked into the likeness of the polymath artist responsible for this growing collection of fibreglass models, tentatively titled *Peers.*

With three projects running concurrently in 2005, JJ is a busy man. Not that this should surprise us, given his career graph since the beginning of the 1990s. The self-taught artist, fiercely independent of cliques or trends, has been a whirlwind of activity since he exhibited his first canvases in 1991. To place in order the primary media employed in his shows since 2000 makes impressive reading: watercolour, sculpture, mixed media, oil on canvas, metal, cement, latex, carpets, mixed media, metal, oil on canvas, steel, and fibreglass.

In the beginning there were the canvas works. His popular series of veiled figures, that date back to the early 90s, were essentially portraits of women from his own community of Bohra Muslims. The twist was that the heavy massing of the musculature under the veils was largely based on JJ's own body. The artist notes that "the figures were coming from a position of authority," and this is clear from the bold sweeps of paint applied to build up the veils. The ambiguous gender of the subjects signposted, at the outset of JJ's career, his interest in critiquing cultures' need to assign and fix roles. By 1993, though, he felt he had said all that he wanted to

JJ professes to enjoy the 'nervousness' of sculpture. Within the context of his practice I take this idea to work both at the operational level of exploring mediums that are constantly mutating, congealing, hardening, cracking, alive, and sensual, as well as a comment on the impact of sculpture and installation on the space around it.

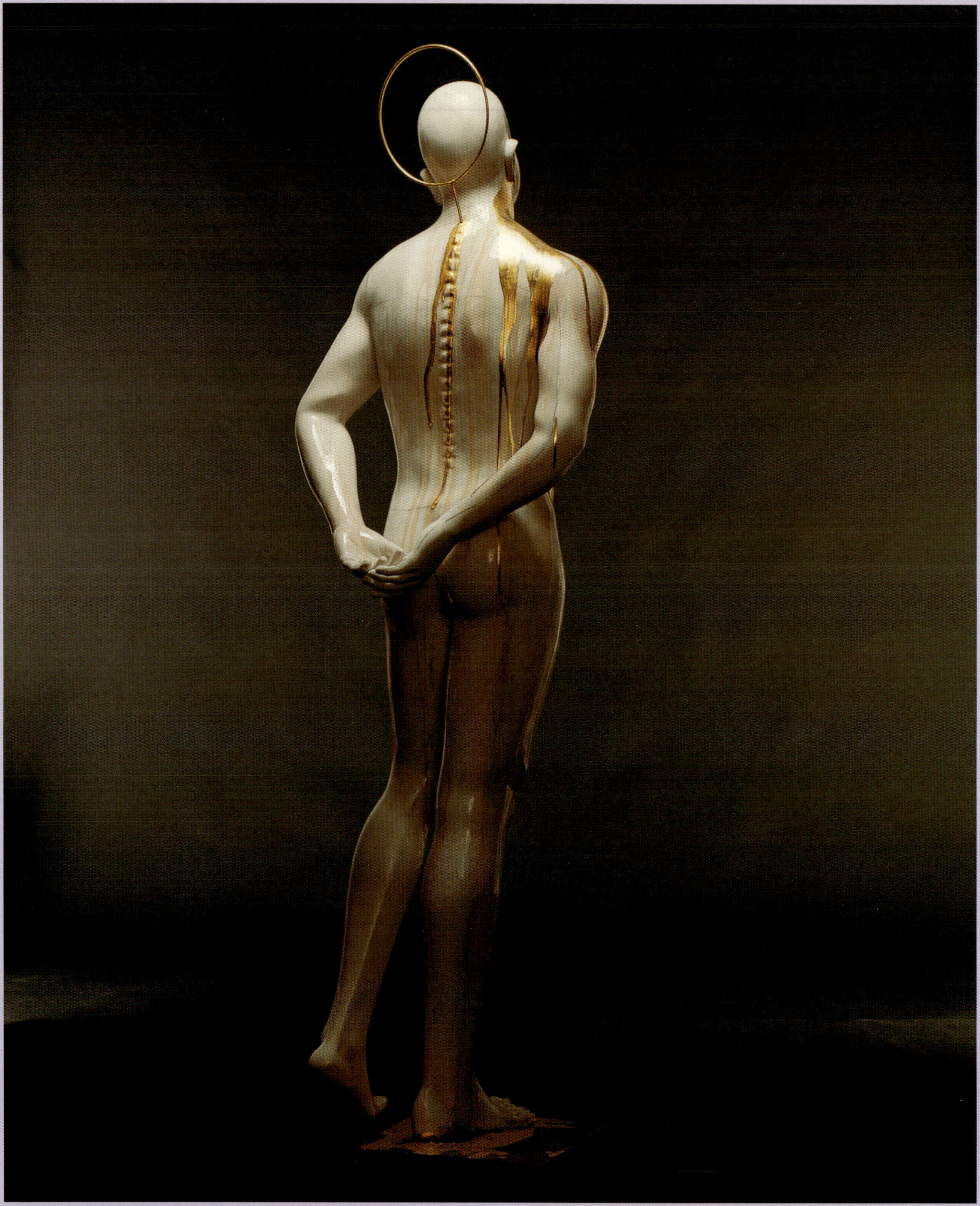

Untitled
Lifesize. Fibreglass, resin, goldleaf and mild steel.
2005

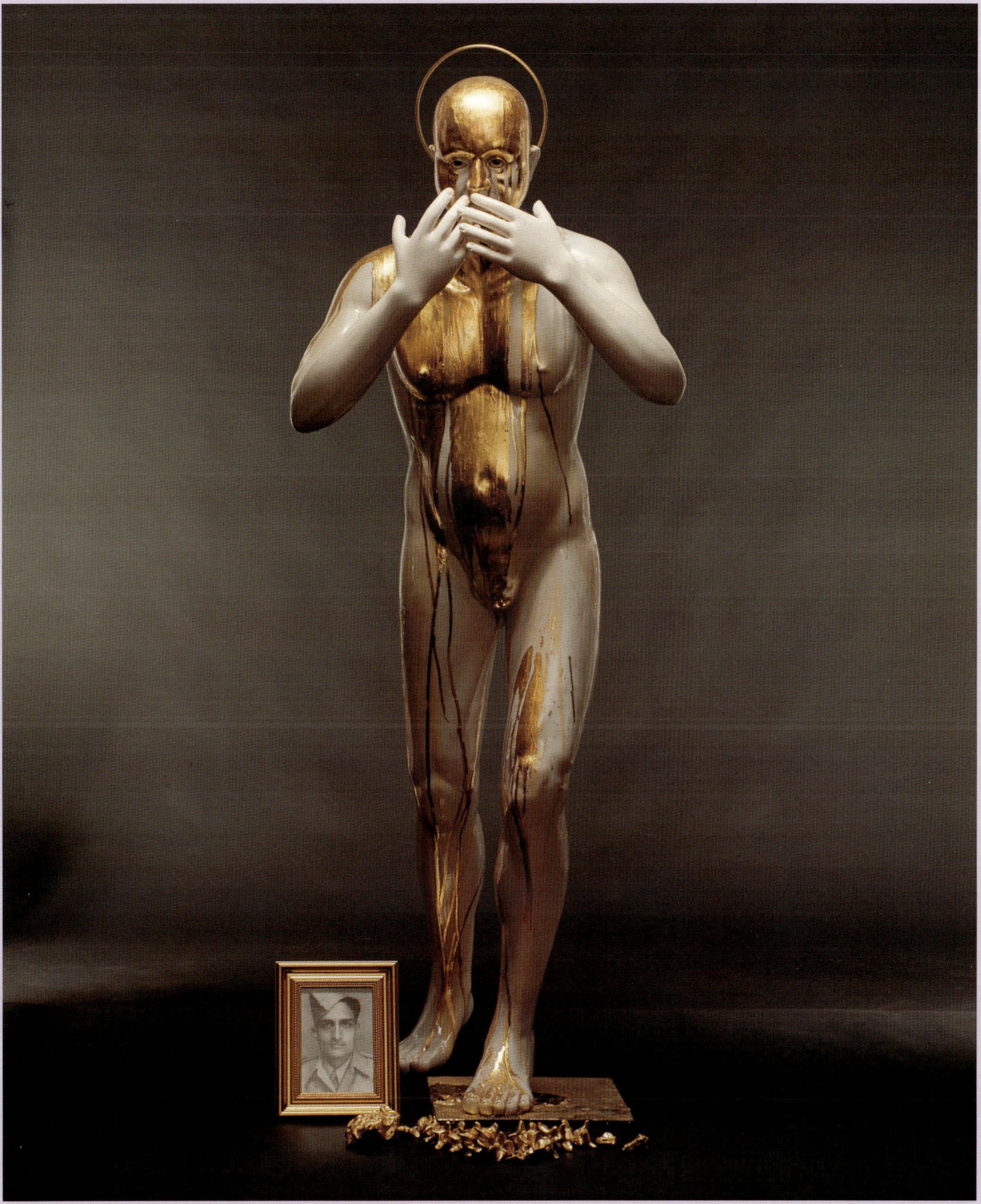

Untitled
Lifesize. Fibreglass, resin, goldleaf, mild steel and photograph.
2005

Much of the sculpture and installation that Jehangir has produced is both confrontational and disturbing. Pain has become a central motif in many of the themes he has been dealing with over the last ten years.

on the subject, and it was not until 2004 that JJ returned to canvas with a show of portraits at the Guild Gallery, Mumbai. "Coming back into painting," in JJ's words, "was an act of exuberance." He was keen to create works more gestural in feel, and to that extent, the 2004 works show a distinct maturing in his abilities as a painter, particularly in his effective use of light. As he says, "My figures (in the earlier canvas works) blocked air: the logical result was sculpture without the baggage of a pictorial frame."

It is testament to Jehangir's self-awareness that he possesses the critical engagement with his work to know when a particular medium is unable to express concepts with which he is concerned with at any particular moment, "I choose the medium of making work and exhibiting for what I want to say; psychologically I hate being bound." So it was that Jehangir broke from painting in the early 90s and moved towards sculpture and installation. Between 1994 and 2001 the most ambitious projects included the seminal *Fairie Tales…A Relook* of 1998 at Jehangir Art Gallery, and the 2001 show, *Stories*, at Gallery Chemould.

JJ professes to enjoy the 'nervousness' of sculpture. Within the context of his practice I take this idea to work both at the operational level of exploring mediums that are constantly mutating, congealing, hardening, cracking, alive, and sensual, as well as a comment on the impact of sculpture and installation on the space around it. JJ points to the fact that he shifted mediums from the ceramic and sheet metal works of *Fairie Tales* (1998), to the fibre-glass figures of *Stories* (2001), because of the limitations of scale inherent in ceramics. The results are larger works that engage the viewer ever more: he enjoys working on a lifesize scale, as he finds that it is at this level that the works become most confrontational (too large, "and they evince awe", a sentiment JJ is averse to conjuring).

Much of the sculpture and installation that JJ has produced is both confrontational and disturbing. Pain has become a central motif in many of the themes he has been dealing with over the last ten years. This may lead a viewer to concluding that the predominant themes supporting the work spring from the darker regions of the artist's consciousness. JJ maintains, "I am searching for beauty," and "my intention is not to disturb you." If it does, however, he hopes to have seduced the viewer with the materiality of the work first.

If JJ's pre-eminent quest is for beauty, it is to the body that he constantly refers, to explore this theme. "My concern

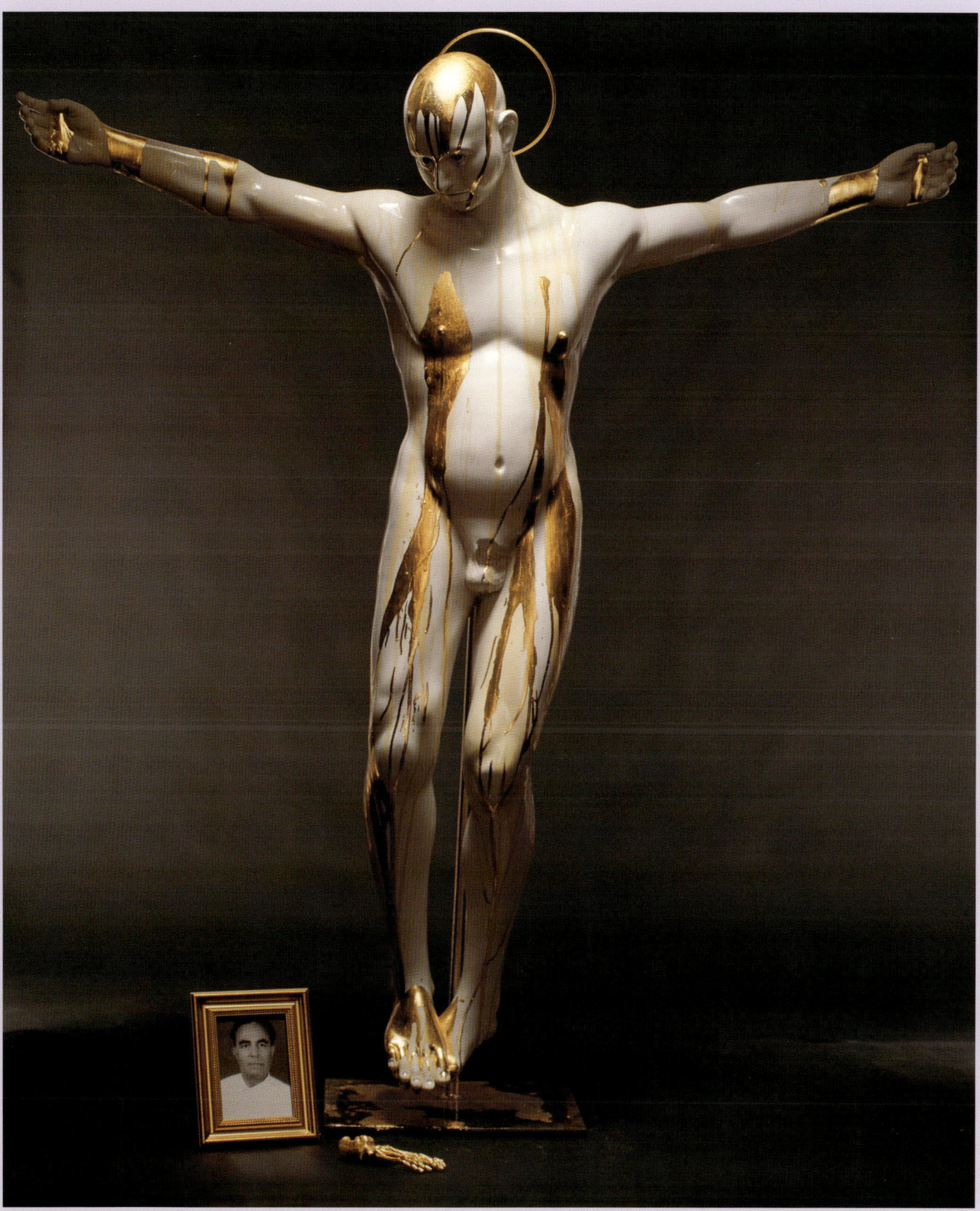

Untitled
Lifesize. Fibreglass, resin, goldleaf, mild steel and photograph.
2005

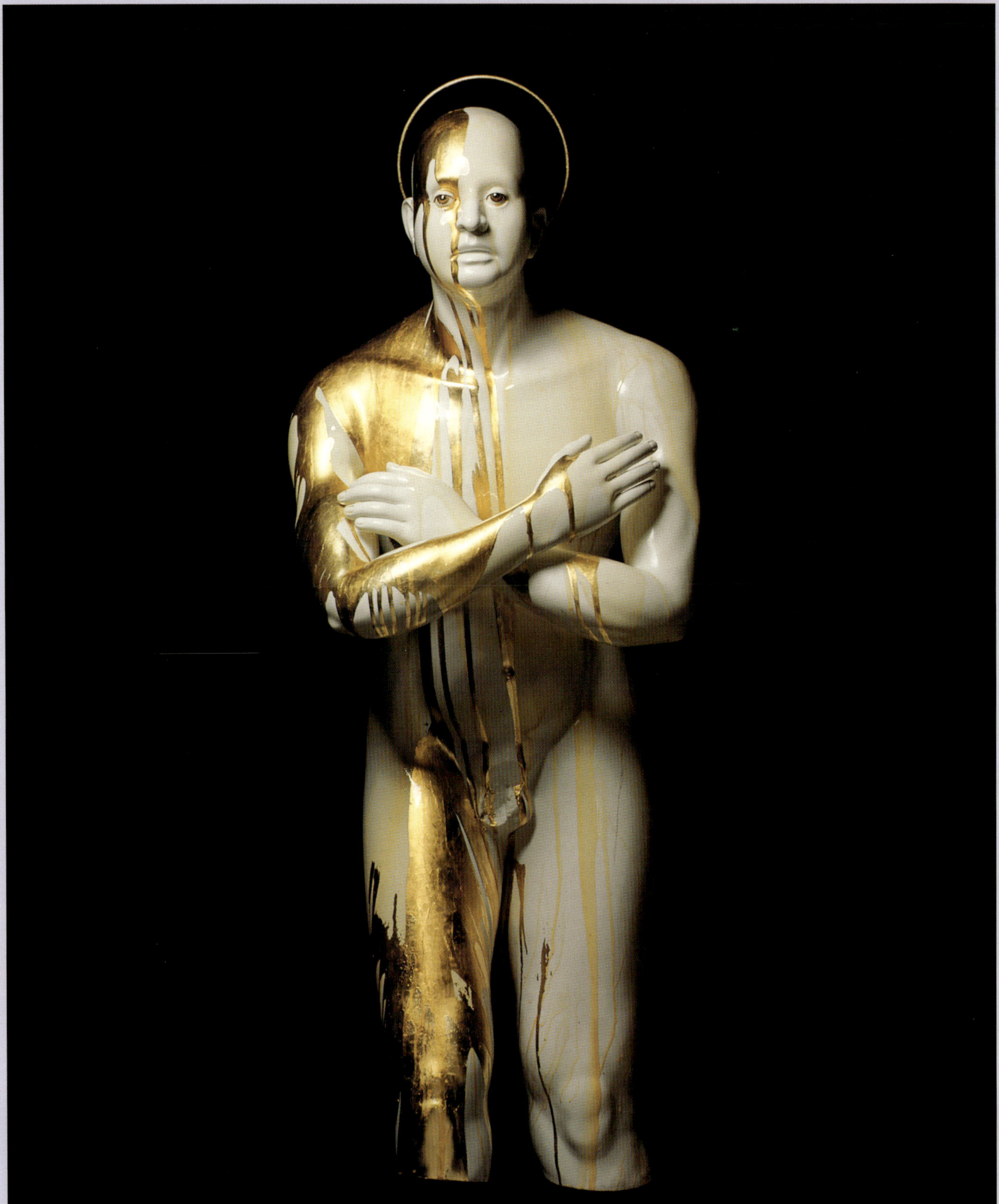

Untitled
Lifesize. Fibreglass, resin and goldleaf.
2005

has largely been the human body and my enquiry into the dynamics of existence. The real body has the capacity to express large truths–of dignity, of pain, of survival of the self–despite the trauma and anxieties which life is fraught with."

Of course, to deal with beauty and pain through the canvas of the body plays strongly to a Christian worldview as epitomised through the life, death, and resurrection of Christ. (Apart from the current series of sculptural references culled from the Bible, JJ entitled one of his works from the 2001 exhibition, *Seven Stations*). The artist describes here how he views the cyclical nature of humanity: "Desire drives one to the quest of a fulfillment in the other…this journey, which desire accelerates, can lead to its thwarting (the agony of fulfilling one's passion) in a bid for a utopian possibility: a triumph of the human being overcoming the travails of the journey with dignity and integrity leads one to being a survivor."

Here we see a strong distinction between pain and suffering. Clearly JJ sees pain as a vehicle through which one can have a much stronger, intense vision of the beauty of existence. In contrast, suffering inhibits this, and it is at this point that JJ's worldview veers away from the traditional Christian doctrine. Ultimately, the most important insight that JJ brings to his work is the idea that "Paradise is here". So we come full circle, back to the fibreglass models of his present series, *Peers*, a play on the English word as well as an allusion to Muslim saints.

A few weeks after visiting his studio, I meet with Jehangir Jani again at a photography session for the finished fibreglass works. The works have taken on an entirely new character: JJ's likeness is now more worked out in the faces; the eyes have been painted; the bodies buffed into a white sheen that accentuates the soft rounding of the bellies; gold leaf has been applied over dripped glue. This perfected quality of the models is a part of JJ's process towards a new sophistication in the sculptures. These are very dignified sculptures; self assured, they neither look down in defeat, nor up in appeal, but rather directly at the viewer. At the same time, the subjects are undeniably fallible, human, and, moreover, middle aged; the stomachs protrude, the faces show weight in the cheeks. In addition, the subjects have all been castrated. JJ's pithy take on his characters is that they have undergone "the shift from the desired body to becoming the desiring body; the body decays yet has the same desires that a teenager has." Here the macabre is intended not as an obvious conceit, but

Clearly JJ sees pain as a vehicle through which one can have a much stronger, intense vision of the beauty of existence. In contrast, suffering inhibits this, and it is at this point that JJ's worldview veers away from traditional Christian doctrine. Ultimately, the most important insight that JJ brings to his work is the idea that "Paradise is here".

These are very dignified sculptures; self assured, they neither look down in defeat nor up in appeal, but rather directly at the viewer. At the same time, the subjects are undeniably fallible...

rather as background noise that constantly plays behind the overt beauty of the buffed, gold-leafed models.

The works will be named after Muslim saints and so there is a new inter-denominational quality to the show. "It is with the Semitic notion that paradise is elsewhere that I question Sainthood in the present sculptures." JJ's subjects are most certainly not victims of their circumstance: he wants his figures to find fulfillment here on earth. Each of the ten sculptures will be placed alone, in their own pools of light, without being in communication with others in the group. The solitary nature of his figures is a constant refrain in JJ's work; he says he is keen "not to narrow down to a relationship." Moreover, by leaving his sculptural figures naked, he negates caste or cadre allegiances that can get in the way of his integral emotions and themes that transcend the pettiness of such allegiances.

In many ways the present series of sculptures provides a meeting point for themes that have variously been investigated in other series throughout the artist's career. At the same time, the centrality of the message, *Paradise is Here,* takes on urgency in reaction to the specificities of our world today, where the message that Paradise is a deferred treat for the faithful, has allowed vested interests to manipulate the emotionally vulnerable. As I leave Jehangir Jani amid his saintly likenesses, I silently applaud the maverick artist for his steadfast belief in a humanity unencumbered by dogma, and for his ability to portray the strength of the human spirit in a most powerful, elegant manner.

Mumbai, August 2005

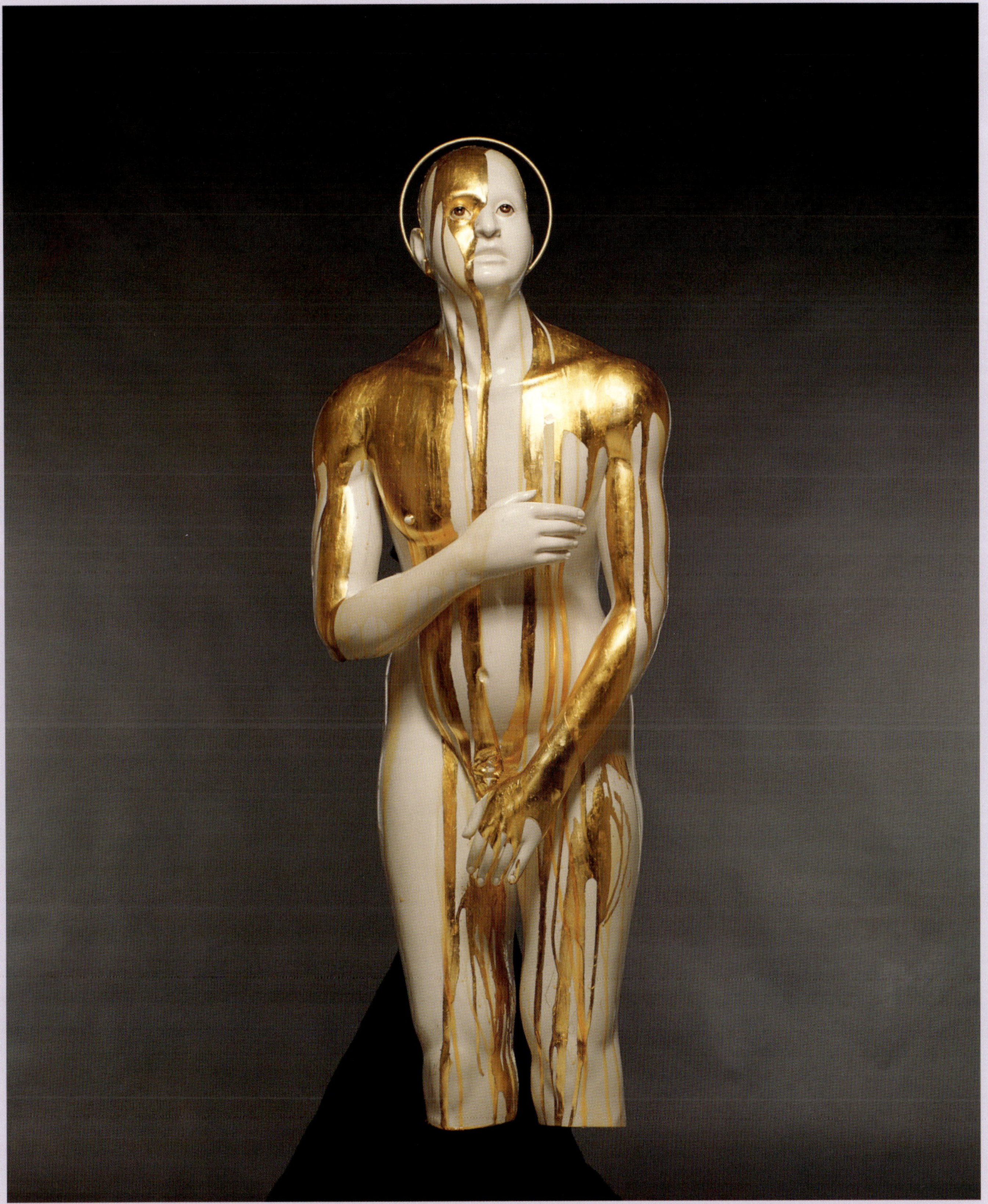

Untitled
Lifesize. Fibreglass, resin and goldleaf.
2005

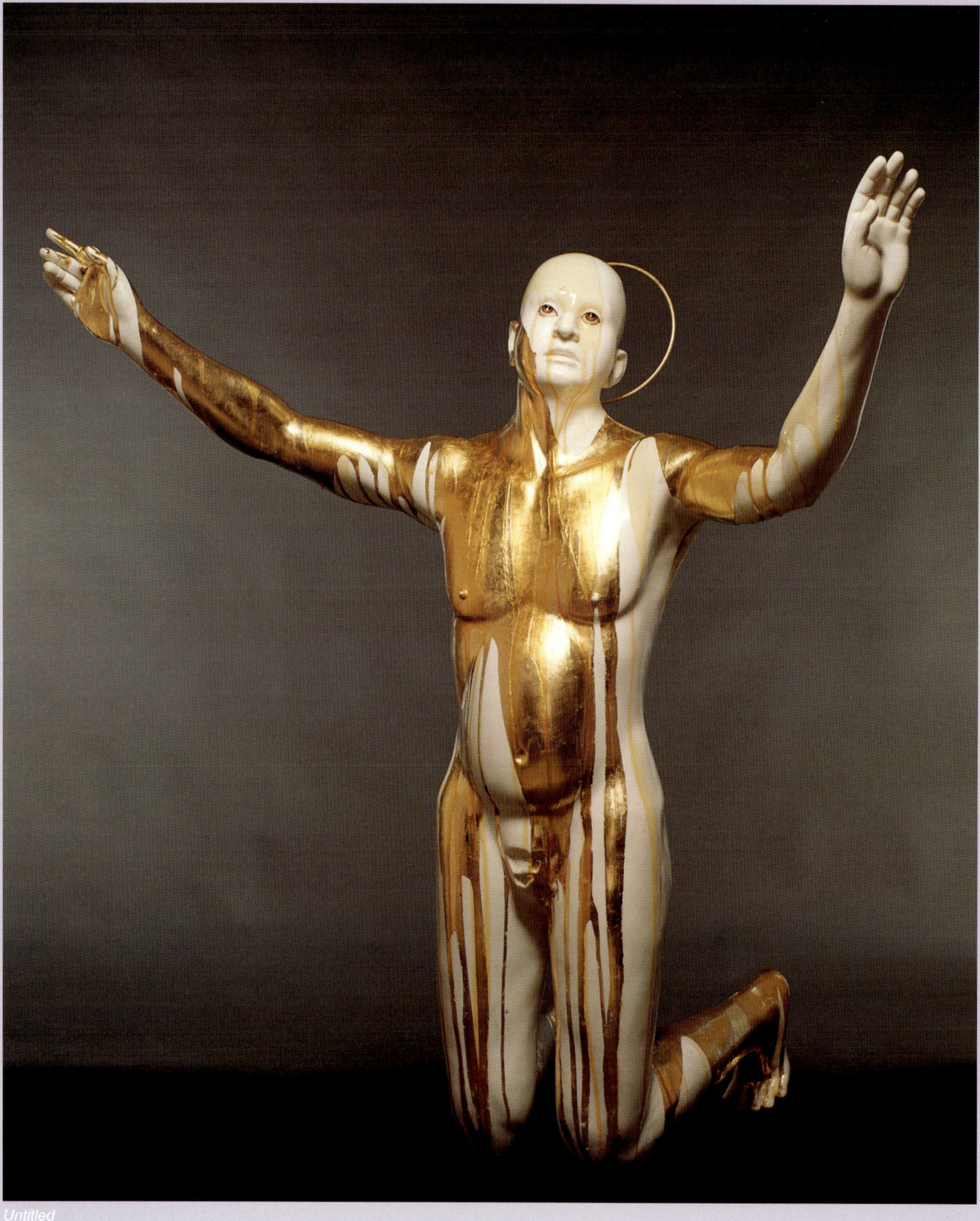

Untitled
Lifesize. Fibreglass, resin and goldleaf.
2005

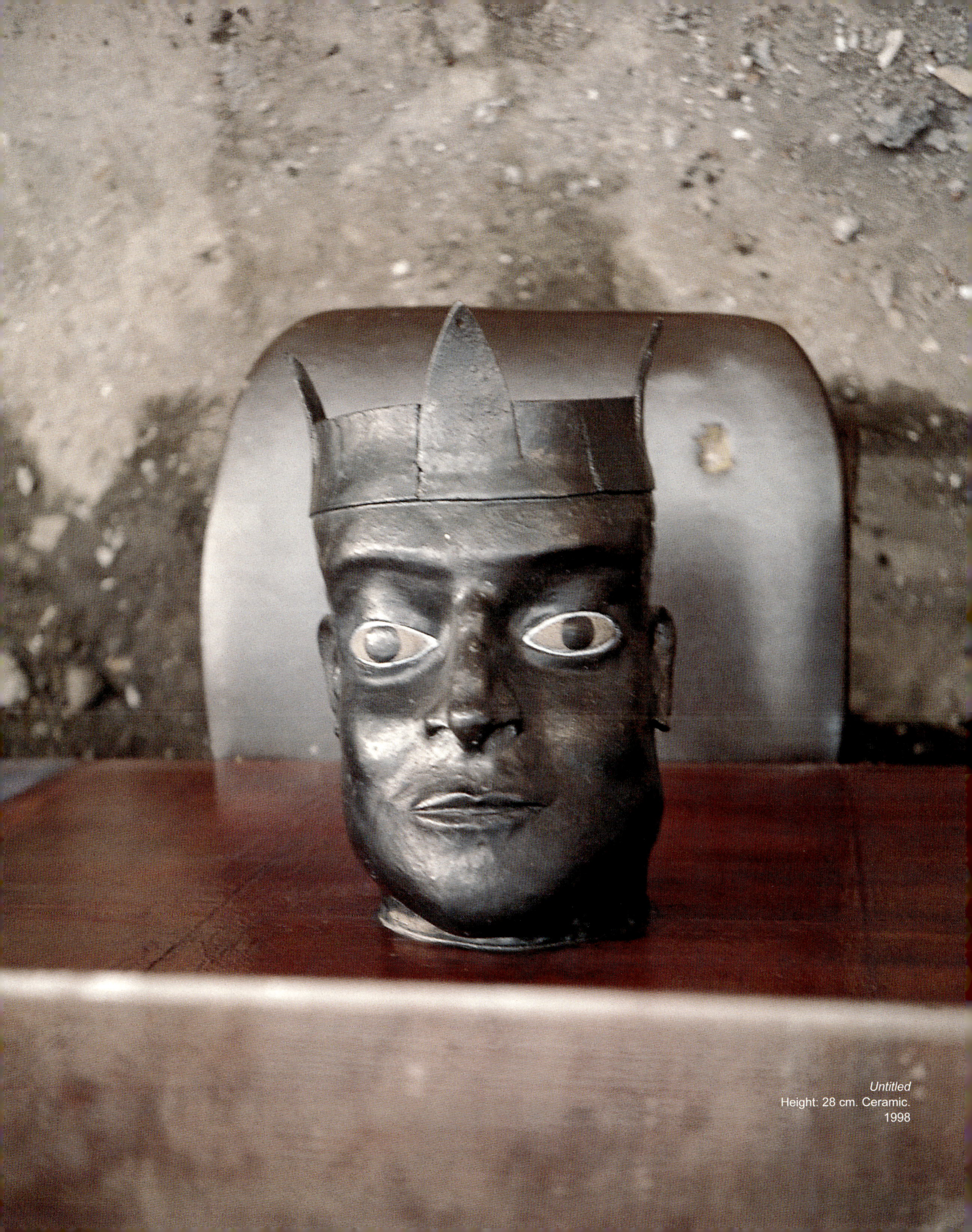

Untitled
Height: 28 cm. Ceramic.
1998

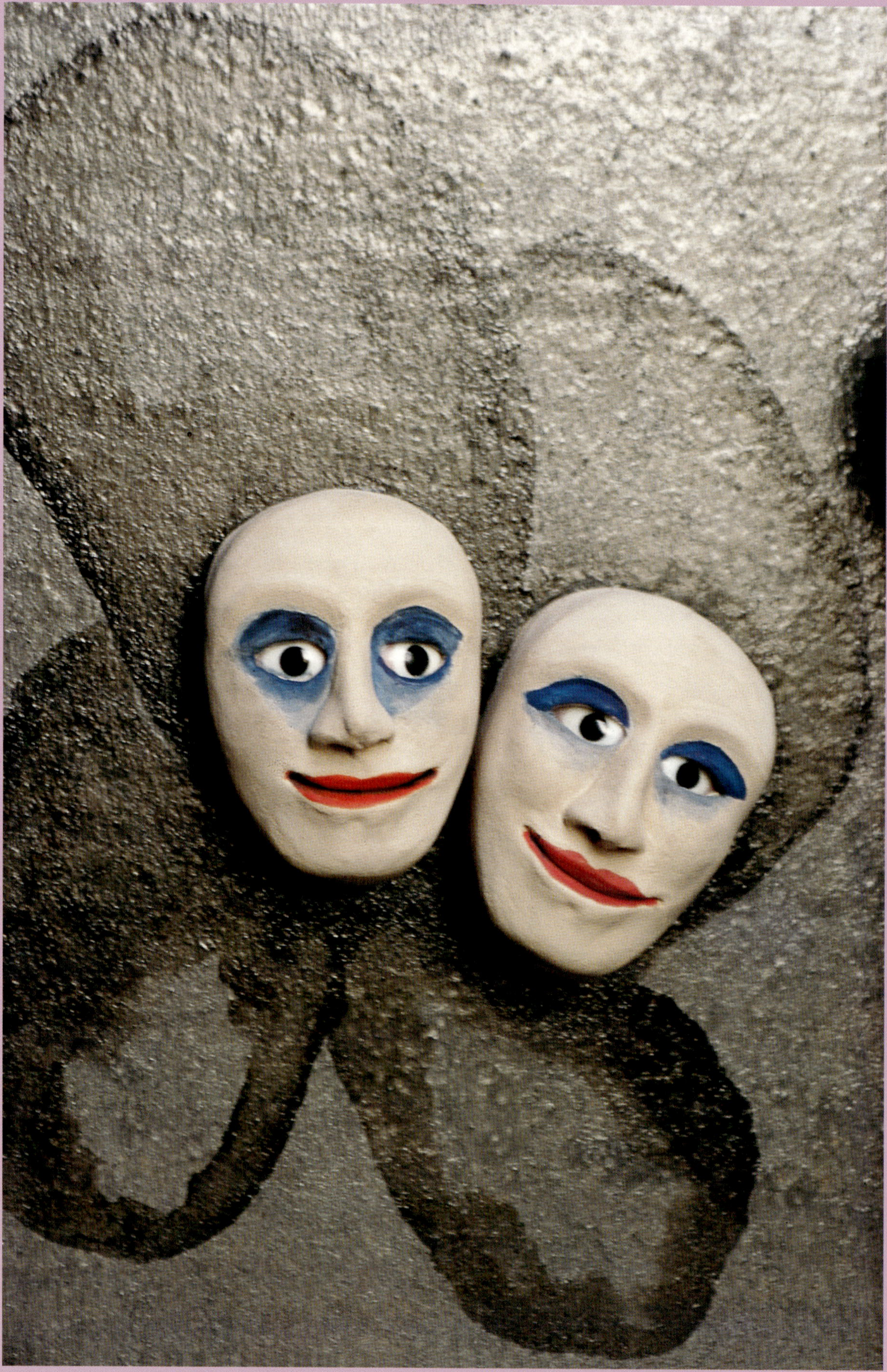

Box of Flowers
46 x 30 x 10 cm. Terracotta, wood, and enamel.
1998

CASTING AN 'INFIDEL' HEAD: RELIEF SCULPTURES BY JEHANGIR JANI

Nancy Adajania

"Where the convexity occurs very near to the [central] point, we have the 'dishonest' nose seen among the Bedouin Arabs. Sometimes this particular nose will appear upon the face of a respectable person who has a fondness for close bargains, but doubtless other organs will offset its dishonest signification."

– Professor Elmer E. Knowles, *Complete System of Personal Influence and Healing* (c. 1920s)

Looking at Jani's head-casts, can you prove that he is a Dawoodi Bohra, a Gujarati-speaking Muslim, a person of alternative sexuality? The head-casts speak for a universal human identity. And yet he is a marked man, a man belonging to a global religion that has been under suspicion and threat in the post-9/11 scenario...

Why do I choose to shock the reader by prefacing an essay on Jehangir Jani's recent relief sculptures with a citation taken from a handbook on physiognomic 'character-reading' popularised by Professor Knowles? I'd like to suggest that JJ's head-casts, mounted on particle boards, mock this fraudulent science based on ethnic prejudice, which has been re-legitimised by police apparatuses at the world's checkpoints in the cause of the War against Terror, since 9/11.

Consider this tragic situation. Every Muslim face is now scanned as a potential threat to world peace (read: America's security). By this logic, Professor Knowles' legislations on the Bedouin Arab's 'dishonest nose' and other ethnic stereotypes, long consigned to the realm of charlatanry, have suddenly re-emerged as essential elements of official state-security wisdom. Looking at JJ's head-casts, can you prove that he is a Dawoodi Bohra, a Gujarati-speaking Muslim, a person of alternative sexuality? The head-casts speak for a universal human identity. And yet he is a marked man, a man belonging to a global religion that has been under suspicion and threat in the post-9/11 scenario, a member of a religious minority whose existence has been endangered after the pogrom in Gujarat, March 2002.

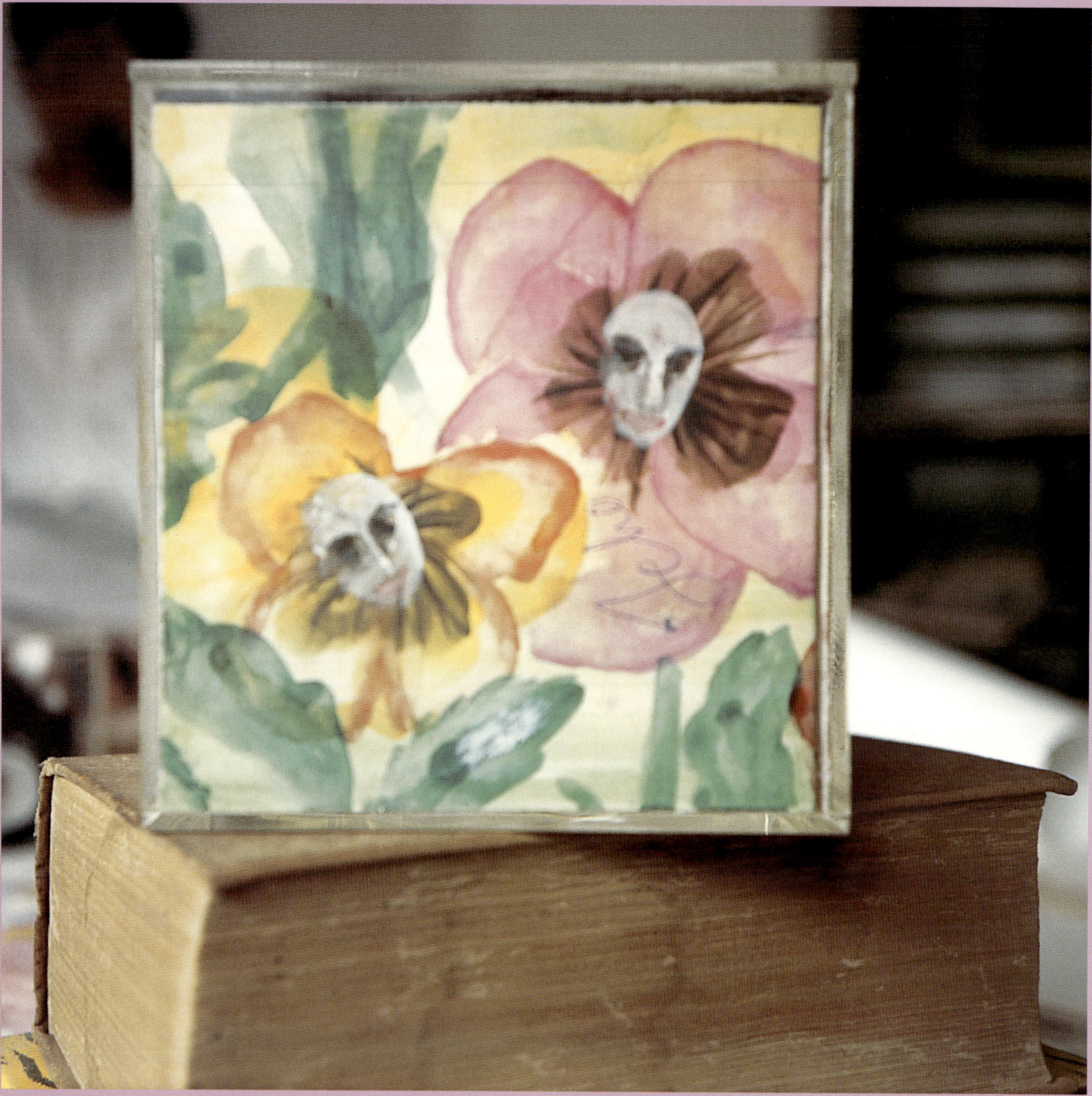

Box of Pansies
15 x 15 x 15 cm. Watercolour, plexiglass and papier mâchè
1997

These themes of unearned suffering may have prompted Jehangir Jani to choose the narrative of Job's ordeal as his leitmotif. JJ has turned the character-reading of the Muslim as 'infidel', the 'other', or the 'enemy' in today's security discourse, into a parable of healing, by subverting the story of Job's monumental suffering and undeserved victimisation.

Job, who appears in both the Jewish and the Islamic scriptures, is a true believer in God; the Devil dares God to a contest in which Job's faith would be severely tested to see if he is led to curse God. It is almost as though Job were being penalised for his faith: this story has exercised the imagination of many writers and artists, because of its moral ambiguity. Vincent Brome paraphrases the psychoanalyst and philosopher Jung, who discusses this dilemma in his book, *Answer to Job:* "If God could allow Adam to be trapped by the serpent in the Garden of Eden, permit Satan to torment Job and demand Abraham's son as a sacrifice, how could he escape the charge of being evil himself." And Jung writes: "I hope...to give expression to the shattering emotion which the unvarnished spectacle of divine savagery and ruthlessness produces in us."

In JJ's personal interpretation, Job becomes an individual searching for universal love, one of the chief values cherished by the Sufis. He imparts a pop-kitsch edge to Job's resilience: his Job is not represented as a solemn, larger-than-life victim, but as an ordinary human being, who goes through the spectacle of everyday savagery with a discreet smile on his face. The major subtext of JJ's relief sculptures, with each of their backgrounds characterising various natural elements and the diurnal cycle of life, is the tension between lack and excess, push and pull, suffering and pleasure.

Each head-cast is framed by a gauze bandage that is layered on the board in an abstract pattern. These bandages connote a sense of healing that comes from confronting pain, not perpetuating it. Their porous weaves quietly meld into the colour of the backgrounds, which are coded with JJ's alternative choices of sexuality and political identity. He uses the figure-ground tension to create moral and political ambiguities, and pursue his personal idiosyncrasies. For instance, in *Love*, the head is bracketed on a glittering, deep-magenta ground that exudes passion and jouissance, but also illuminates JJ's alternate sexuality. The bandage is arranged around the head to look like a liberatory star. Fittingly, this Sufiesque toleration of difference is coded in the kitschy pink environment of a discotheque.

JJ has turned the character-reading of the Muslim as 'infidel', the 'other' or the 'enemy' in today's security discourse, into a parable of healing...

> JJ rescues the significance of the 'infidel' position from the no-man's-land of derogation: the defiant infidel here is the marked man who rejects the call to surrender or succumb, the seeker who refuses to subscribe to the outward pieties of any orthodoxy, and who, therefore, individuates himself, much as the Sufis did.

While in *Love* the background paint is applied informally, to connote warmth and intimacy, in *Fire*, the bandage itself becomes the absorbent ground covering the whole board. Here, there are no purificatory flames that will consume the death and darkness visited upon Job. Instead, the work aspires to a Rothkoesque meditative crimson lake with ivory-black background.

In *Night*, the bandage becomes a tantalising veil bathed in glitter; beneath it, the facial contours of Job become more angular. We are bewitched by this oneiric synaesthesia. Under the veil of darkness, trespassing becomes easier and hierarchies soften. But even as night democratises, its offensives strike out: blood drips into the gauze-glitter.

JJ accentuates this sense of indeterminacy by working the background in many layers. The rice paper on board is painted with a combination of acrylic with the artisan's binders or stainers. The domestic materials, mixed with the ersatz of glitter, suggest intimacies of emotional context.

This series does not inhabit a demonstrative space of blame. In Jehangir Jani's portrayal, Job is an 'infidel' because he breaks the contract of the narrative of suffering, and dares to smile even when he is supposed to be plunged in despair. By doing this, JJ rescues the significance of the 'infidel' position from the no-man's-land of derogation: the defiant 'infidel' here is the marked man, who rejects the call to surrender or succumb, the seeker who refuses to subscribe to the outward pieties of any orthodoxy, and who, therefore, individuates himself, much as the Sufis did.

Mumbai, September 2002

Essay for the catalogue of Jehangir Jani's exhibition, 'JOB'; Jamaat Art Gallery

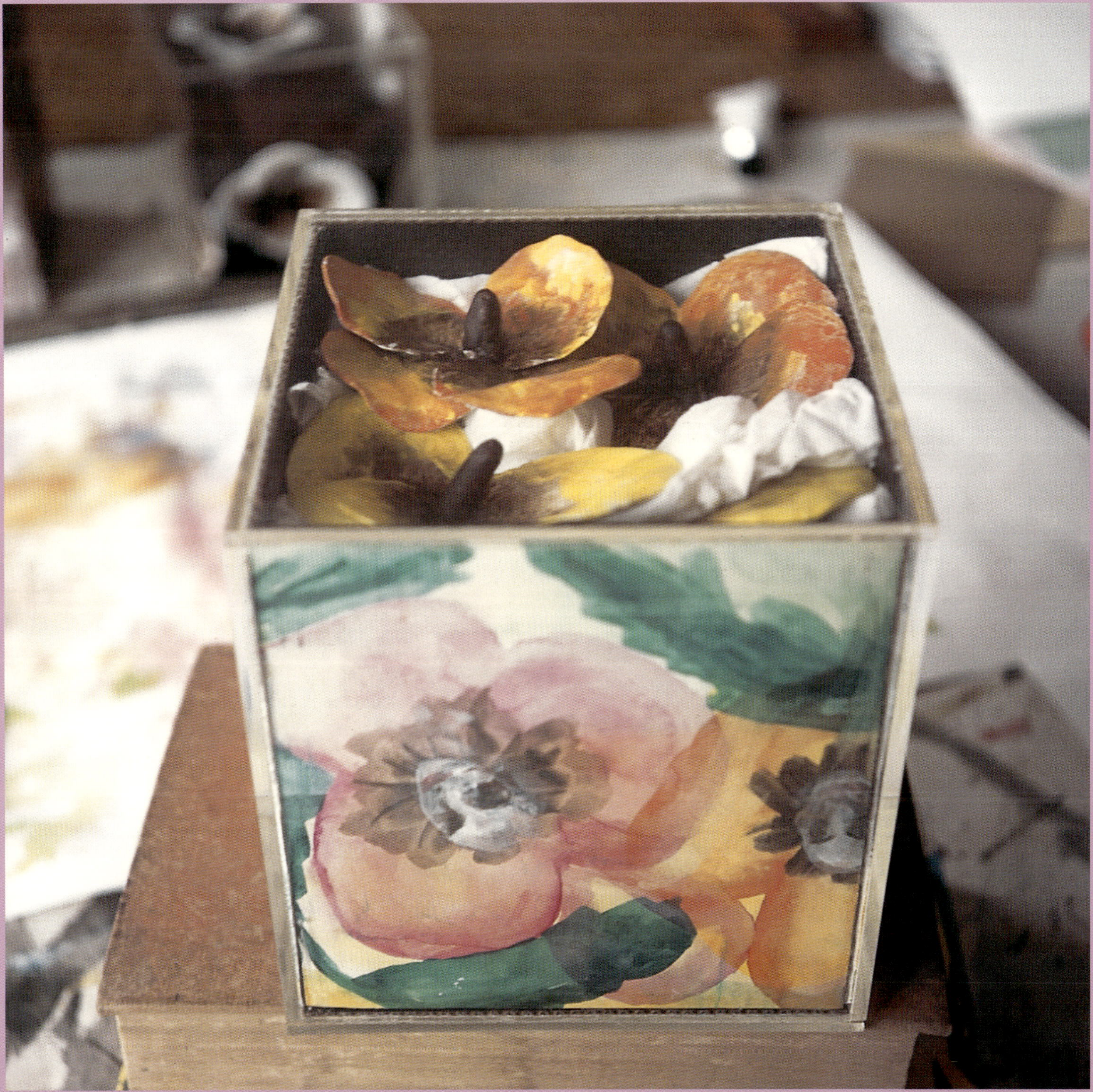

Box of Pansies, Gift for India
15 x 15 x 15 cm. Watercolour, plexiglass and papier mâchè
1997

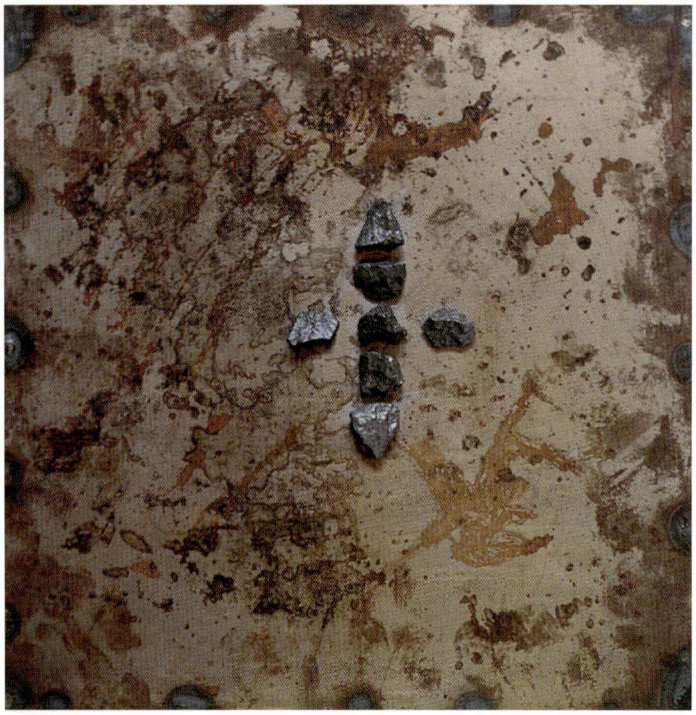

VOWels
31 x 31 x 3 cm. Sheet metal and basalt.
2001

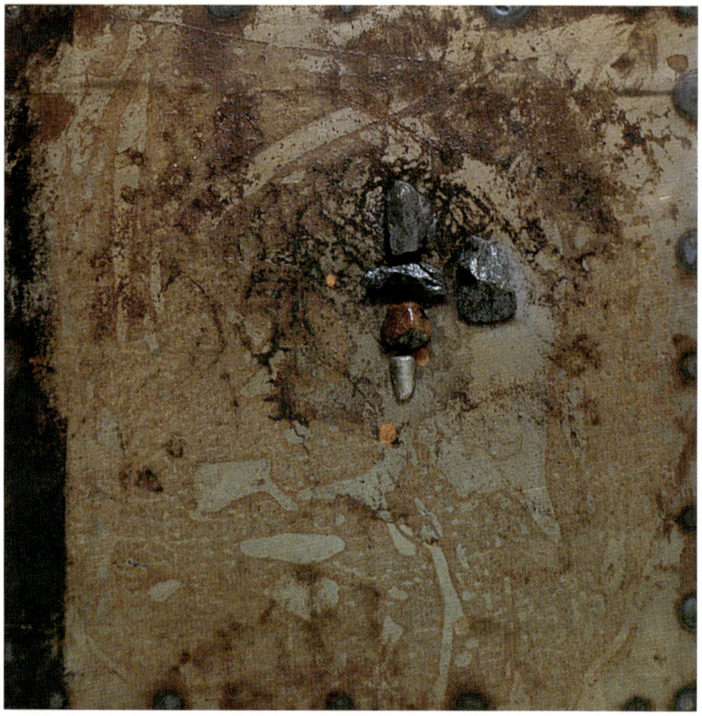

VOWels
31 x 31 x 3 cm. Sheet metal and basalt.
2001

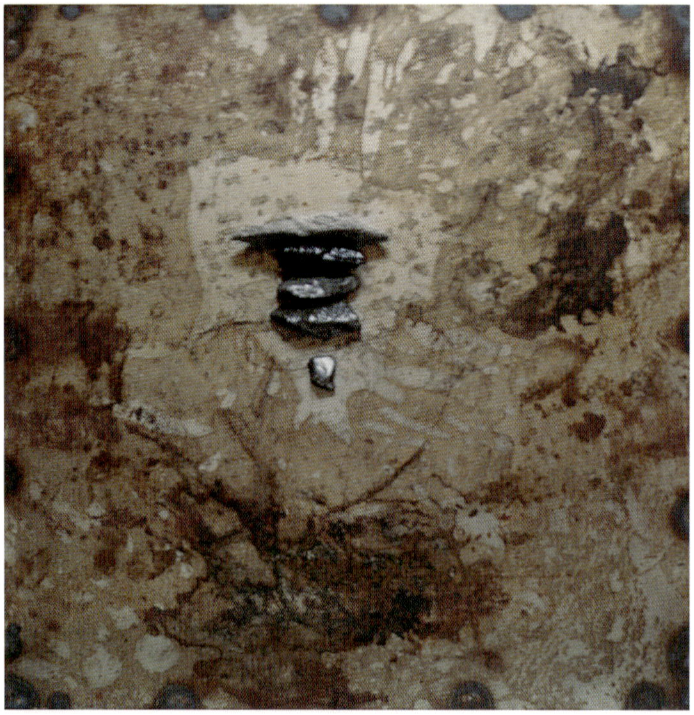

VOWels
31 x 31 x 3 cm. Sheet metal and basalt.
1999

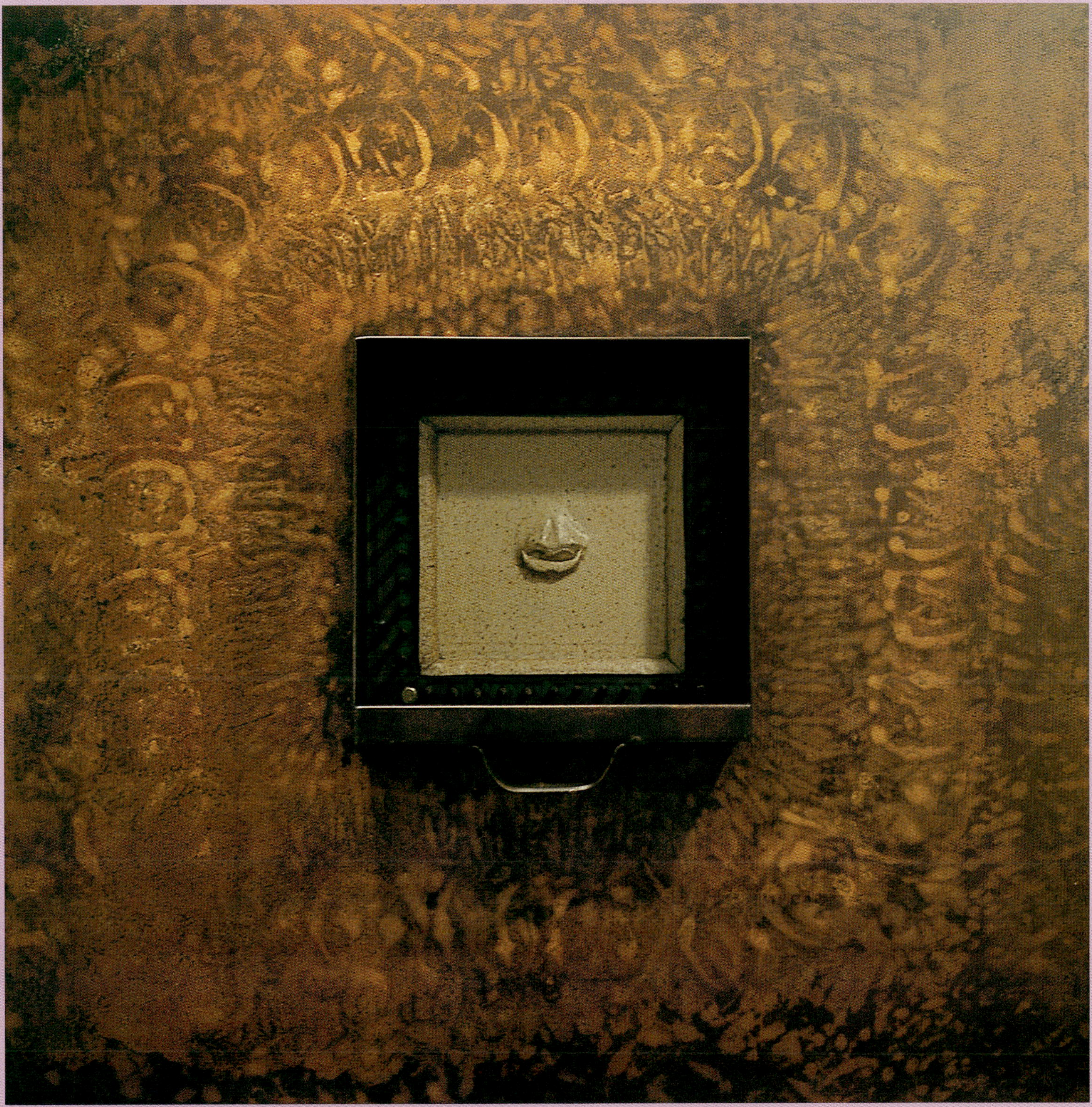

Anonymous
122 x 122 cm. Sheet metal and ceramic.
1999

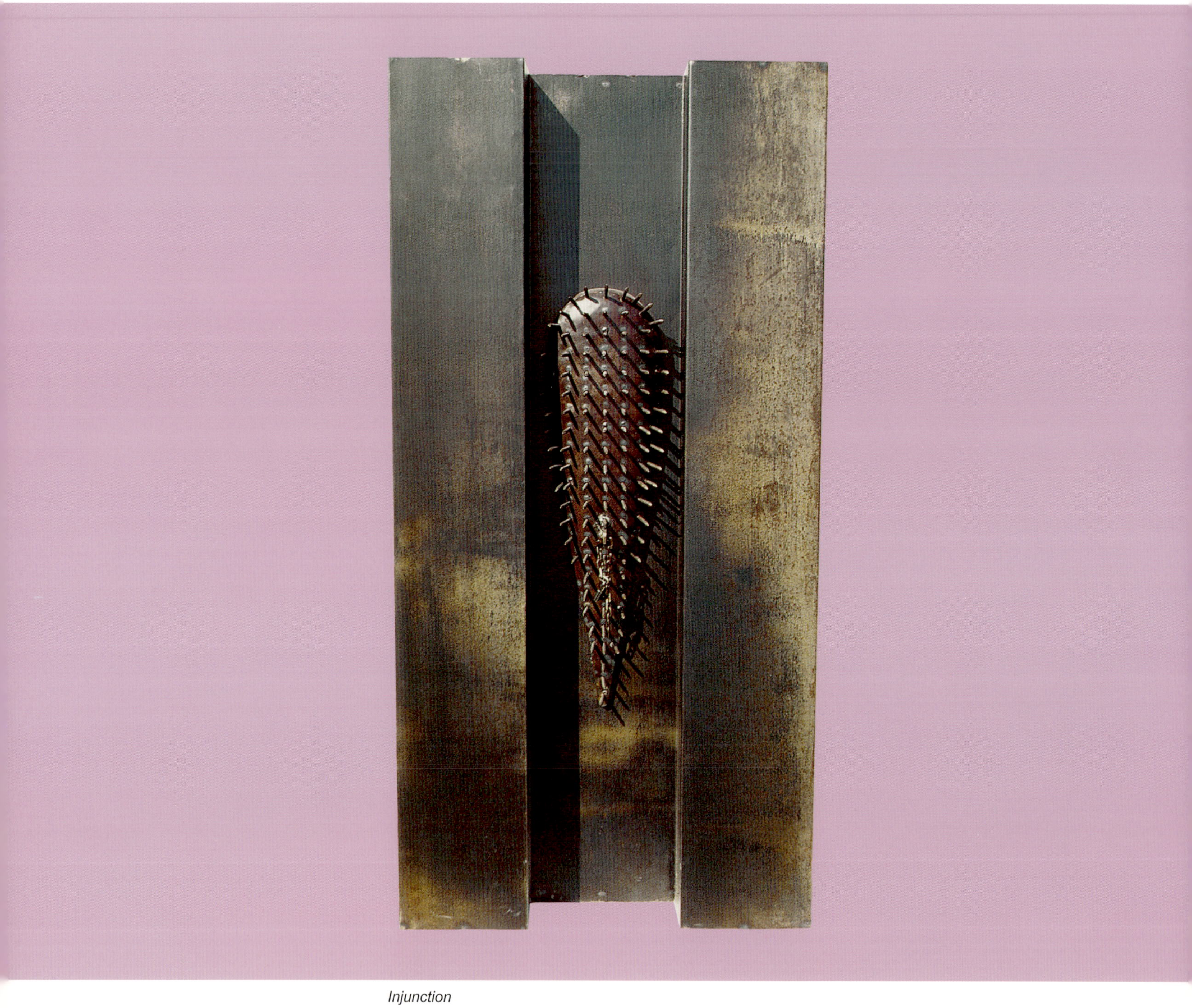

Injunction
122 x 61 cm. Mild steel.
1999

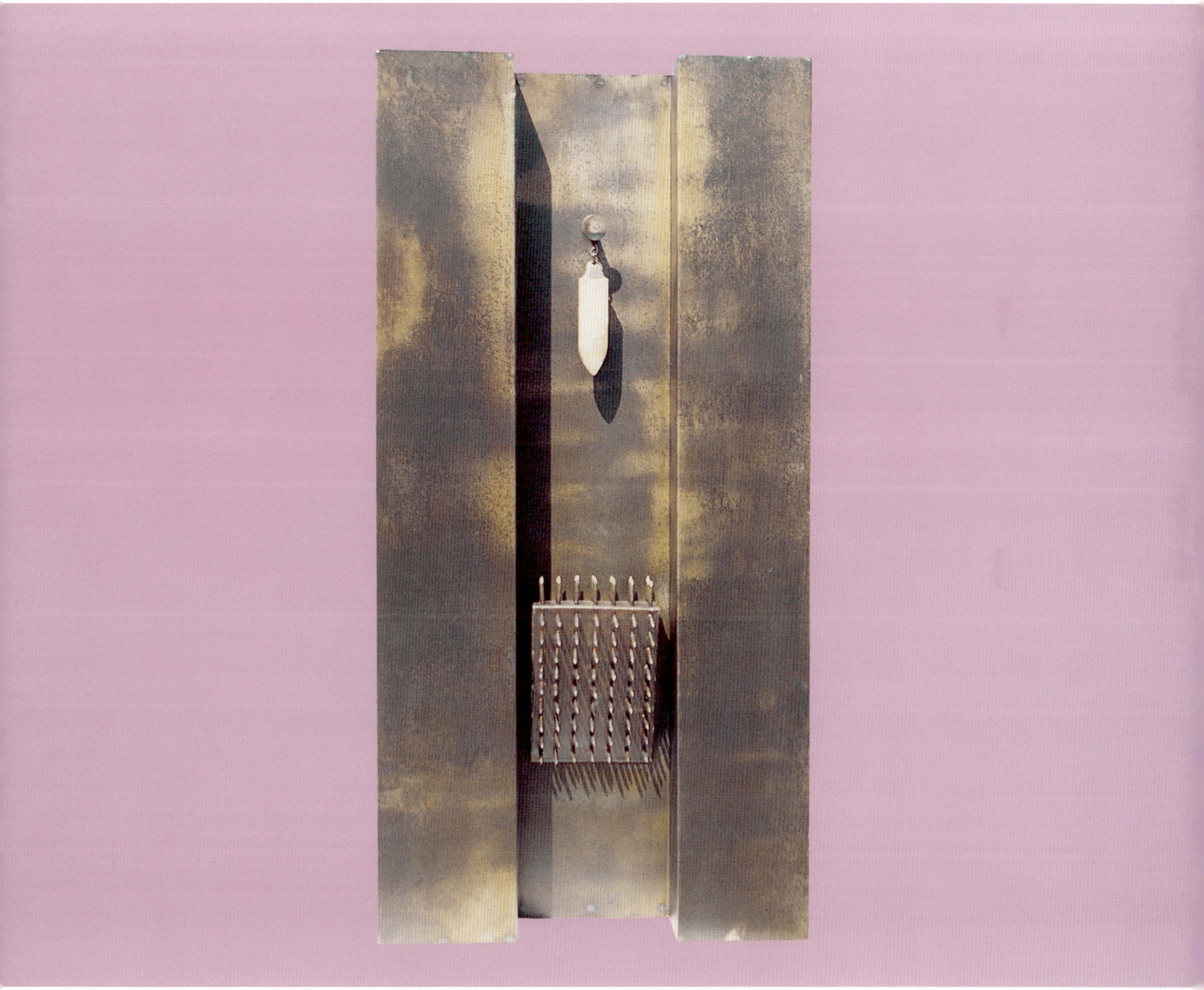

Injunction 1
122 x 61 cm. Mild steel and ceramic.
1999

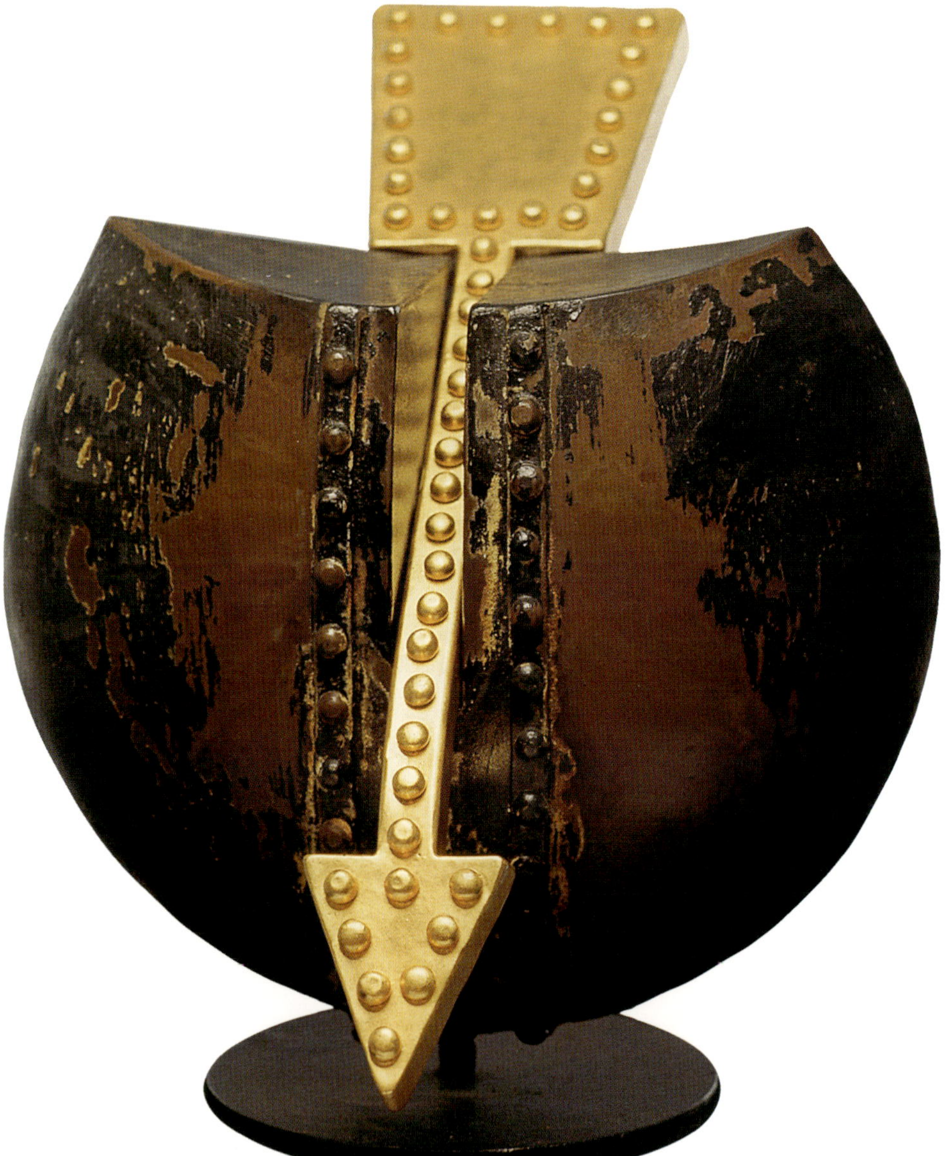

Habil
31 cm diameter. Sheet metal and gold leaf.
2004

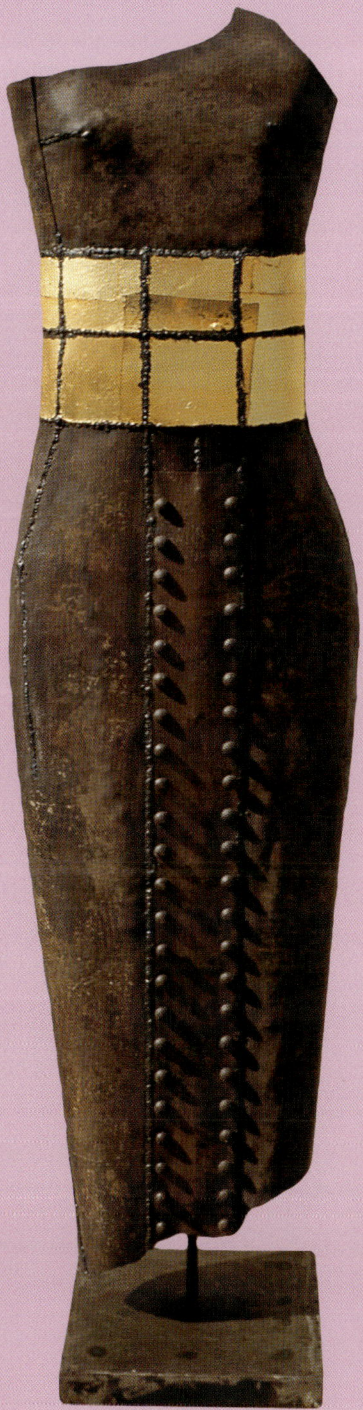

Untitled
183 x 183 x 20 cm. Sheet, metal and gold leaf.
2005

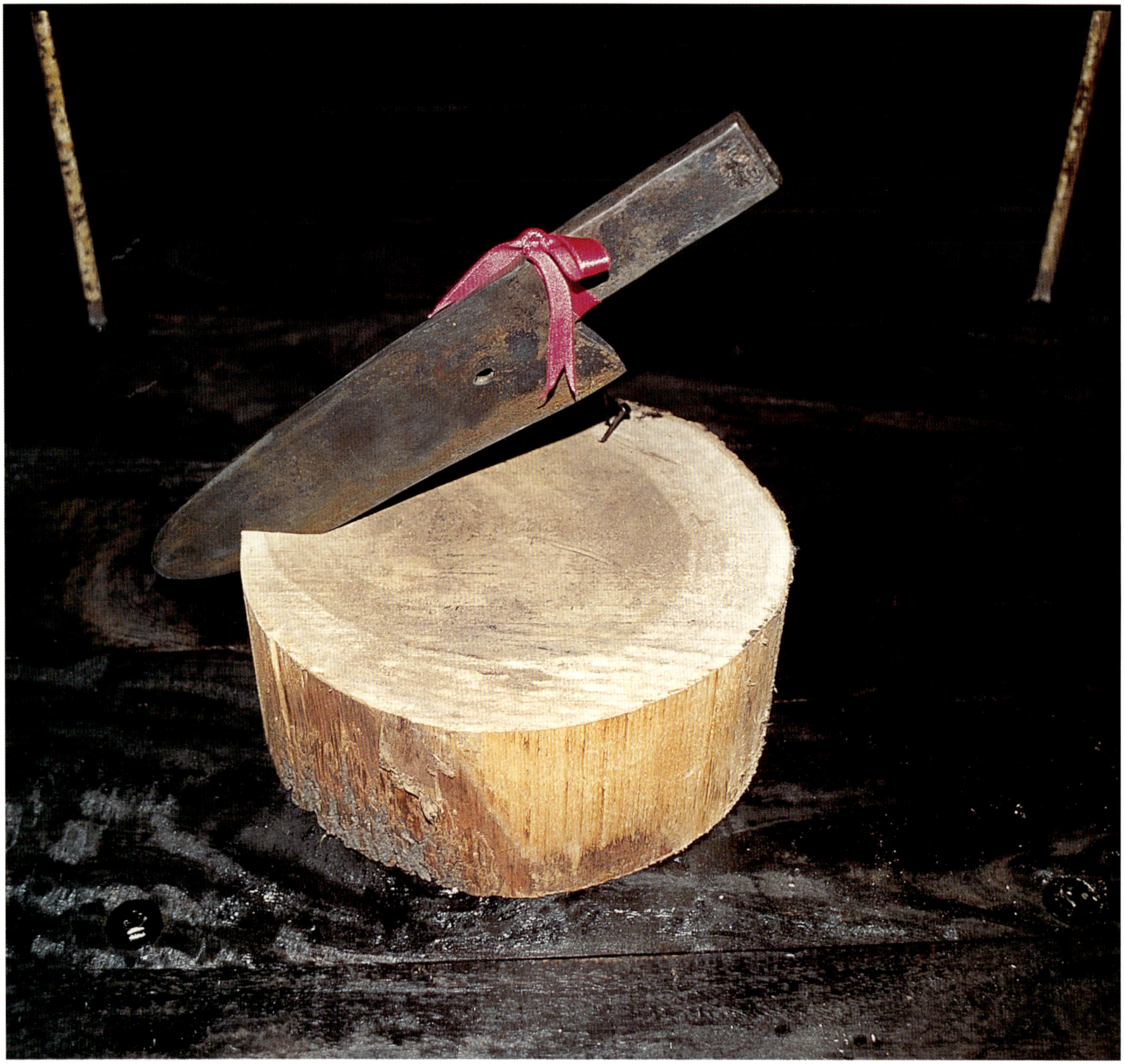

Manish/A Colaco Divas
46 x 25 x 53 cm. Mild steel, wood and silk.
2001

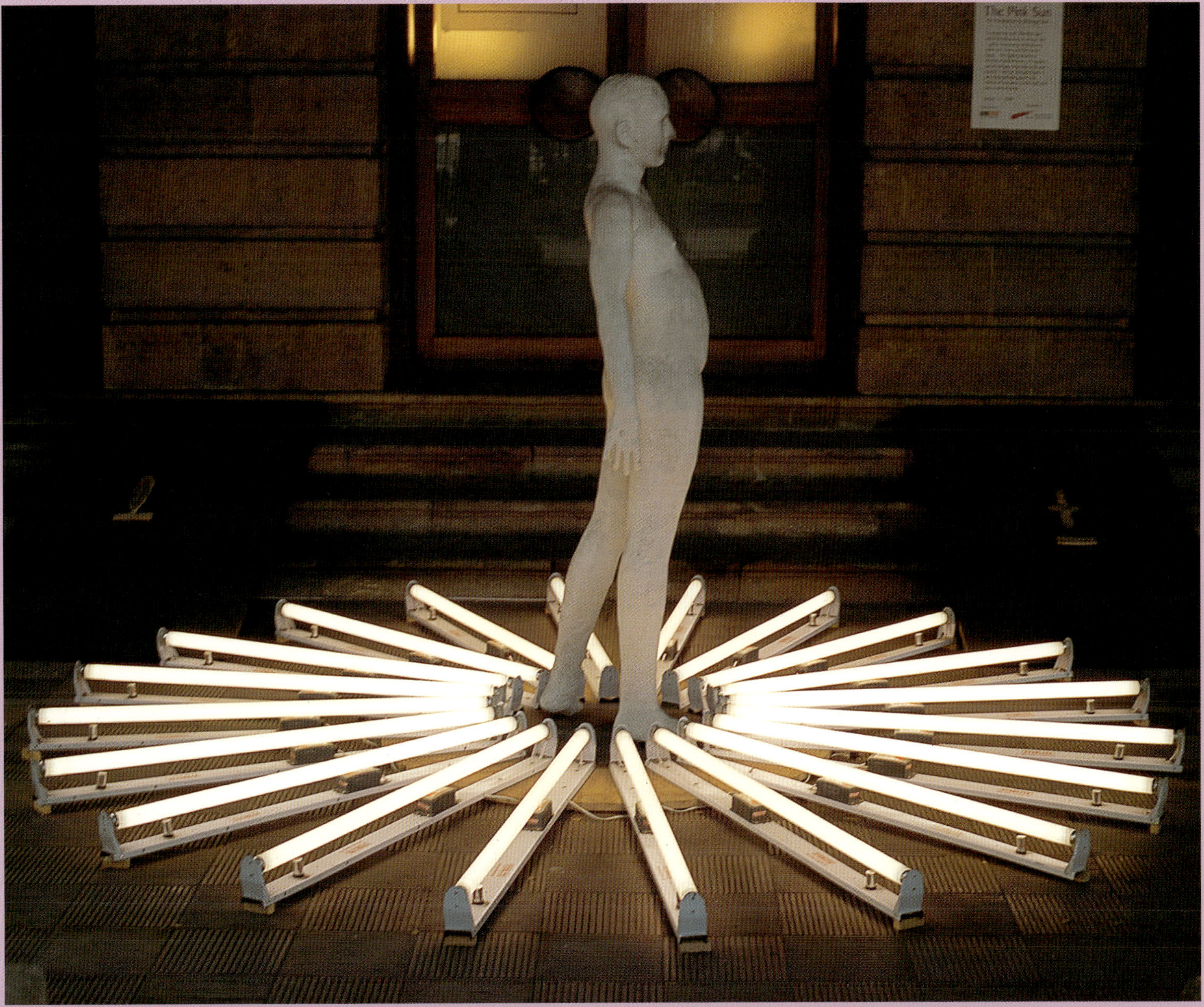

Pink Sun
183 x 305 cm. Plaster of Paris and neon lights.
2000

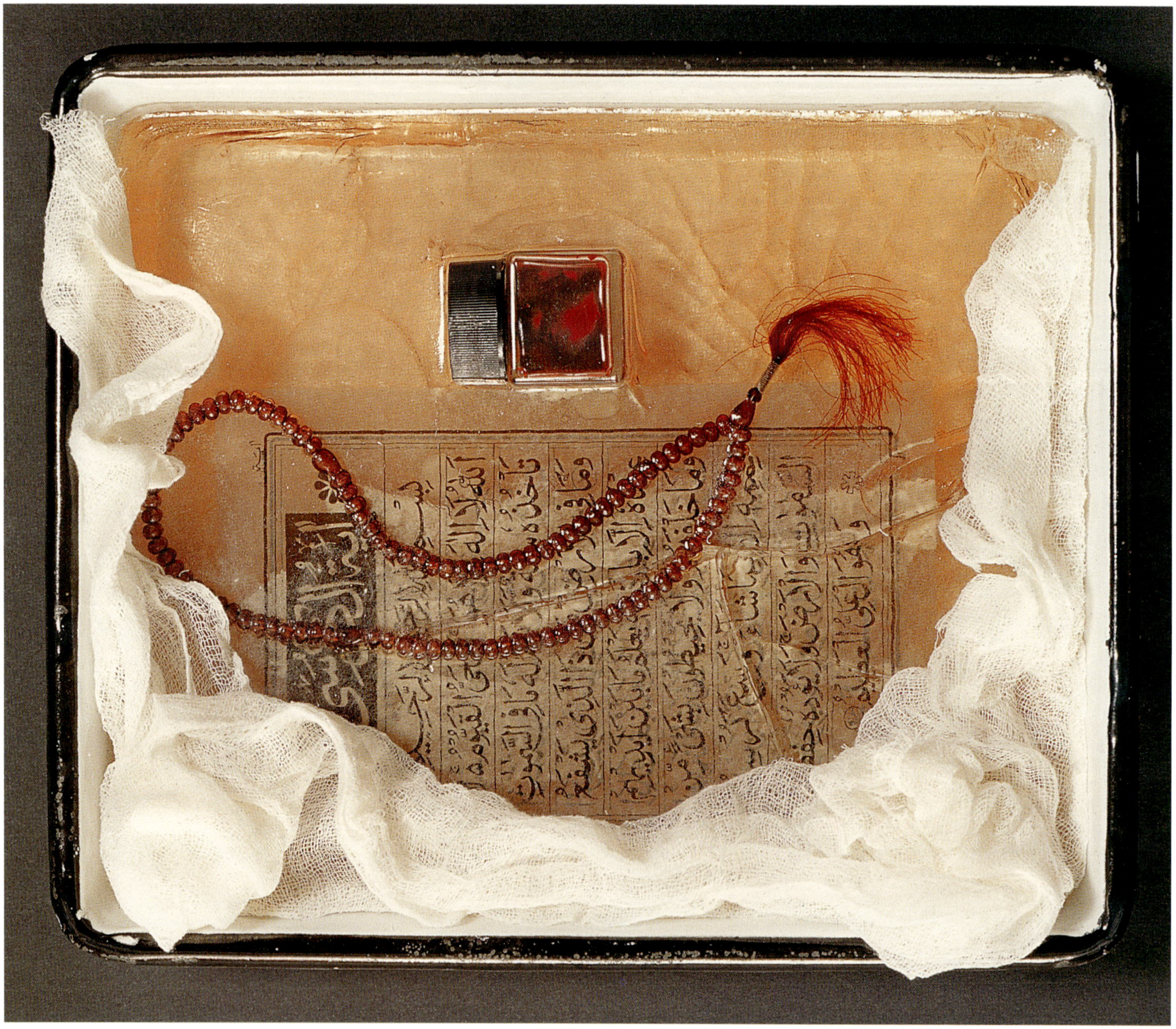

6 Trays
Detail. Enamel, resin, plastic, glass, pigment and surgical gauze.
2004

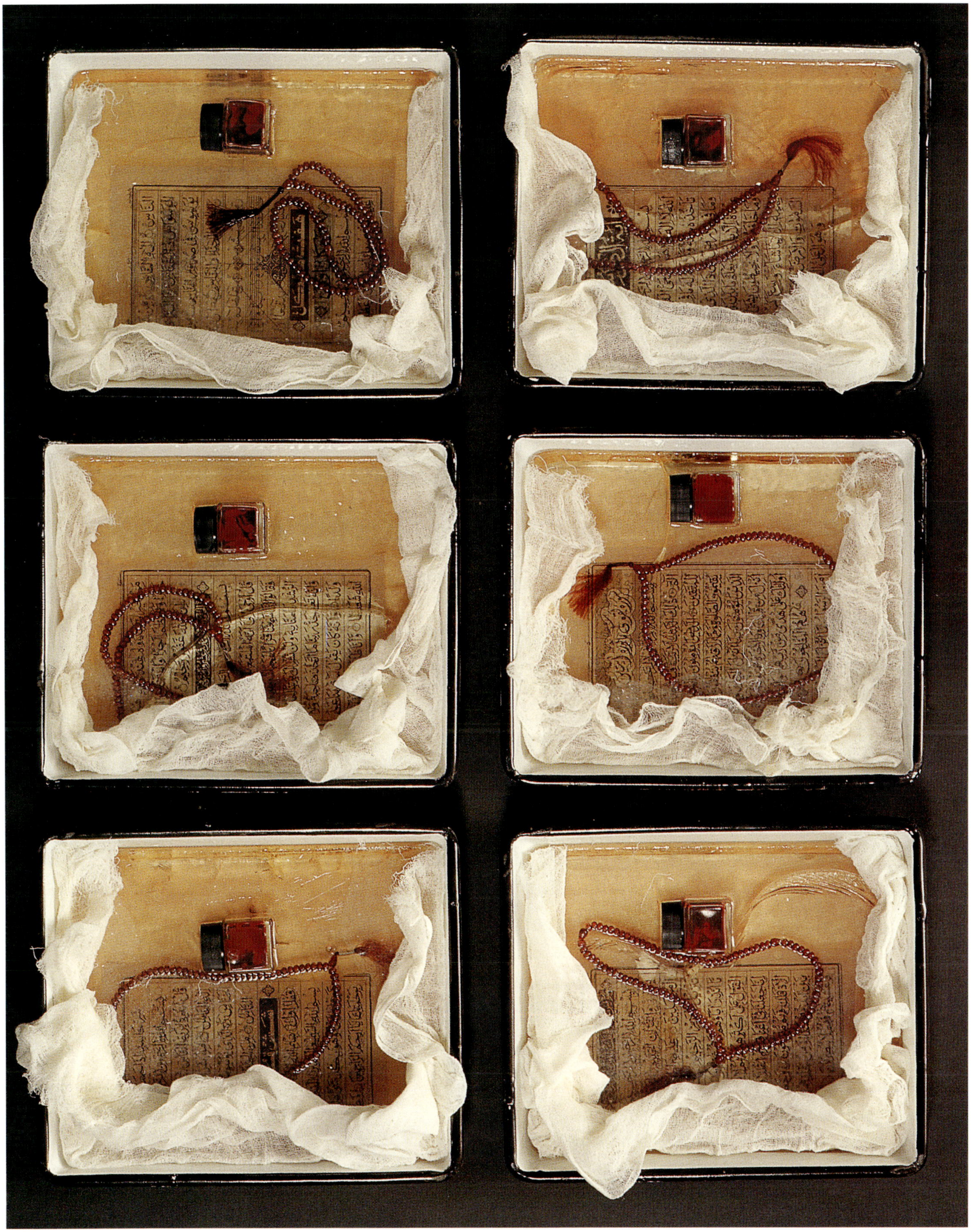

6 Trays
Variable. Enamel, resin, plastic, glass, pigment and surgical gauze.
2004

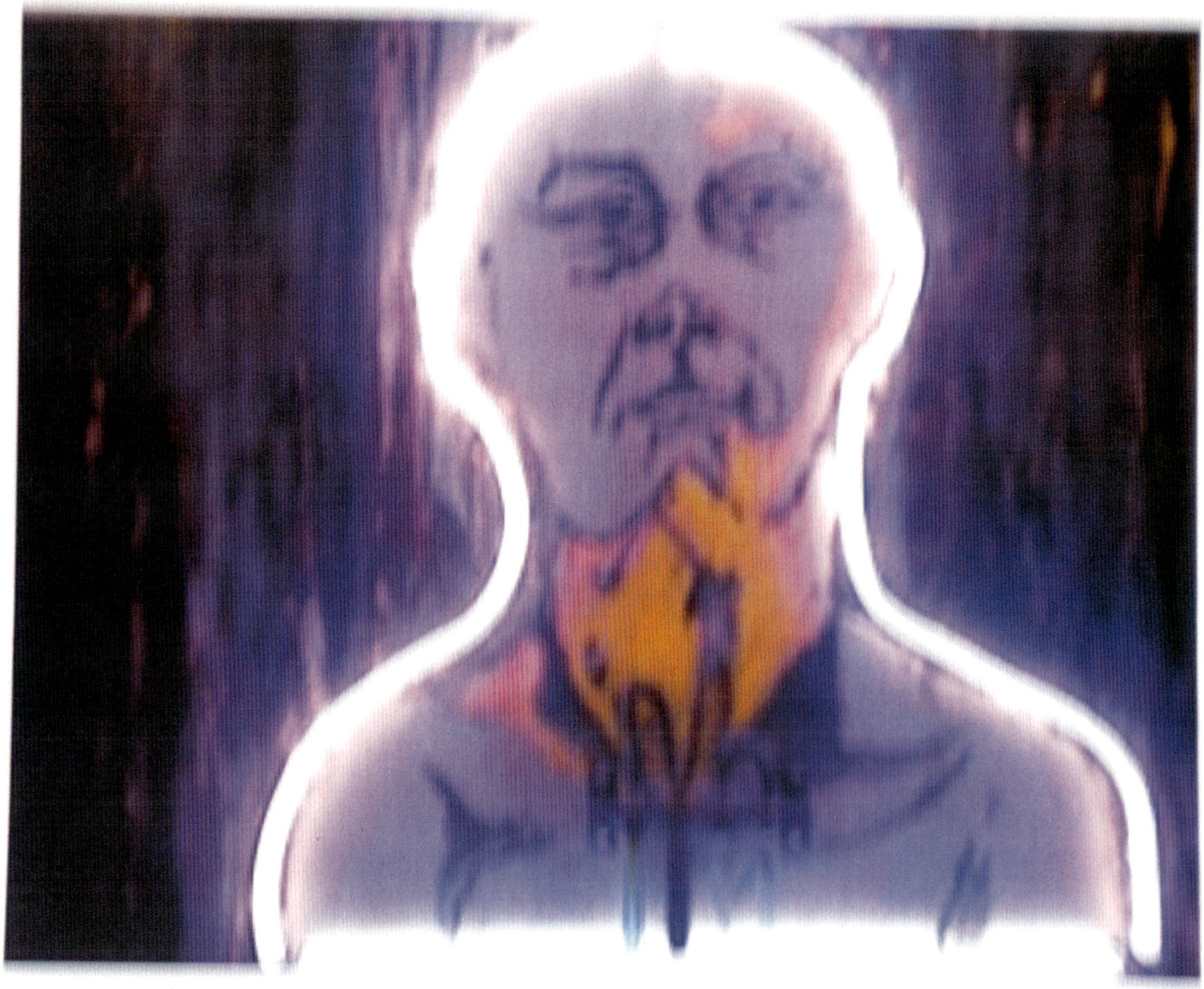

The Alchemist 2
92 x122 cm. Sheet metal, gold leaf, neon light and glass.
2001

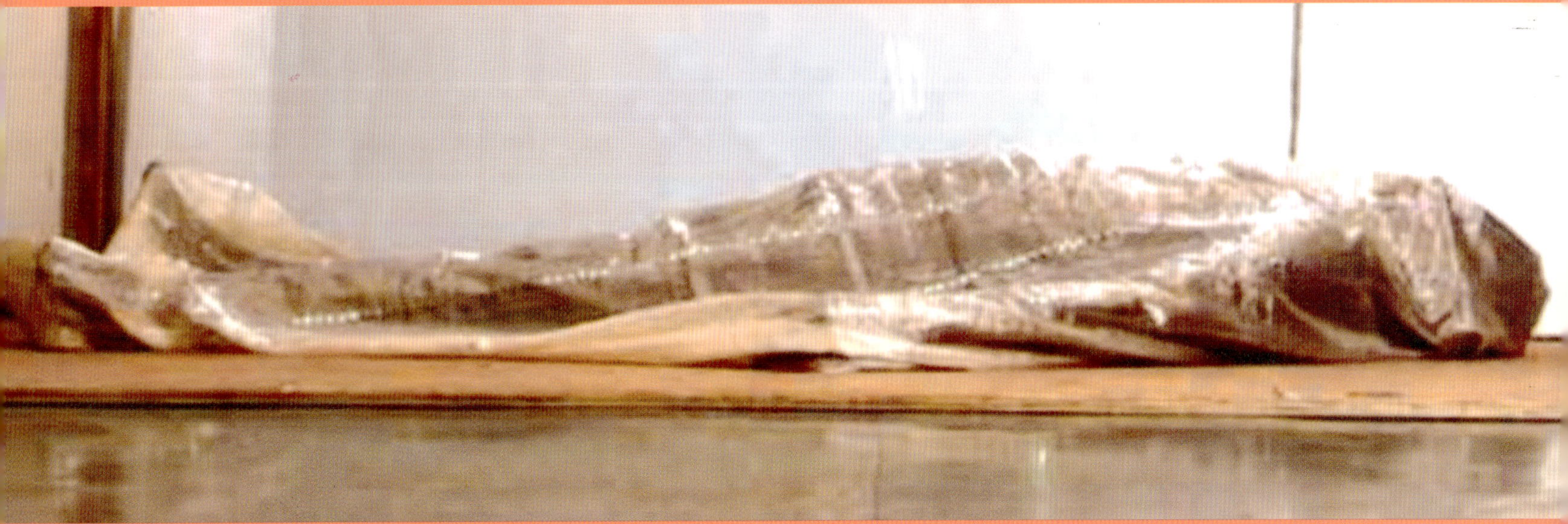

Lazarus
183 x 91x 91 cm. Cast latex, fabric and sequins.
2005

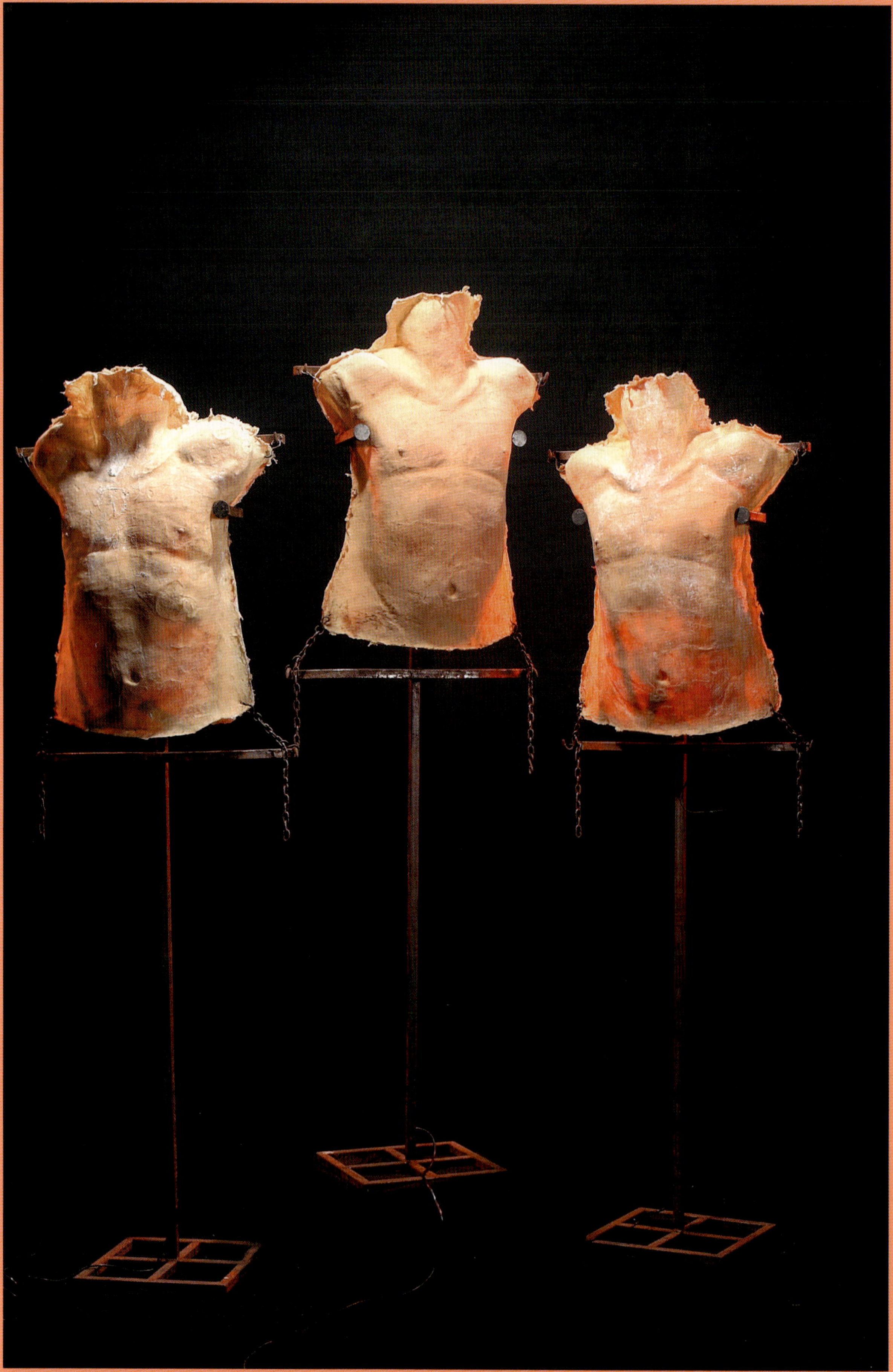

Three Wise Men
Variable. Latex, mild steel and argon lights.
2002

The Dancer in the Tomb: Jehangir Jani's Transgressive Gesture

Ranjit Hoskote

Jehangir Jani's recent installation strikes us with decisive emphasis; despite assuming the form of sophisticated theatre, it conveys the charge of raw affront. Unlike many installations produced in India – which serve as illustrations of political intent rather than as provocations making visible the totems and taboos of society, its invisible access codes, and oppressive hierarchies – here is an art-work that exposes the artist to a genuine measure of risk. In what does the specific risk of JJ's work reside? Not only does it oblige us to face the discomfiting reality of death, and the uncertainty of resurrection, but it also throws our pieties into confusion by interweaving death with beauty, the elegiac with the sensuous. Above all, as I will argue in this brief reflection, JJ enters the extraordinarily fraught territory of religious belief.

In what does the specific risk of JJ's work reside? Not only does it oblige us to face the discomfiting reality of death, and the uncertainty of resurrection, but it also throws our pieties into confusion by interweaving death with beauty, the elegiac with the sensuous.

In this public demonstration, he deploys gestures associated with burial rituals normally conducted in privacy. He draws on elements of Shi'ite ceremonial to create an iconography, defying the interdict against graven images in Islam. And so he comes, in several ways, into conflict with the mandates of the ethnic group and religion to which he belongs by birth. In contemporary India, its public life strained by civil dissension and unrest generated by politicised religiosity, only the mad or the brave would adopt such a position – or perhaps the Sufi, who knows that the paths of revelation are often mapped through the terrain of seeming lunacy.

As we part the blinds and step into the installation, we find ourselves in an environment suggestive of a mausoleum: a body lies shrouded on a table; columns of severed hands mount guard near it; bare torsos address us, skewered on stands; and we are struck by a grid of 92 pink, glowing night-lamps that resemble miniature TV screens. We attune ourselves to the beat of drums; gradually, we realise that they are the rhythmic sounds of ritual breast-beating. JJ's installation is dramatised between two intimately related, but opposed figures: Lazarus and Anarkali, the mummy-wrapped corpse, waiting in the tomb to be delivered back to life, and the vivacious court dancer, chained inside a tomb, watching as the mason lays the last bricks that will choke off her breath. We never meet the rotting corpse and the

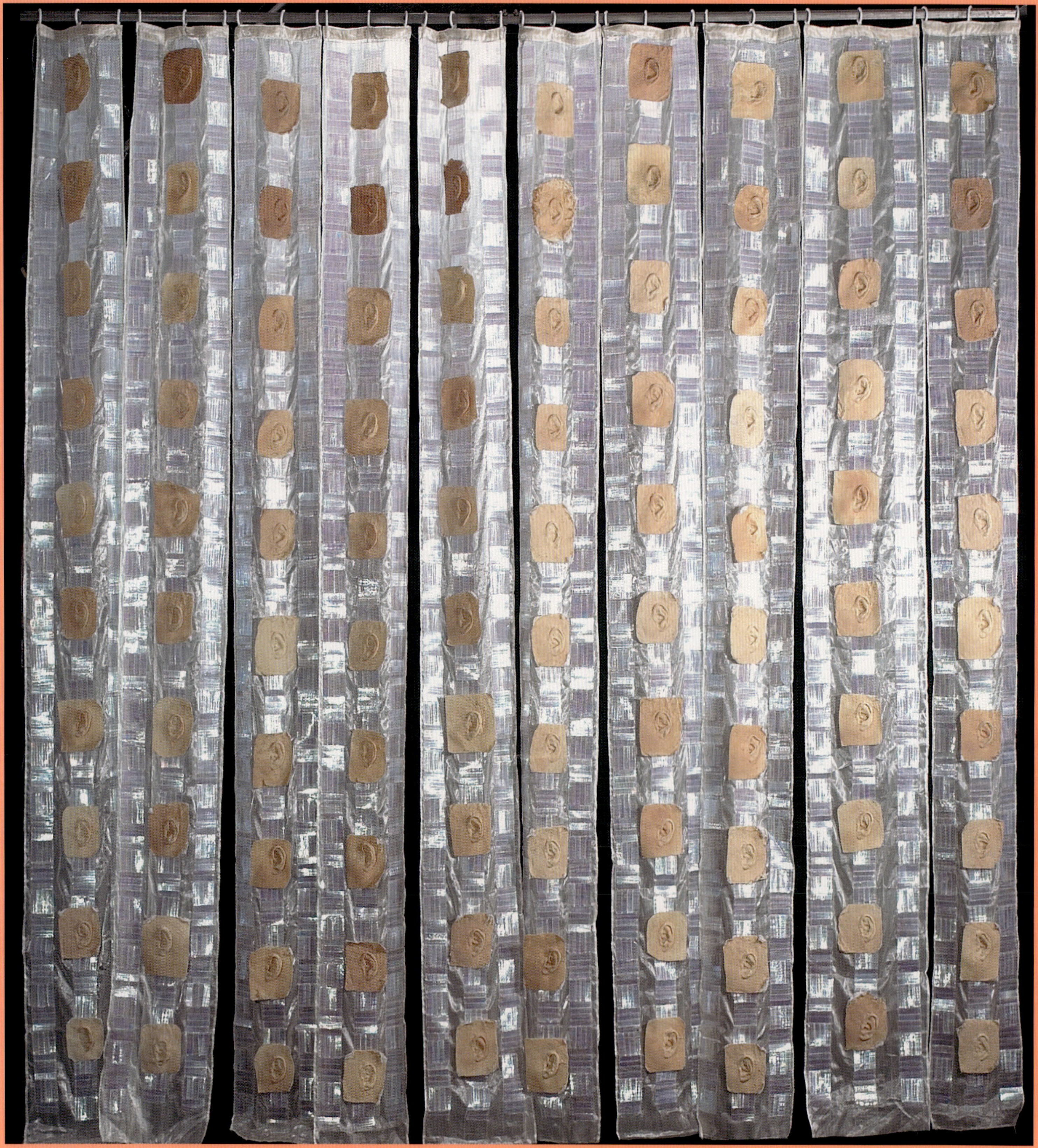

Curtain of a 100 Names
274 x 274 cm. Latex, resin, fabric and sequins.
2002

gilt-spangled dancer as Exhibits A and B: they are implied presences, tropes, allusions traced through colour, sound, and body-cast.

Our eyes get used to the subtleties of JJ's light arrangements. The tomb reveals itself as a site of meditation signed with the flourish of the carnival. The trophies of mortality are everywhere, but held in counterpoint by the seductive. We turn, and find that the blinds through which we entered are studded with multiple casts of the artist's ear: by implication, JJ extends our awareness of the sensorium beyond vision and touch; he also encodes a playful reference to the mythology of the artist legislating violence on himself. JJ's focus is the body subjected to the violence of mutilation and betrayal: the vulnerability of this sacred token of existence is tragically echoed by the fragmentation of the invocation to God, written in Gujarati rather than Arabic calligraphy, in the 92 components of the light piece, which can be switched on and off by the viewers. Again, these fragments are simulacra, details photographed from a watercolour inscribed with the prayer.

JJ's focus is the body subjected to the violence of mutilation and betrayal: the vulnerability of this sacred token of existence is tragically echoed by the fragmentation of the invocation to God...

Jehangir Jani's installation demands nothing less than that we abandon our aesthetic preconceptions about the universality of art. His installation derives its special, unnerving, subversive power, not from its aspiration to universality of meaning, but precisely from its rejection of the vacuity of generic abstractions. It insists on the import of a specific religious and ethnic milieu, and the history of the development of a private self in such an ethos. In the aftermath of the genocidal violence enacted against the Muslim minority in Gujarat, during March 2002, by Hindu pogromists, the portents of JJ's installation are unmistakable. He invests the artwork with his pain and sense of betrayal as an Indian of Gujarati Dawoodi Bohra ethnicity; he layers it with the realisation of outsiderness forced upon him. And yet, in another swift slippage, the various elements of his work are threaded together by the joyous shade of pink, a reference to his alternate sexuality.

JJ takes up his place in an adversarial isolation; but this is not the melodramatic stance of the romantic. Rather, his is the transgressive gesture of continuous resistance, which invites others to share in the opposition to the various aggressions promoted in the cause of pure religious, regional, and sexual identities.

Mumbai, September 2002

Essay for the catalogue of Jehangir Jani's exhibition, 'Lazarus'; The Fine Art Resource / Jehangir Art Gallery in Mumbai

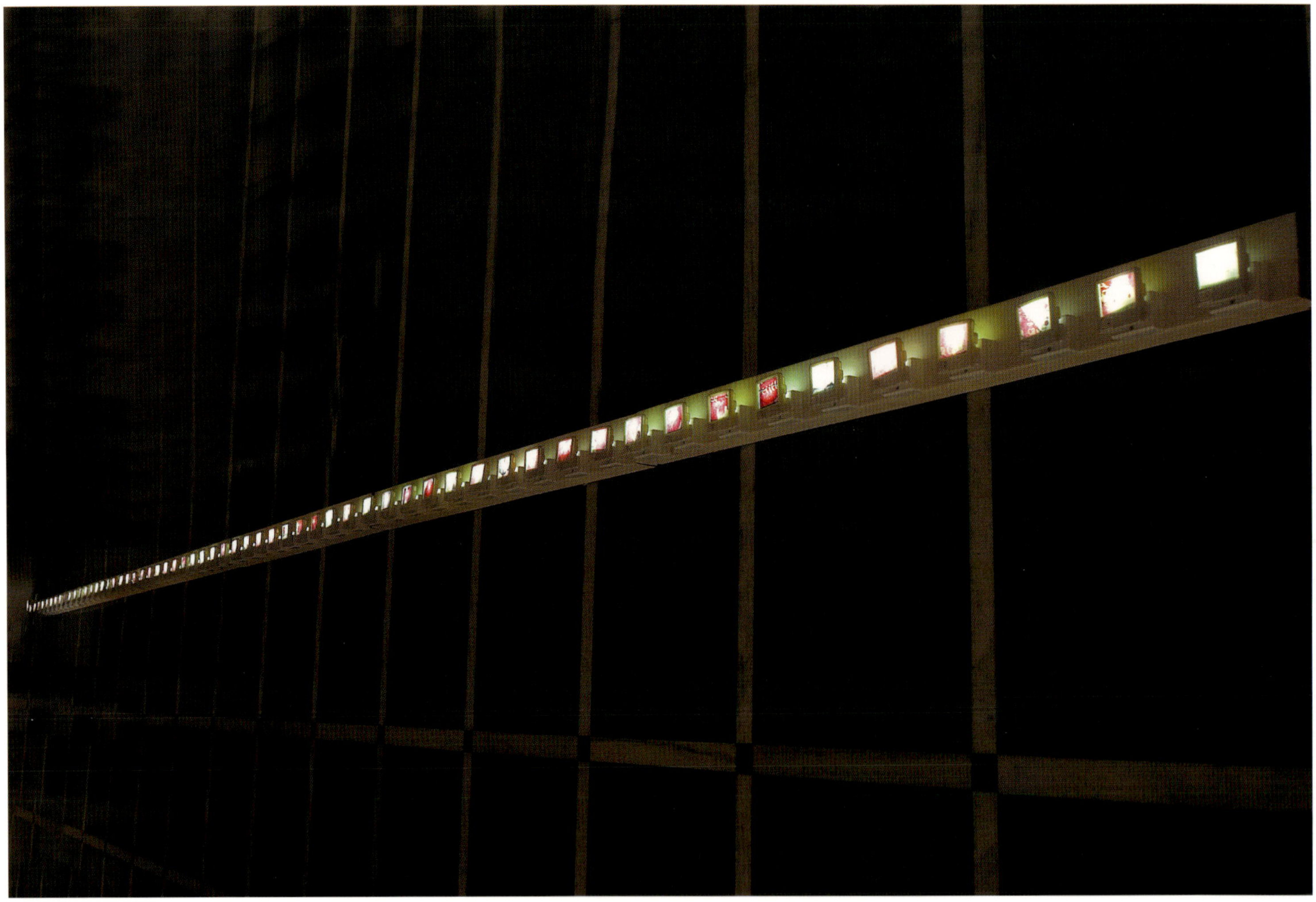

100 Eyes of Karim
Variable. Argon lights, rubber sheet, chip board and translites.
2002

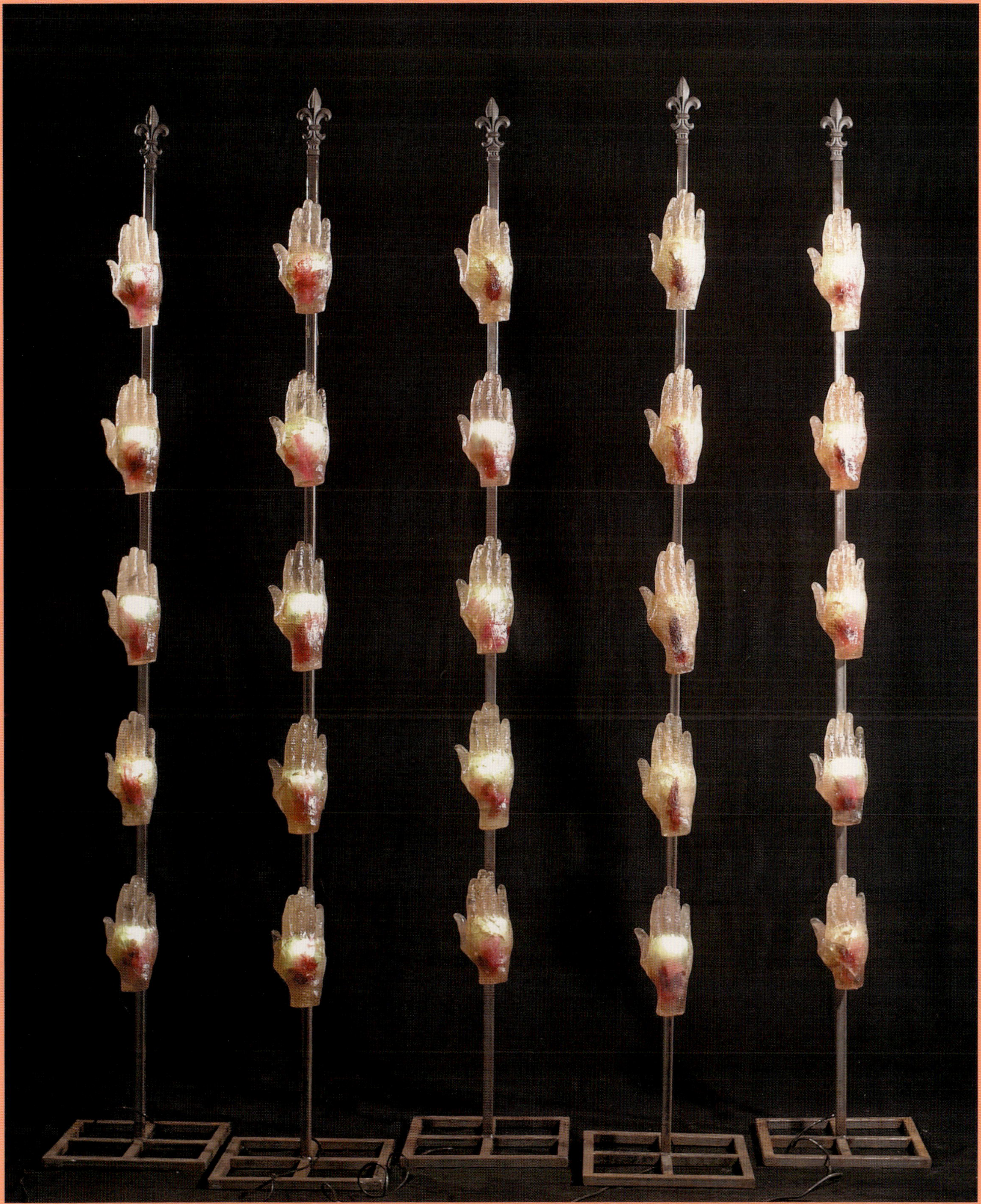

The Five Faithful
183 x 183 x 30 cm. Resin, feathers argon lights and mild steel.
2005

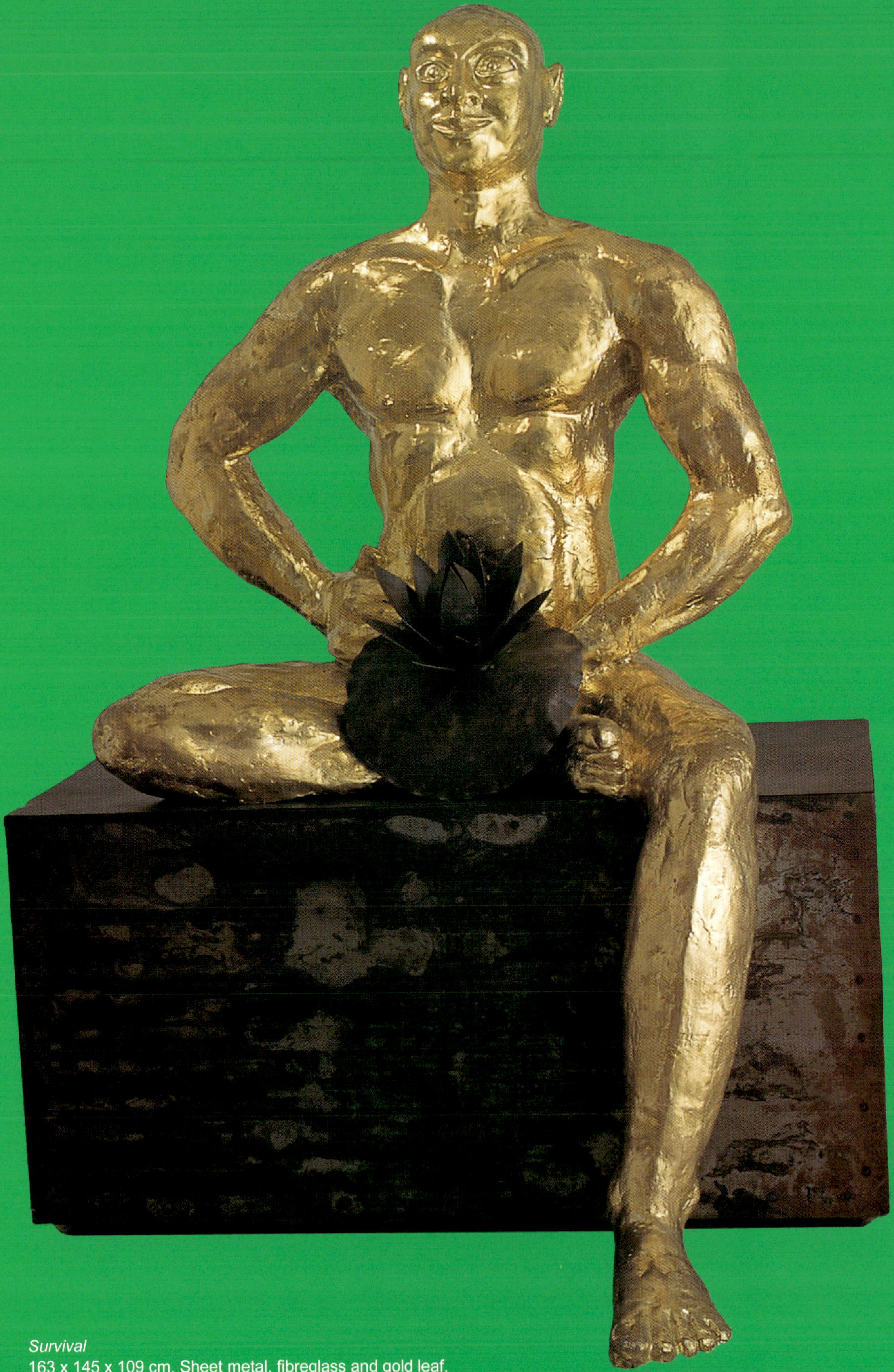

Survival
163 x 145 x 109 cm. Sheet metal, fibreglass and gold leaf.
2000

RELIGIOUS SCORES, NEW-AGE TECHNO CULTURES AND MUSEAL TALES

Nancy Adajania

...The same museal understanding of the devices of the new art is present in Jehangir Jani's sculptures: treating the space of the gallery as a space where the museum is both created and deconstructed, subverting the norms of permanence, security and authority of meaning.

By astutely recreating a museum ethos for his figural sculptures, JJ mocks the whole business of museum display: the high-cultural commodity with its classicism, conservatism and monoculturalism. The clues of alternative modes of being are inserted into this: alternative sexuality, alternative perception of the male body, readings of fertility and virility myths, and androgyny in place of macho heroism.

For instance, he uses the museal logic of serving the past as an exoticised fragment separated from its original cultural and historical context in Passion (the story of the bull and the horn); note the chipped nose and armless torso, the figure set on the pedestal. The twist in this phallo-centric tale comes from the fact that Jehangir Jani turns the logic of fragmented display into his own principle of construction – an abstract poetry of detachment through which he tells his own modern fables of sexual transgression and cultural identity...

Mumbai, October 2005

Extract from: Nancy Adajania, '*Auf dem Weg zu einer neuen folkloristischen Imagination*/ Towards A New Folkloric Imagination', in Gerald Matt, Angelika Fitz and Michael Woergoetter, eds., *Kapital und Karma: Aktuelle Positionen indischer Kunst/ Capital and Karma: Recent Positions in Indian Art* (Kunsthalle Wien/ Hatje Cantz Verlag: Vienna/ Ostfildern-Ruit, 2002).

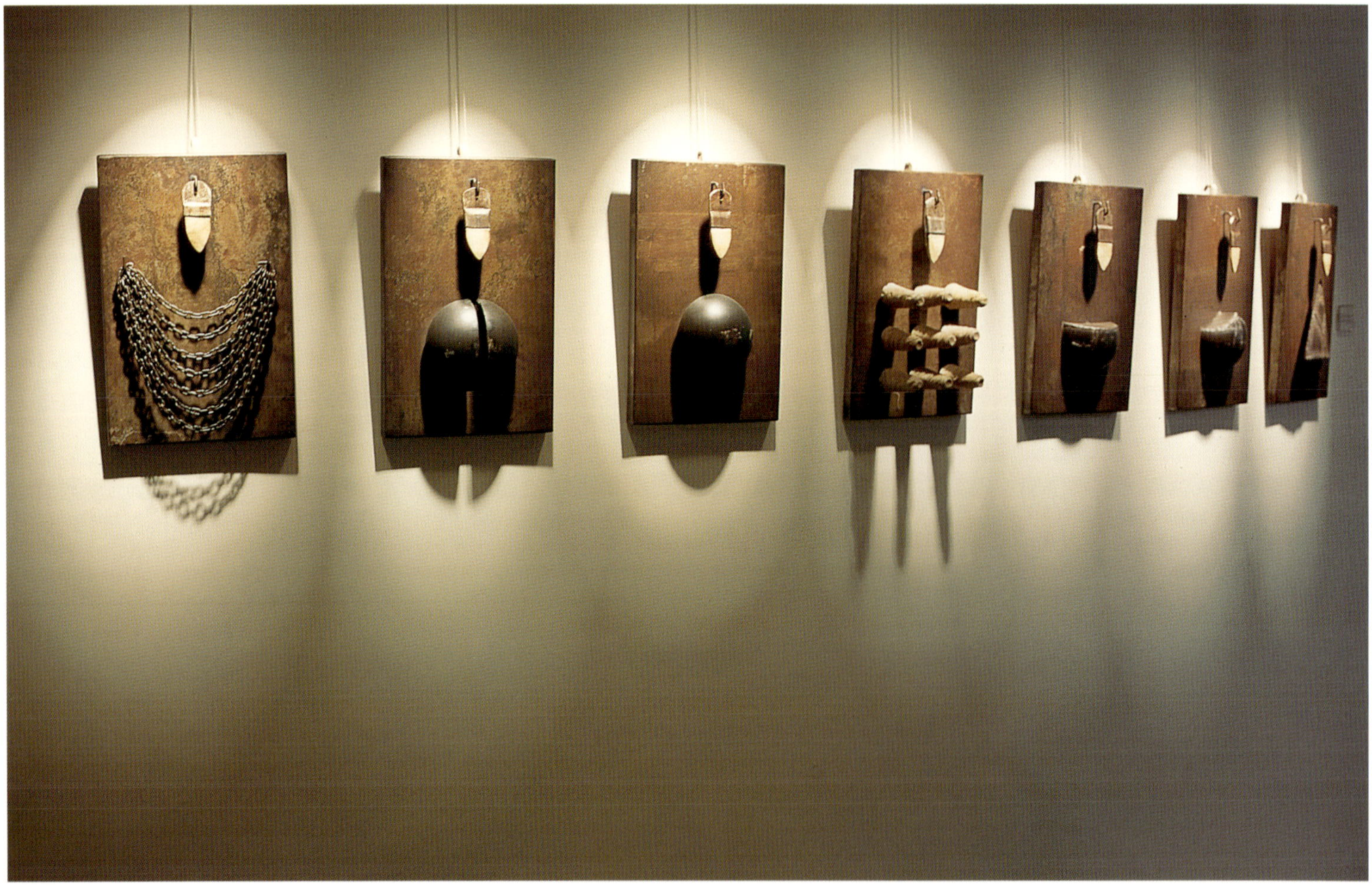

Seven Stations
46 x 31 x 10 cm each. Sheet metal and ceramic.
2000

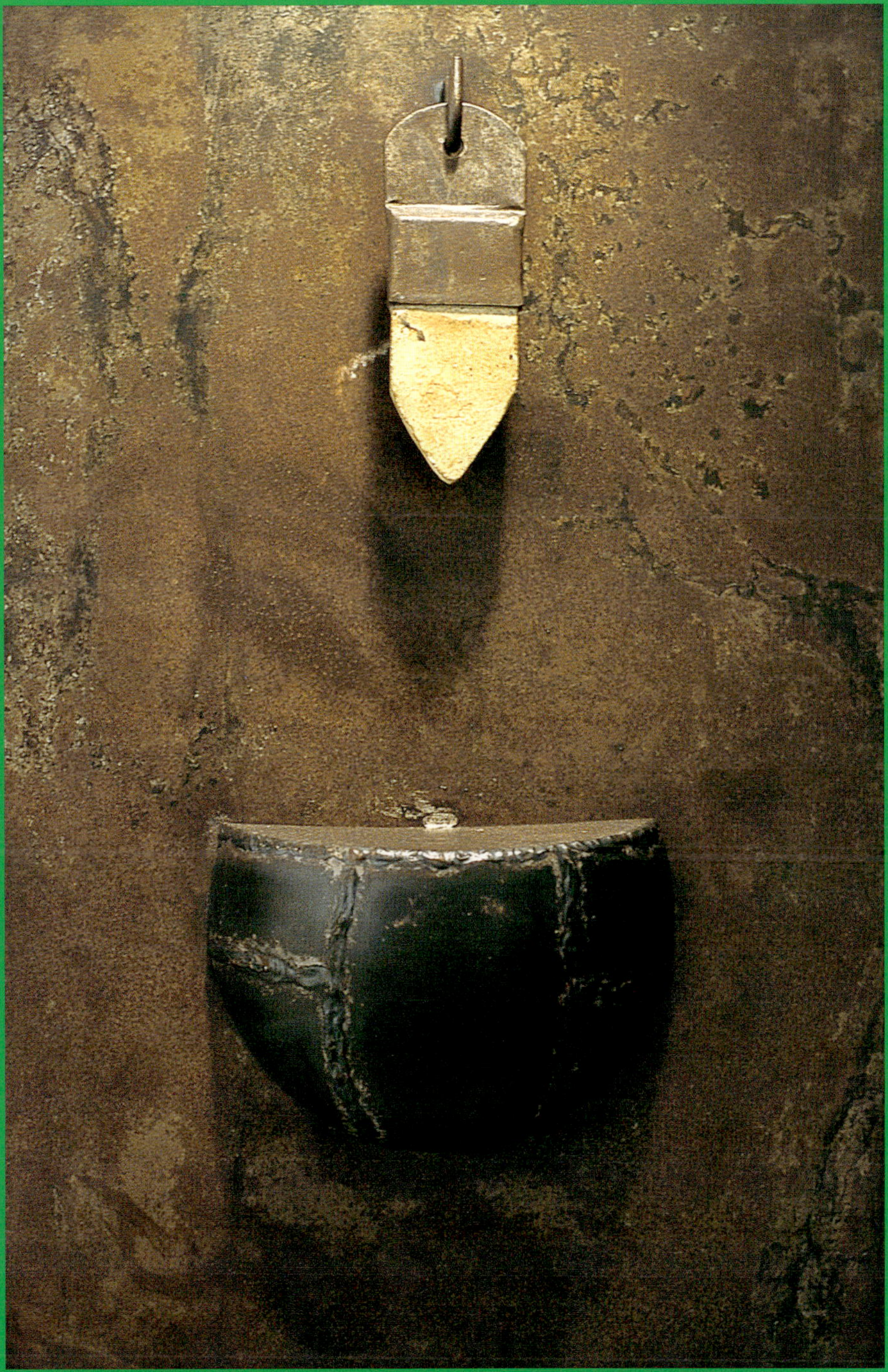

Seven Stations
Detail, 46 x 31 x 10 cm. Sheet metal and ceramic.
2000

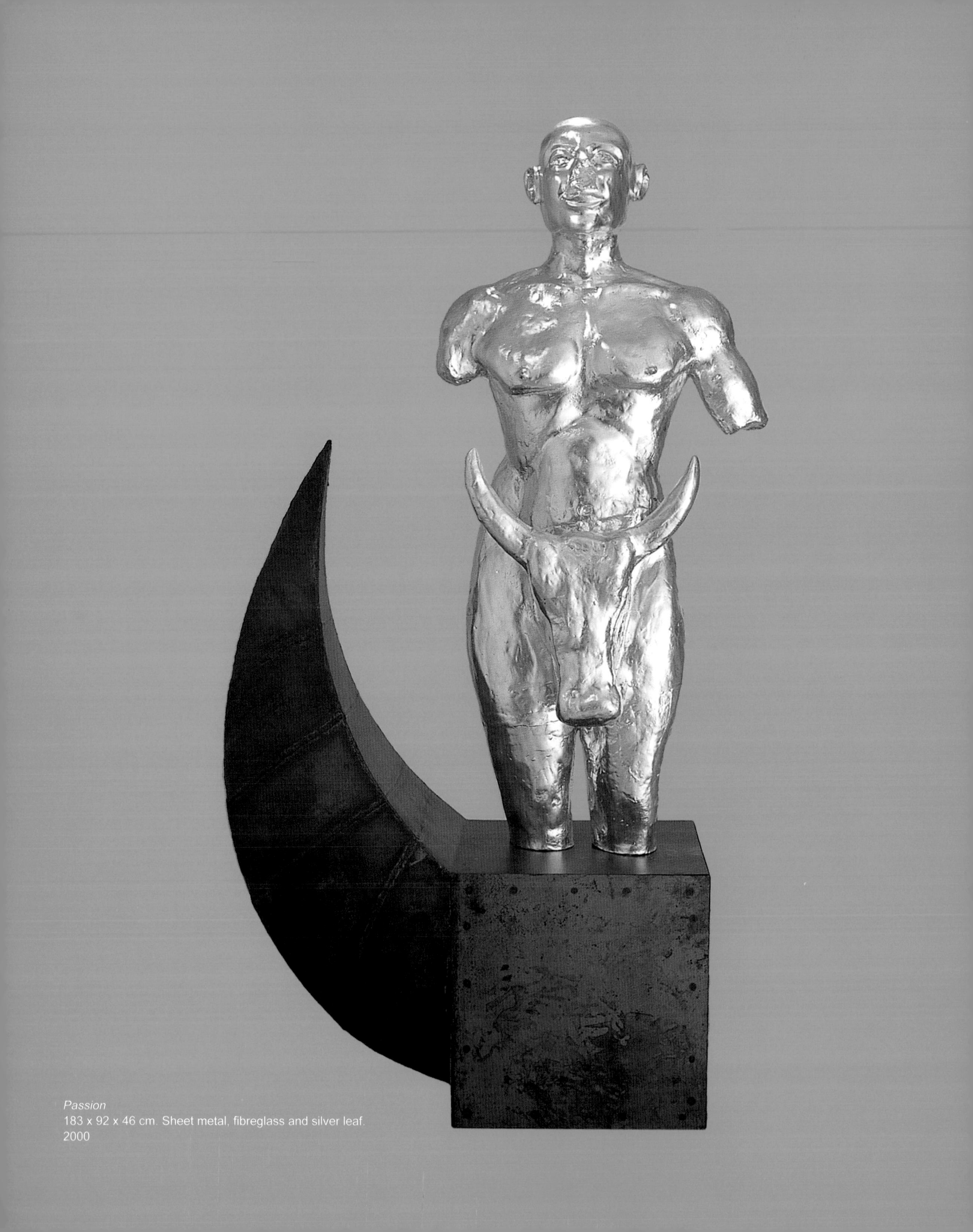

Passion
183 x 92 x 46 cm. Sheet metal, fibreglass and silver leaf.
2000

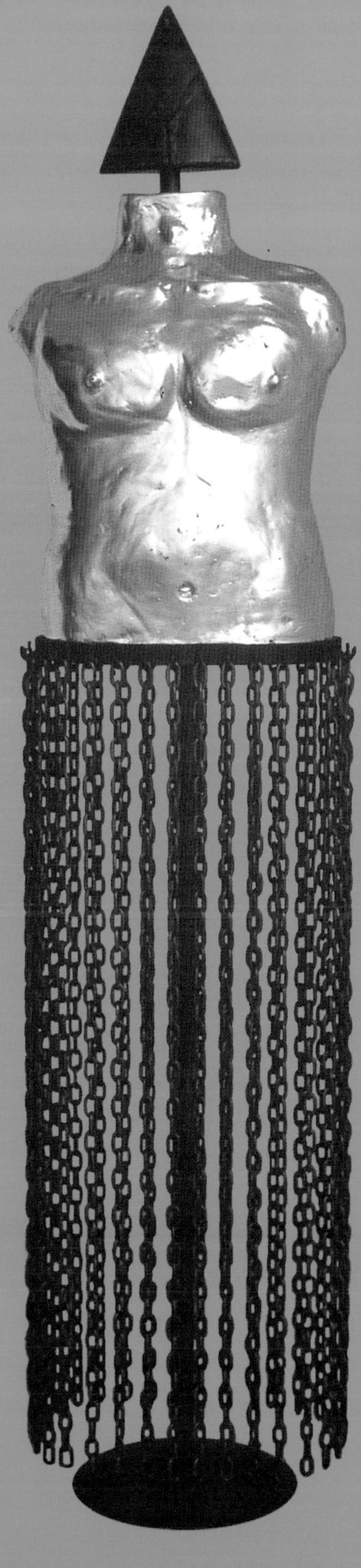

Agony
183 x 38 x 20 cm. Mild steel, fibreglass and silver leaf.
2000

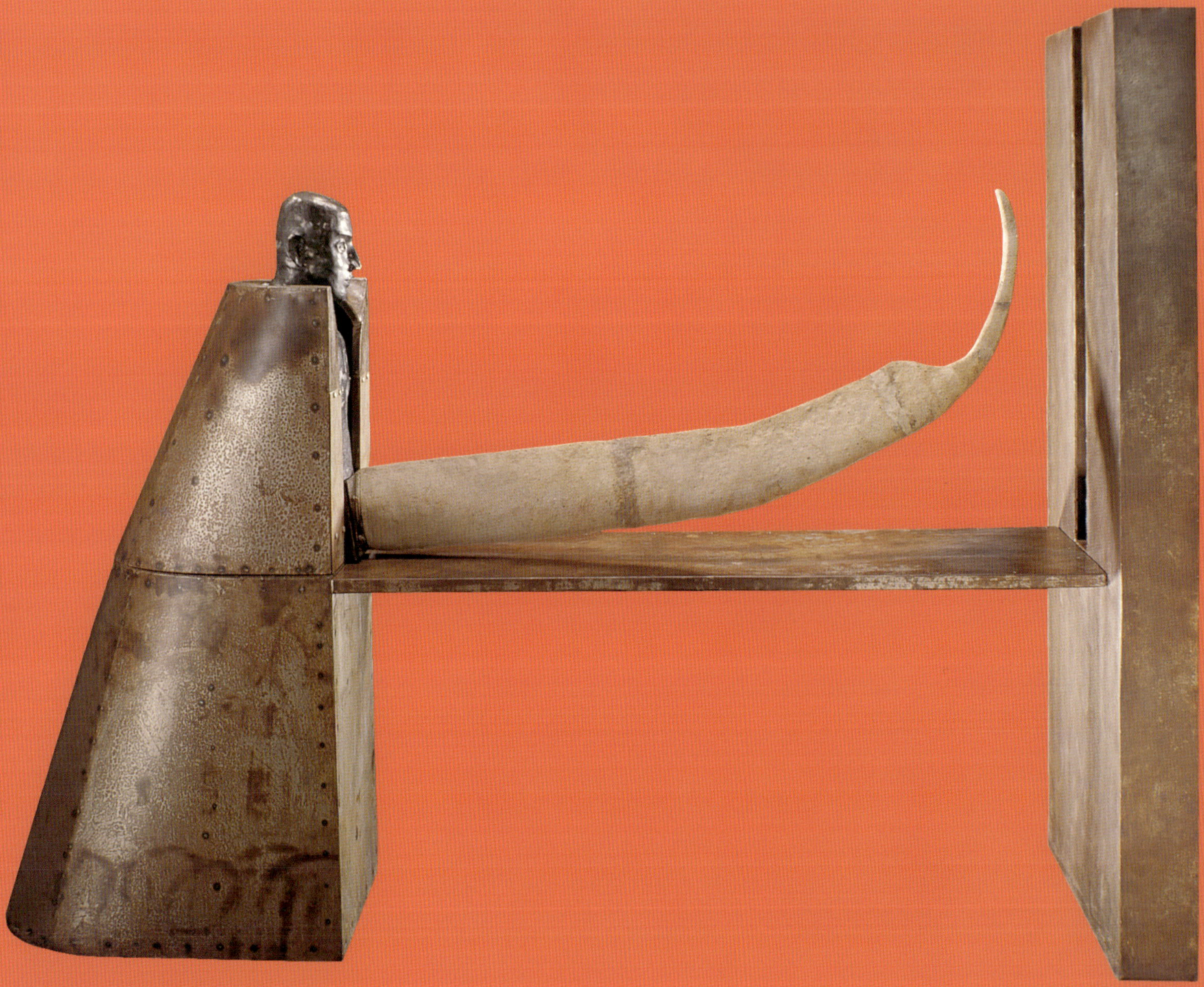

QUEEN NUR, His Wand and the Wall
183 x 244 x 91 cm. Ceramic and steel metal.
1998

MARKED BY RESTRAINT

Girish Shahane

Jehangir Jani's protagonists inhabit a Foucaltian world, where desire and power face off without any apparent mediatory possibilities. And some of the titles of his work in *Faerie Tales…A Re-Look (CHakka, CHakka, CHakka, CHakka, CHakka, CHakka; Naked Flowers/Pansies)* themselves hint at an immediate response on the part of the artist to the slings and arrows of convention. But JJ's creative effort, a parallel to Foucault's authorial voice, is altogether more considered than those in your face titles, or the first shock of facing his outrageously phallic constructions, might lead us to believe.

JJ's characters – trapped, manacled, racked – are restrained from journeying to the untravelled world which gleams through the arch of experience, but we, the spectators, can move beyond our initial shock to the more subtle details apparent in his work. The stoic countenances that the artist has crafted, some of them modeled on his own face, counter any attempt to place his work in a kinetic-rebellious category. While these shackled characters cannot transcend their situation, they seem to posses, like Sisyphus in Camus' vision, an awareness, a consciousness of their state.

Satre considered Camus' view too dark to be genuinely existentialist, and the consciousness JJ's figures possess also seems a small compensation for the tortures they are subjected to, for the restraints that have marked, scarred, mutilated them, for the immobility which is a sign of their helplessness. The clay body, of desire, is overmatched by the metal of a soul, of society…

Mumbai, September 1998

Excerpt from an essay for the catalogue of 'Faerie Tales…A Re-Look'

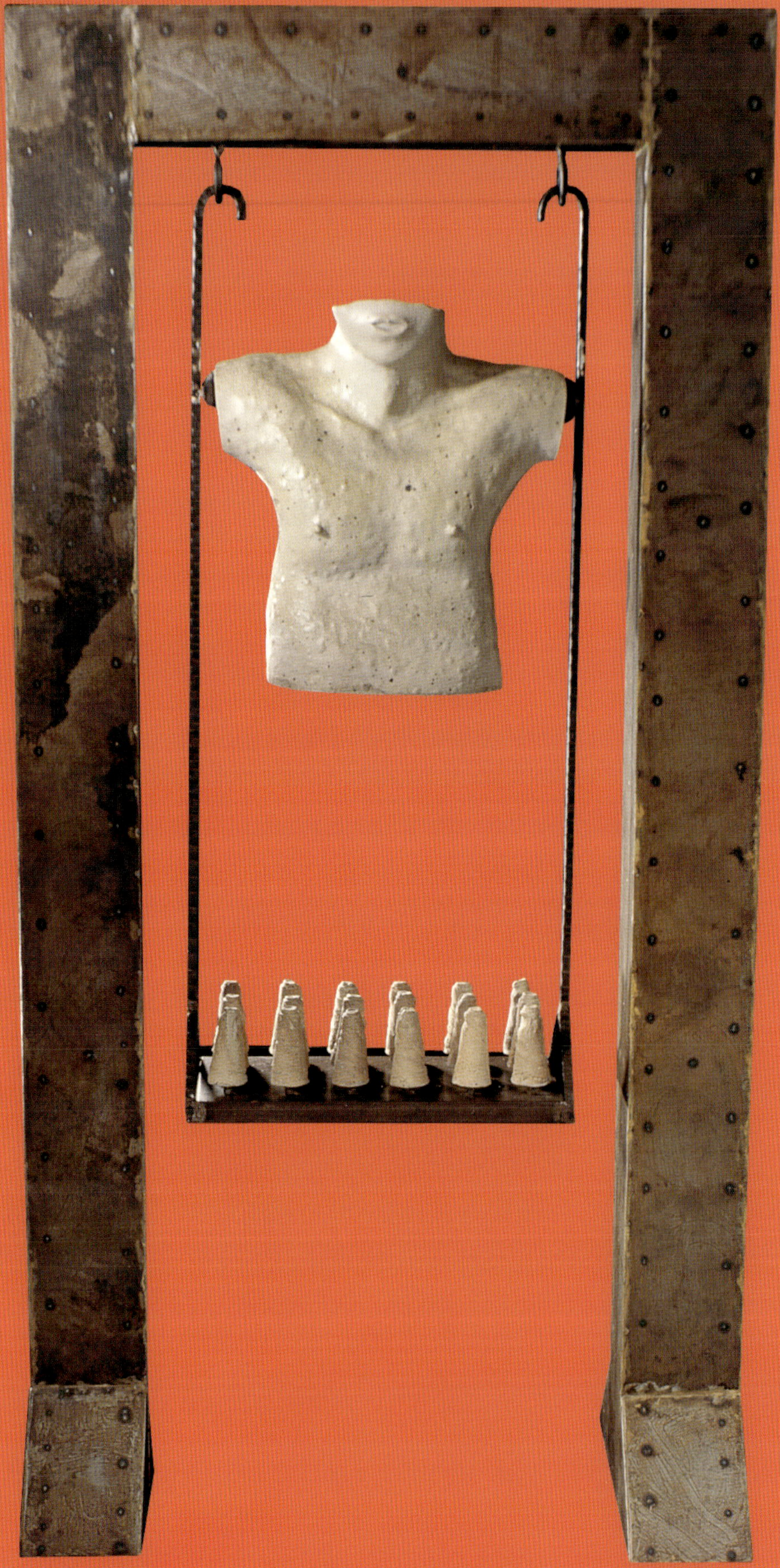

SISSY/Phus's Swing
183 x 91 cm. Ceramic and steel metal.
1998

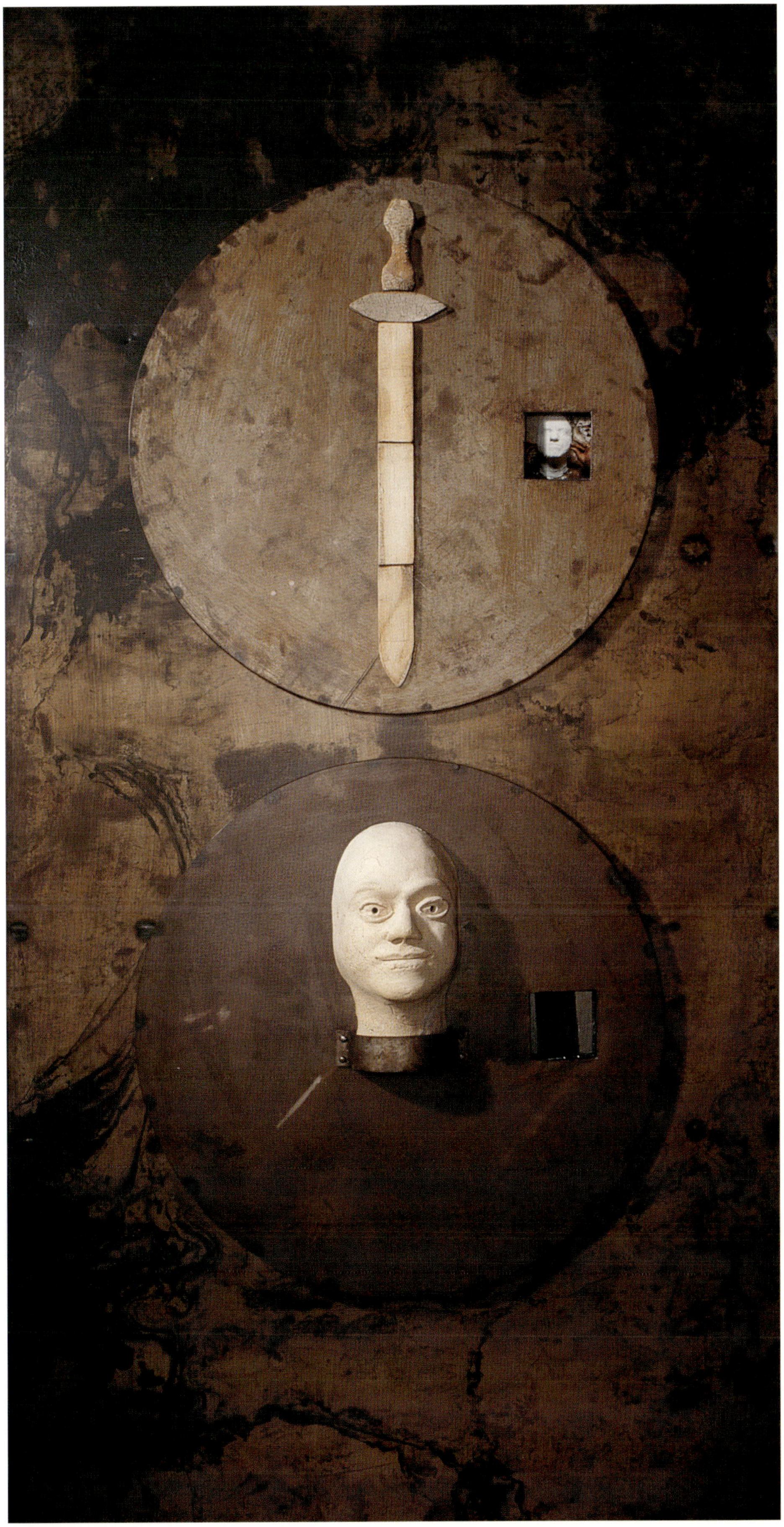

MOOSA/isa
183 x 91 cm. Ceramic and steel metal.
1998

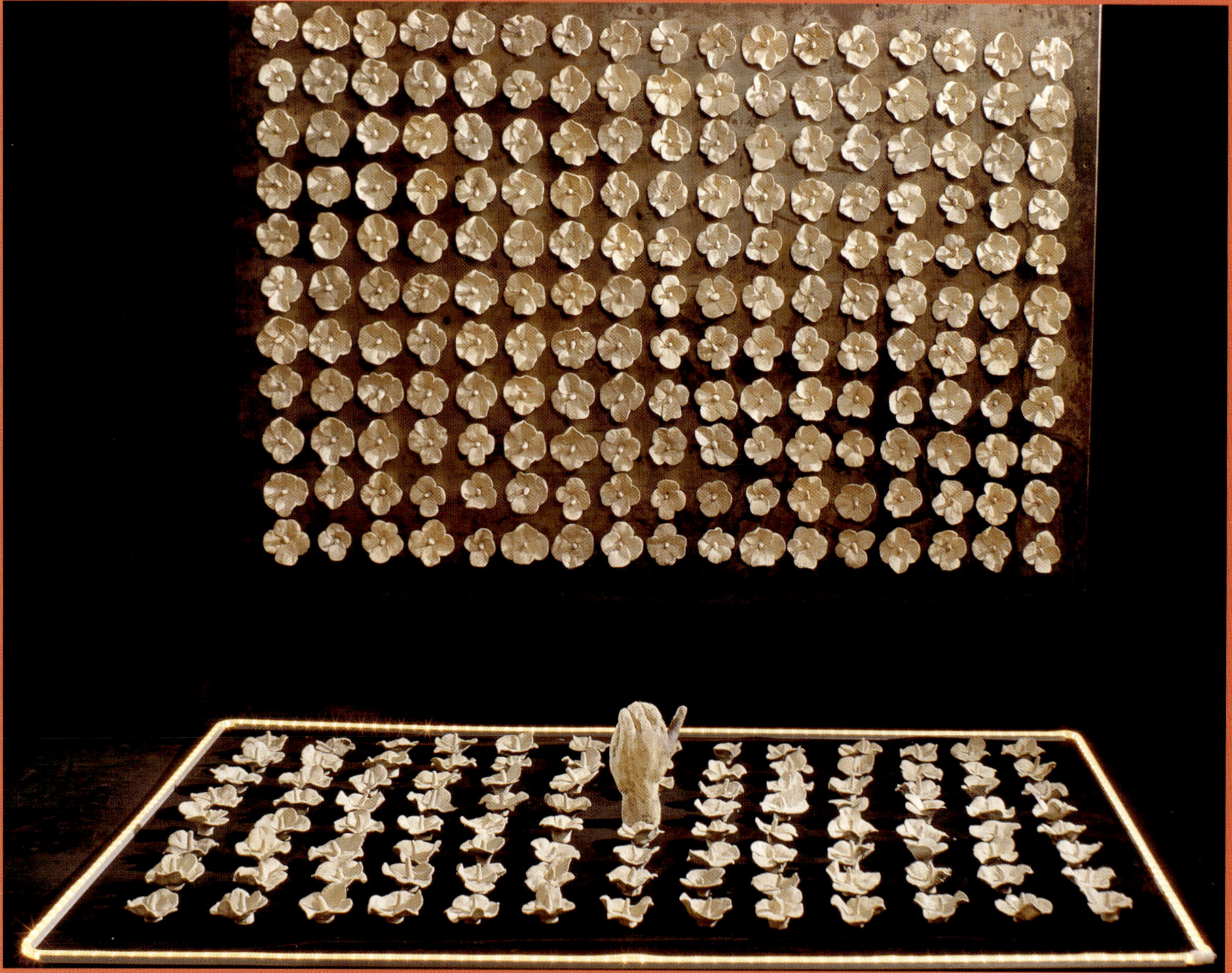

NAKED Flowers/Pansies
183 x 122 x 183 x 122 cm. Ceramic and steel metal.
1998

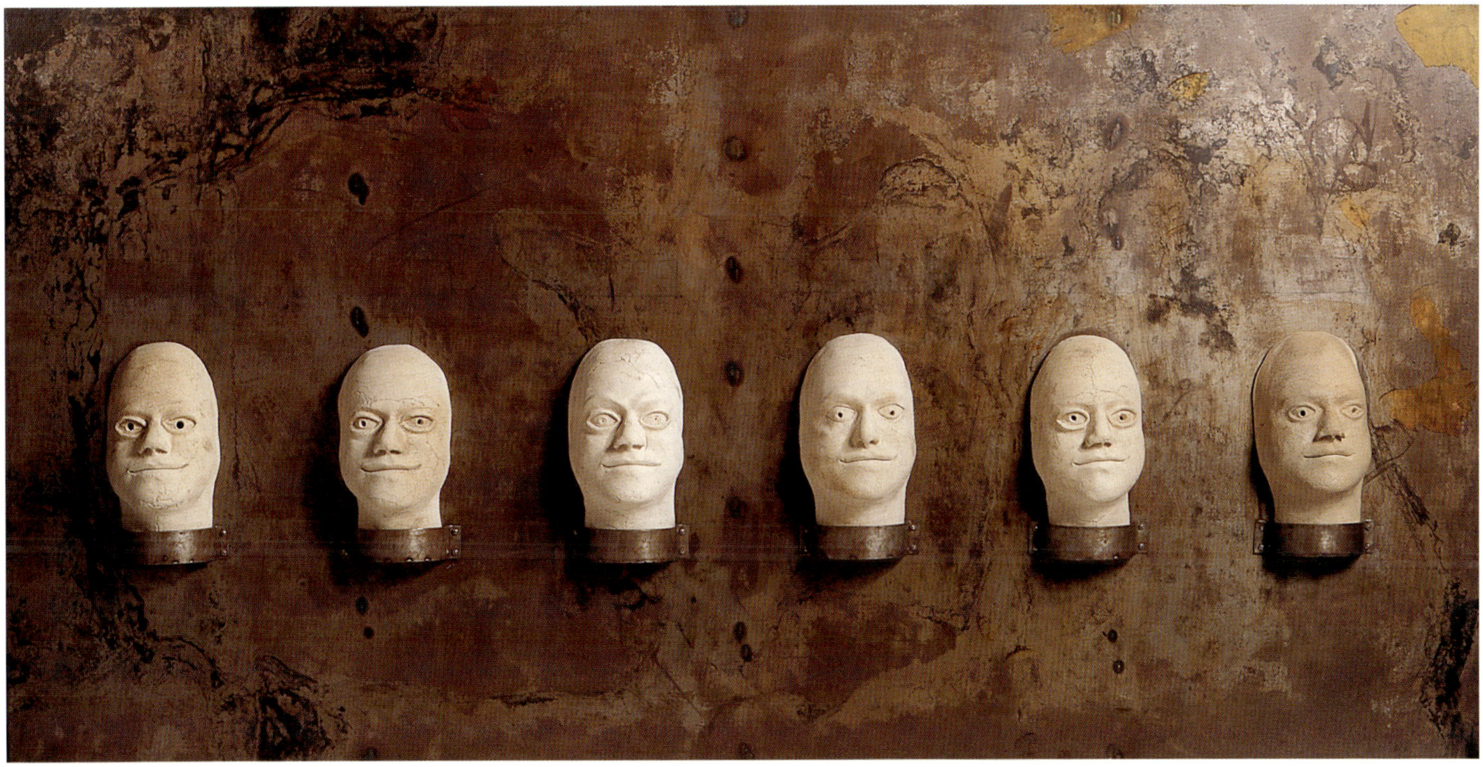

CHakka, CHakka, CHakka, CHakka, CHakka, CHakka
183 x 91 cm. Ceramic and steel metal.
1998

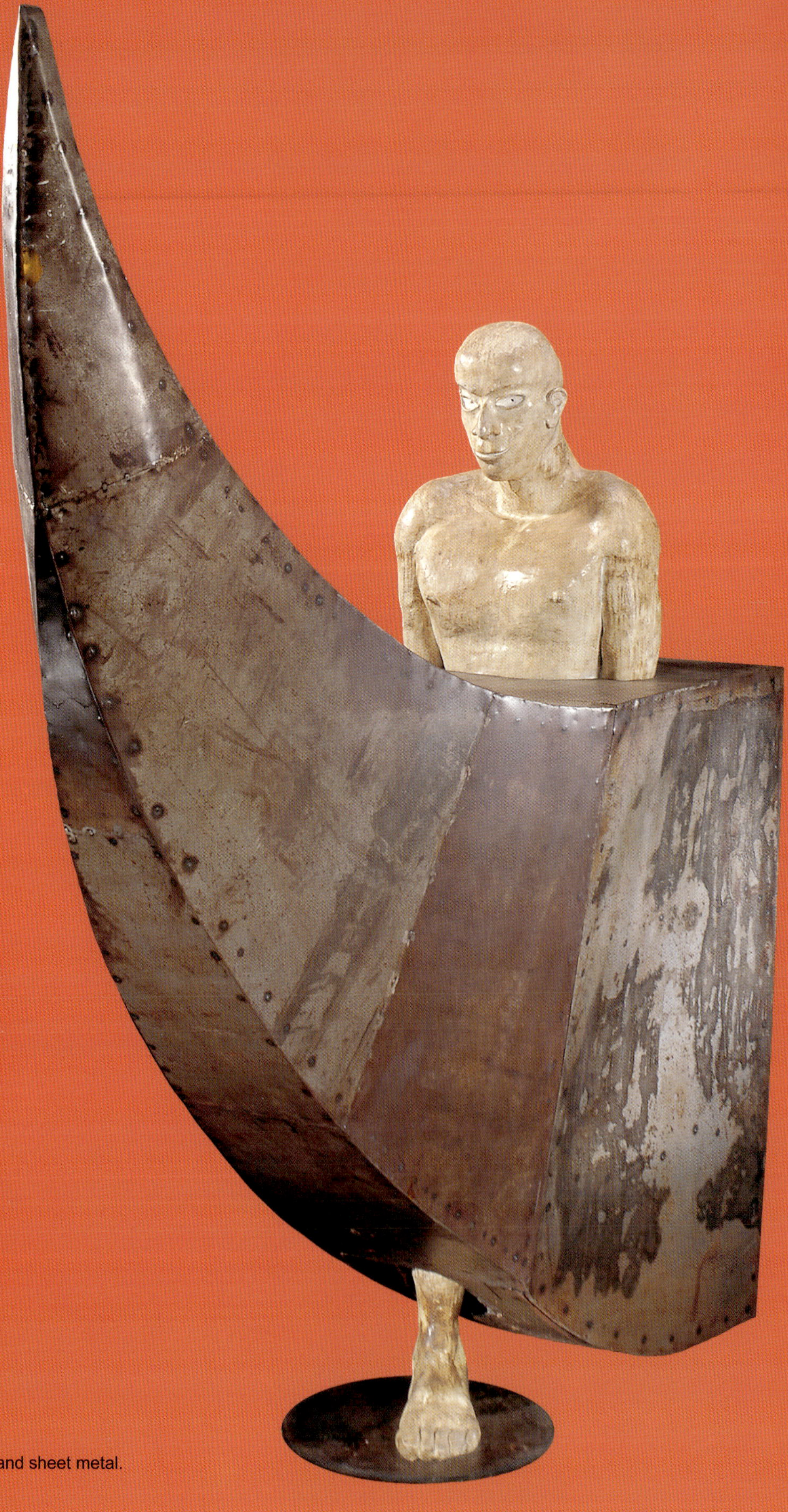

NU'S Boat
244 x 213 x 61 cm. Ceramic and sheet metal.
1998

Nu's Boat
244 x 214 x 61 cm. Ceramic and sheet metal.
1998

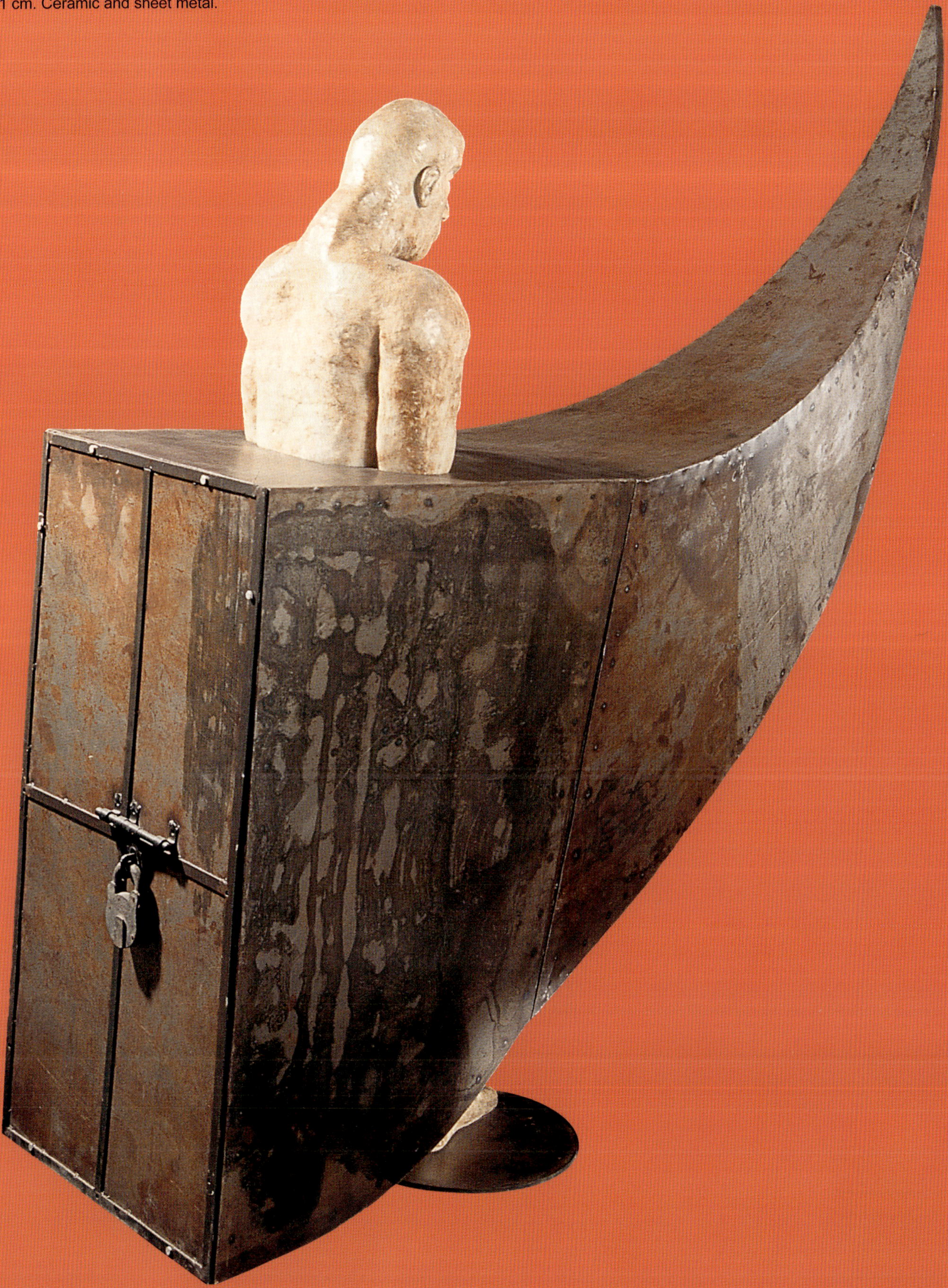

CANVAS

THE OTHERNESS OF THE SELF

JEHANGIR JANI'S RECENT PAINTINGS:

Ranjit Hoskote

During the last decade, Jehangir Jani has extended his artistic practice in a variety of directions: he has experimented with sculpture and assemblage, investigating the expressive possibilities of ceramic, sheet metal and steel; he has committed himself to installation and inter-media works, as well as to collaborative performances; he has developed figurative suites in watercolour. Through these forms, in each of which he has played between declarative candour and oblique allusion, JJ has involved his viewers in an unfolding drama of the narrative self: a self that performs its predicaments, conflicts and irresolutions through a sequence of symbolic gestures, asides, half-veiled self-portraits. In the process, JJ has demonstrated himself to be a protean artist dedicated to the exploration of expressive strategies, rather than motivated by any desire to master a single image-making method, or a constraining fixity of style. Diverse as they may appear, however, JJ's formal departures are elaborated around a central concern: the male figure cast, not as the defiant hero who overcomes the conspiracies of circumstance, but as the survivor who endures the wounds of choice, as well as the stigmata imposed on him by society. If his works have been veined by a certain romanticism, it is one that marks the isolation of the reluctant martyr, not the flamboyance of the decadent.

Significantly, the only medium that JJ renounced during his decade of experimentation was the one with which he began his career: oil on canvas. Perhaps he felt impelled to break out of the constraints of this historical matrix and the elevated antecedents that it presumes, which are so impressive as sometimes to become oppressive to a contemporary practitioner. Perhaps he wished to escape the weight of the formal necessities that the medium brought with it, and to improvise with informal, heterodox, and playable materials instead. At any event, the present exhibition marks his return to his starting point after a hiatus of eleven years. He has not, of course, merely picked up the medium where he left it off. He returns to it transformed and fortified by his extremely productive excursions into other media. His concerns with the figure, with the body and self it incarnates, have deepened. He has acquired a flexibility of approach through his treatment of diverse material resources. He has acquired sensitivity to the social semiotics of the image, by reading

JJ's formal departures are elaborated around a central concern: the male figure cast, not as the defiant hero who overcomes the conspiracies of circumstance, but as the survivor who endures the wounds of choice, as well as the stigmata imposed on him by society.

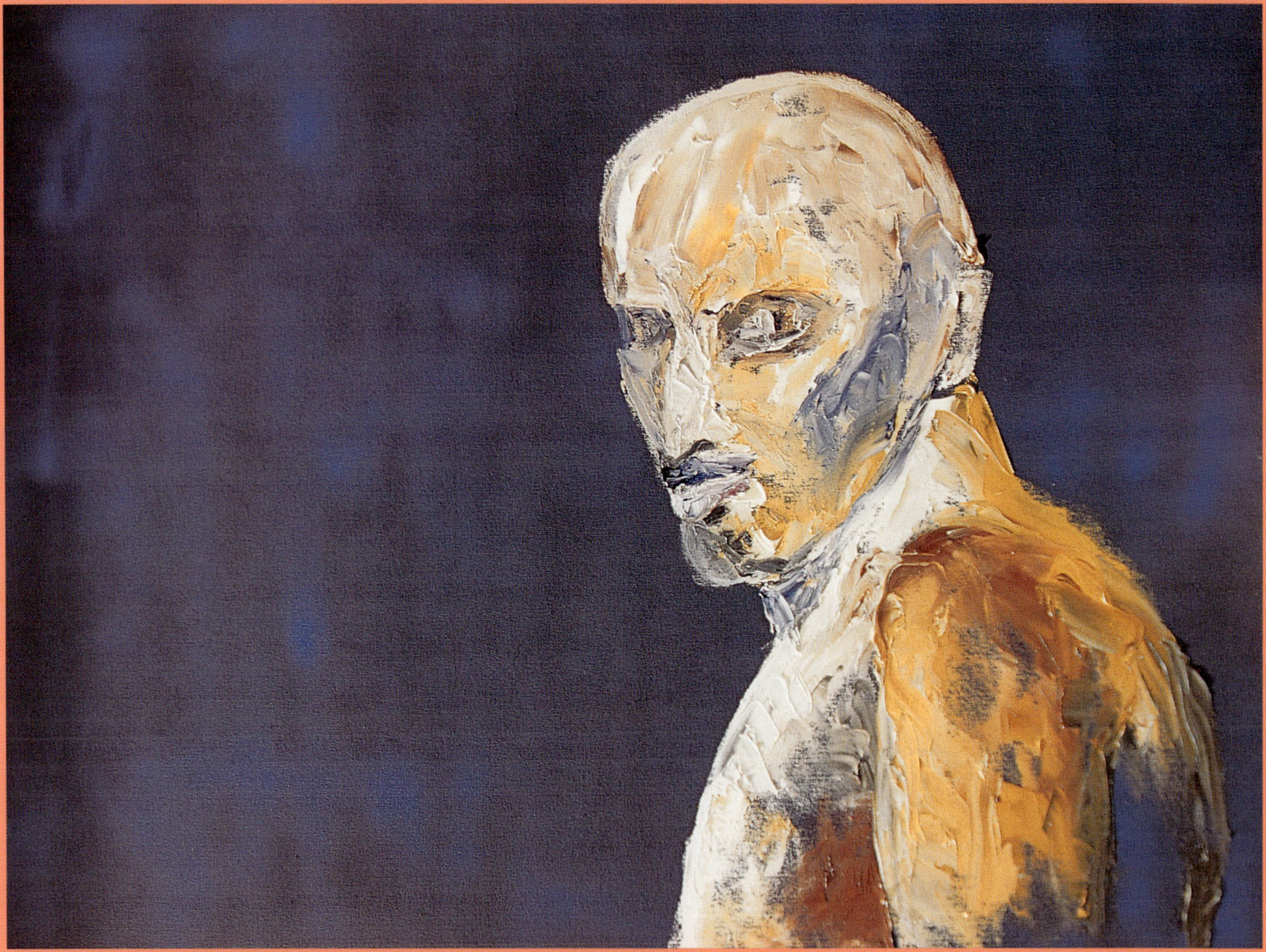

Untitled
92 x 122 cm. Oil and acrylic on canvas.
2005

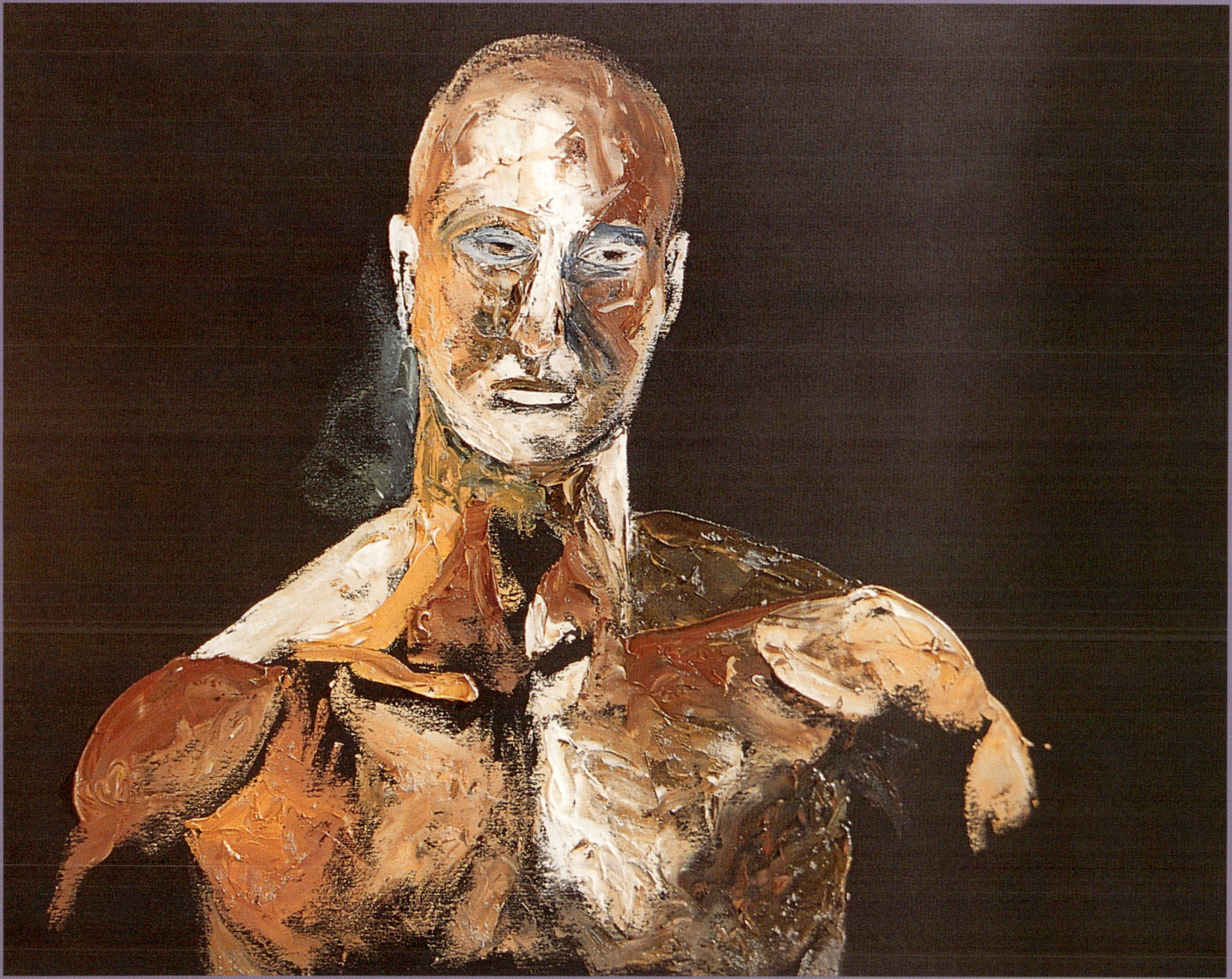

Untitled
92 x 122 cm. Oil and acrylic on canvas.
2005

Indeed, whether human or animal, many of these portraits function at some level as self-portraits, mythic surrogates for the self.

These figures seem to achieve the stillness of the eternal, as though memorialised on the wall of a cave and seen by torchlight; but we find them convincing only because they are quickened by the tremor of the ephemeral.

artworks in their theoretical and institutional contexts. As such, we view JJ's oils on the far side of a period of intense, and intensive, experiment: they display that paradoxical combination of nervous vitality and confident repose that distinguishes such a position.

Since the figure has always been central to JJ's elaborations – in painting and sculpture, installation and performance – he has studied its strengths and vulnerabilities, examined how it resists and survives its conditions, how it disintegrates. In these recent oils, he employs a black acrylic field as his stage, with a portrait or a group of figures set dramatically against it; or, in an alternative reading, emerging from it. The protagonists include both humans and animals: the head of a bull, a group of deer heads, and male torsos that approximate to self-portraiture. Indeed, whether human or animal, many of these portraits function at some level as self-portraits, mythic surrogates for the self. As in his sculptures, JJ's painted figures are powerfully contoured; the strokes of the palette knife are emphatically impasto, and the palette is uniform, consisting of ochre, burnt sienna, Naples yellow, and whites of varying intensity. With the artist, we dwell on loci of specific sensuous delight: the light on a shoulder blade, the flick-away gesture of an antler, the blunt curve of a bull's horn. He has shaped this suite of paintings with self-assured movements that wax in energy; and yet there is an apprehension, in them, of bodily changes and the insidious operation of time, of ageing and waning. These figures seem to achieve the stillness of the eternal, as though memorialised on the wall of a cave and seen by torchlight; but we find them convincing only because they are quickened by the tremor of the ephemeral. JJ's animal heads are imbued with an element of the totemic and the ritual, even in the moment of sacrifice and death; similarly, his human heads, torsos, and standing figures convey a hieratic presence that is shot through with vulnerability, an assurance shadowed by mortality.

At first glance, these images seem spare, austere, and cut away from all but the most ancient shamanic contexts. On closer examination, though, they yield several lineages of reference. Some of them allude to the artist's own stylised combination of deity and totemic animal, which echo the slyly votive popular iconography of Kalighat. Others rhyme with Joseph Beuys' early neo-shamanic animal drawings and watercolours, distinctively rendered in ferric chloride. Following these clues, we find ourselves inquiring further into the implied histories of the images that JJ conjures before us, the resonances they carry. The logic of these paintings commits them to retracing the male image at the intersection of several aesthetic and political trajectories, including formalism, idealisation, masculinity, and a gay

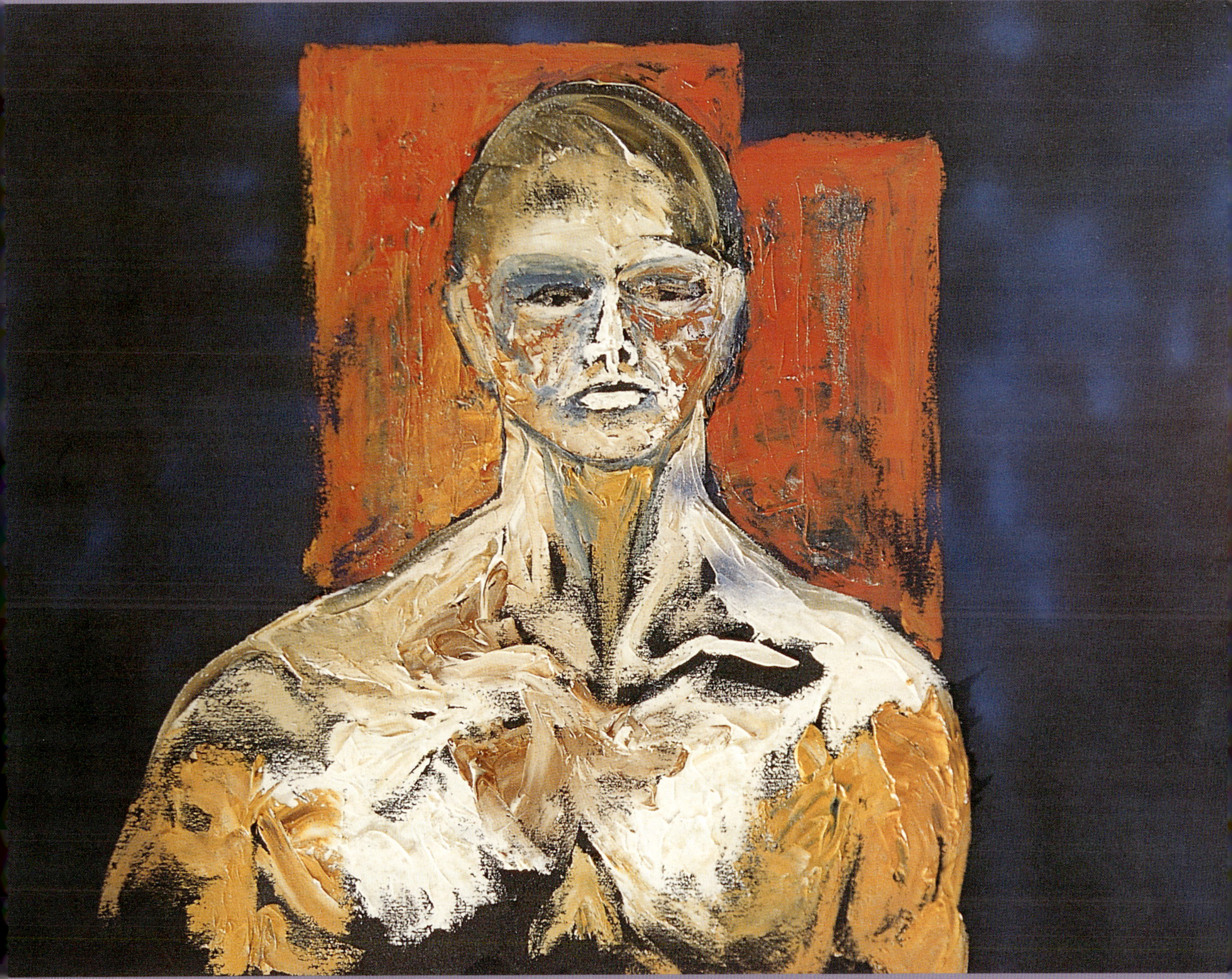

Untitled
122 x 92 cm. Oil and acrylic on canvas.
2005

The logic of these paintings commits them to retracing the male image at the intersection of several aesthetic and political trajectories, including formalism, idealisation, masculinity, and a gay identity.

These paintings are imprints, records of images that have burned themselves into the artist's consciousness, presences which he must confront on this threshold of transition as he re-shapes, yet again, his pictorial language.

identity. We may note that JJ's exemplars, while executing these paintings, include the refined priest-king of Mohenjo Daro and the elegant Bodhisattvas of Ajanta; the present works also constitute an act of homage to the radiant, otherworldly personae of Akbar Padamsee's stately Prophets series of 1960s.

Such references may well impart a deceptive simplicity of ambition to this suite of works. To the casual eye, it might appear that JJ desires little more than a nostalgic recovery of the monumental, even iconic, single image of modernist figuration. That course of action would merely have led the artist back to the formalist, universalist, and transcendentalist aesthetics that has been substantially abandoned by several generations of Indian artists, from the 1960s onward, including its early proponents. It is true that JJ's figures are not especially anchored in particularities here; and yet, neither do they float in a comfortably vague darkness. Let us look closely at these frames: the background is no incidental backcloth for the staging of the figure's magnificence. Instead, its darkness interpenetrates the figure, which is more trace than assertion of will; their contest is fought out through variously brushy, blurred, and sharp lines, and through the quiet waves of energy rippling along the velvet, planed-down blackness. In revisiting earlier concerns, JJ does not simply re-score the old music; rather, he invites us to undertake a journey of retrieval with him, trusting to our knowledge that he has steered his figuration by postmodern and postcolonial maps of insight.

To the extent that Jehangir Jani's human figures in this suite are of an androgynous nature, we find a hint of the gay politics of representation with which the artist engaged during the 1990s, but which he now recognises as a possible dead end. Even as he steps beyond the potential sectarianism of a sexual minority, the artist braces it in the mode of inquiry. This duality of attitude is symptomatic of the liminal space, the space of betweenness that JJ's figures occupy: while proposing portraiture of the self, they also point to the permanent 'otherness' implicit in that self. Rendered in the current moment, coded with its anxieties, they yet encrypt ancestral psychological realities, recall the deep cave of primitive consciousness. These paintings are imprints, records of images that have burned themselves into the artist's consciousness, presences which he must confront on this threshold of transition as he re-shapes, yet again, his pictorial language.

Mumbai, July 2004

Essay for the catalogue of Jehangir Jani's exhibition, 'Portraits' at The Guild Art Gallery, Mumbai

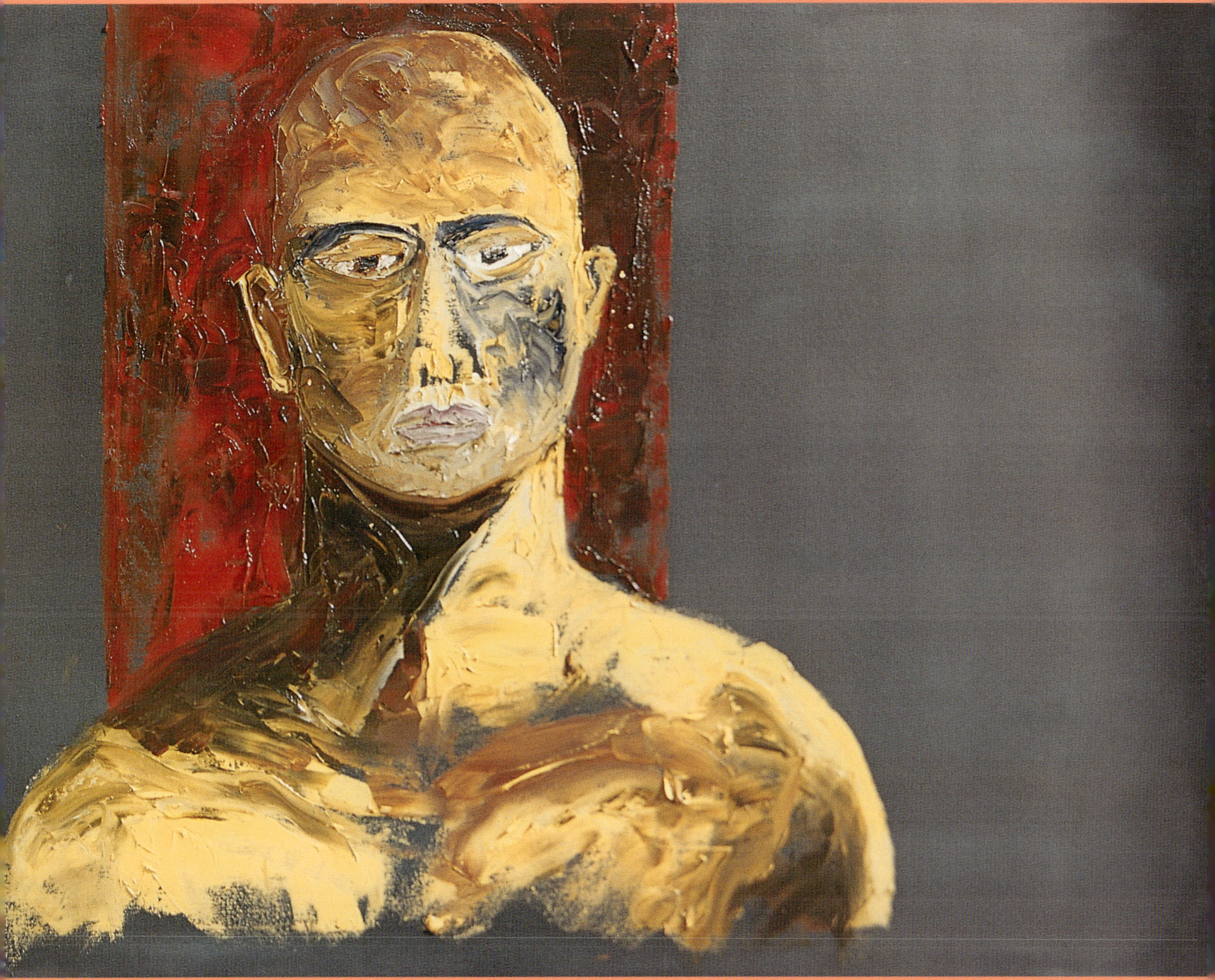

Untitled
92 x 122 cm. Oil and acrylic on canvas.
2005

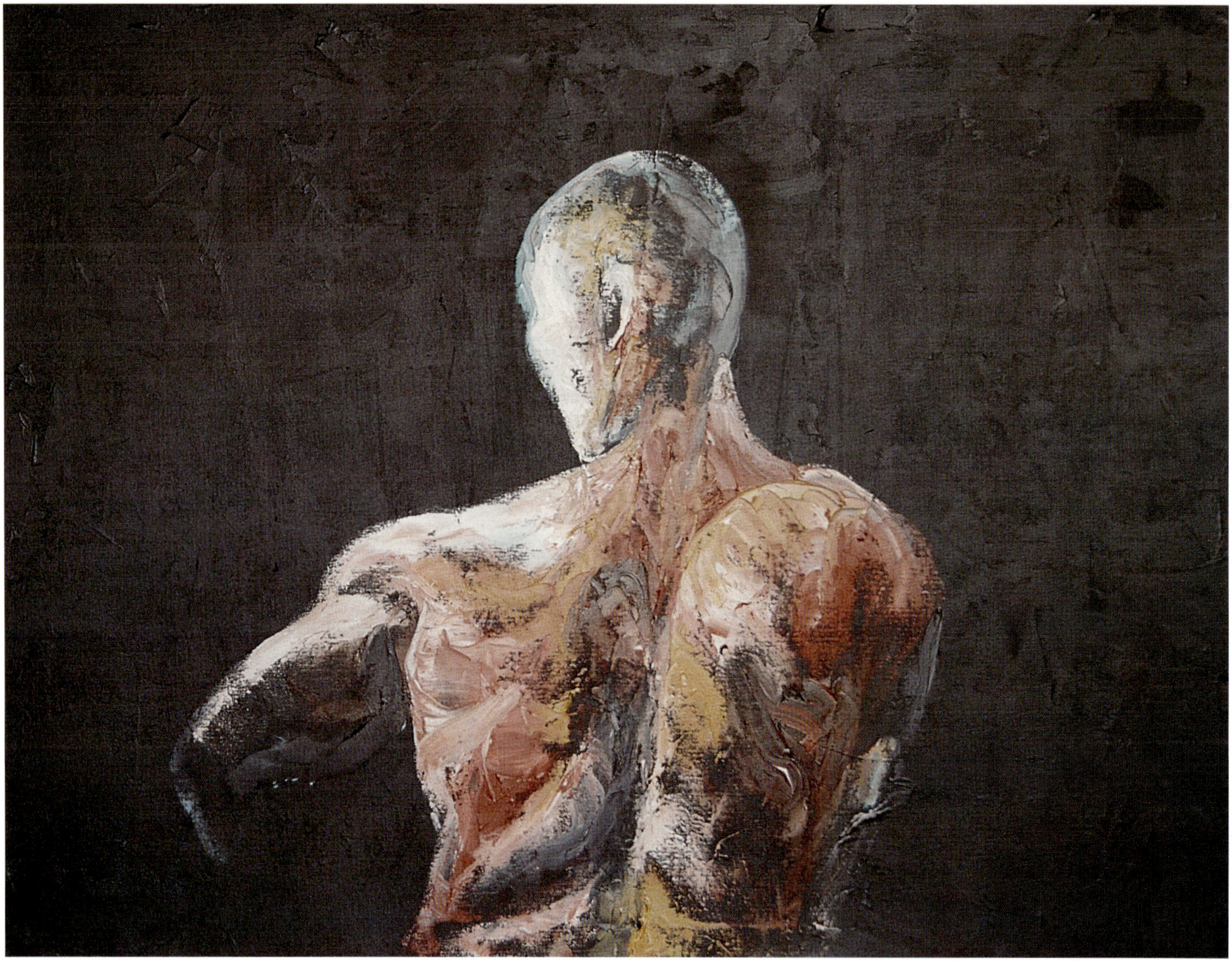

Untitled
92 x 122 cm. Oil and acrylic on canvas.
2005

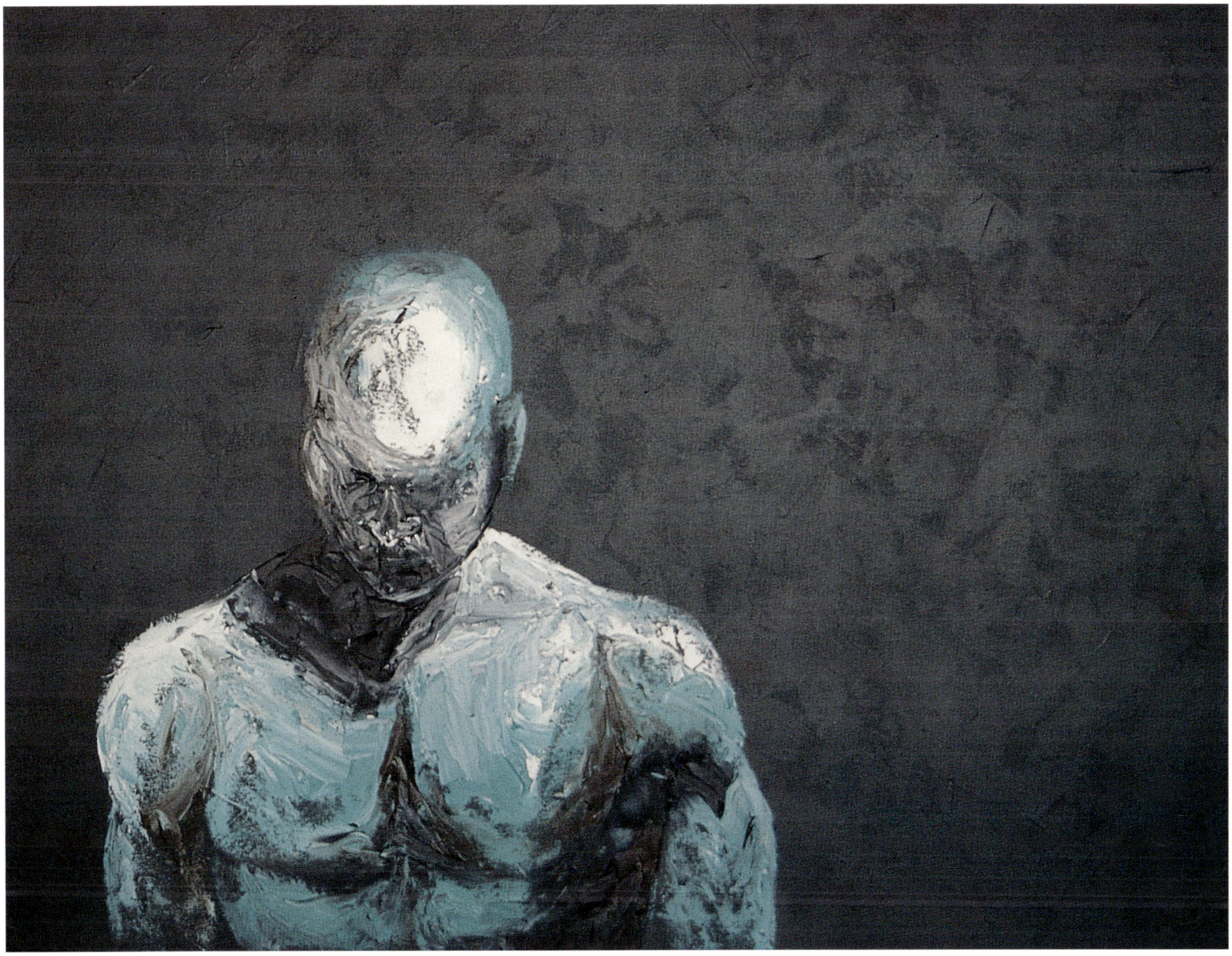

Untitled
92 x 122 cm. Oil and acrylic on canvas.
2005

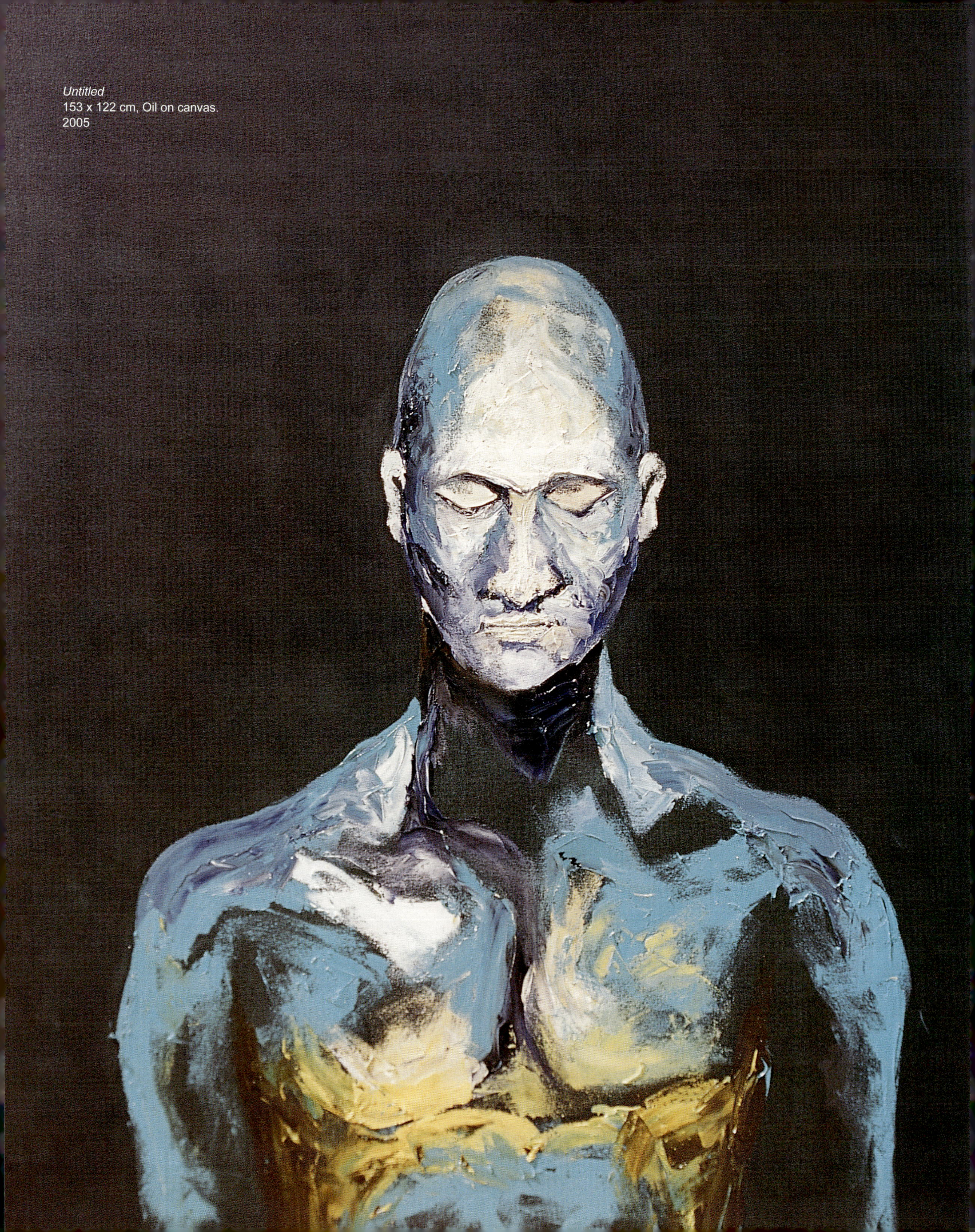

Untitled
153 x 122 cm, Oil on canvas.
2005

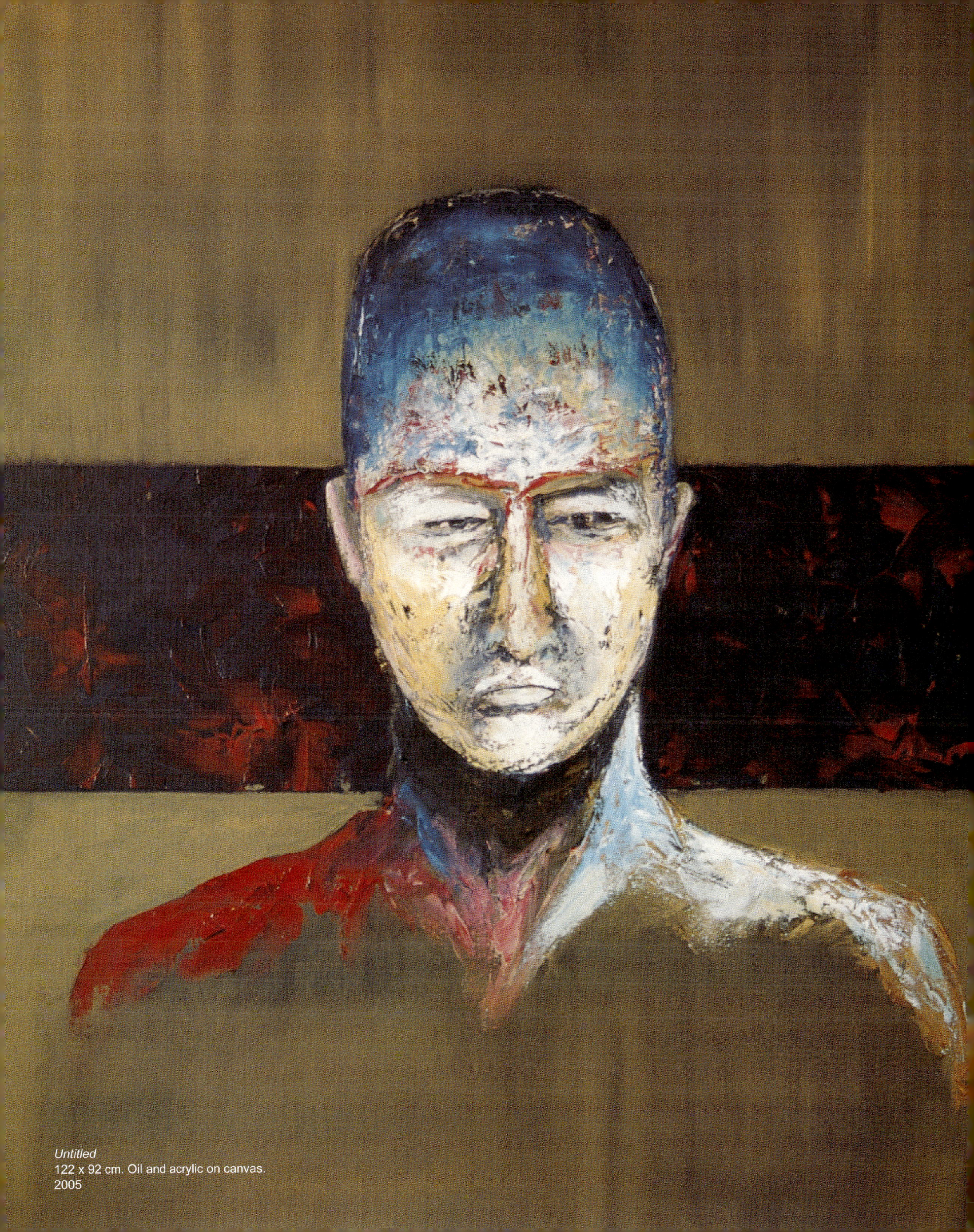

Untitled
122 x 92 cm. Oil and acrylic on canvas.
2005

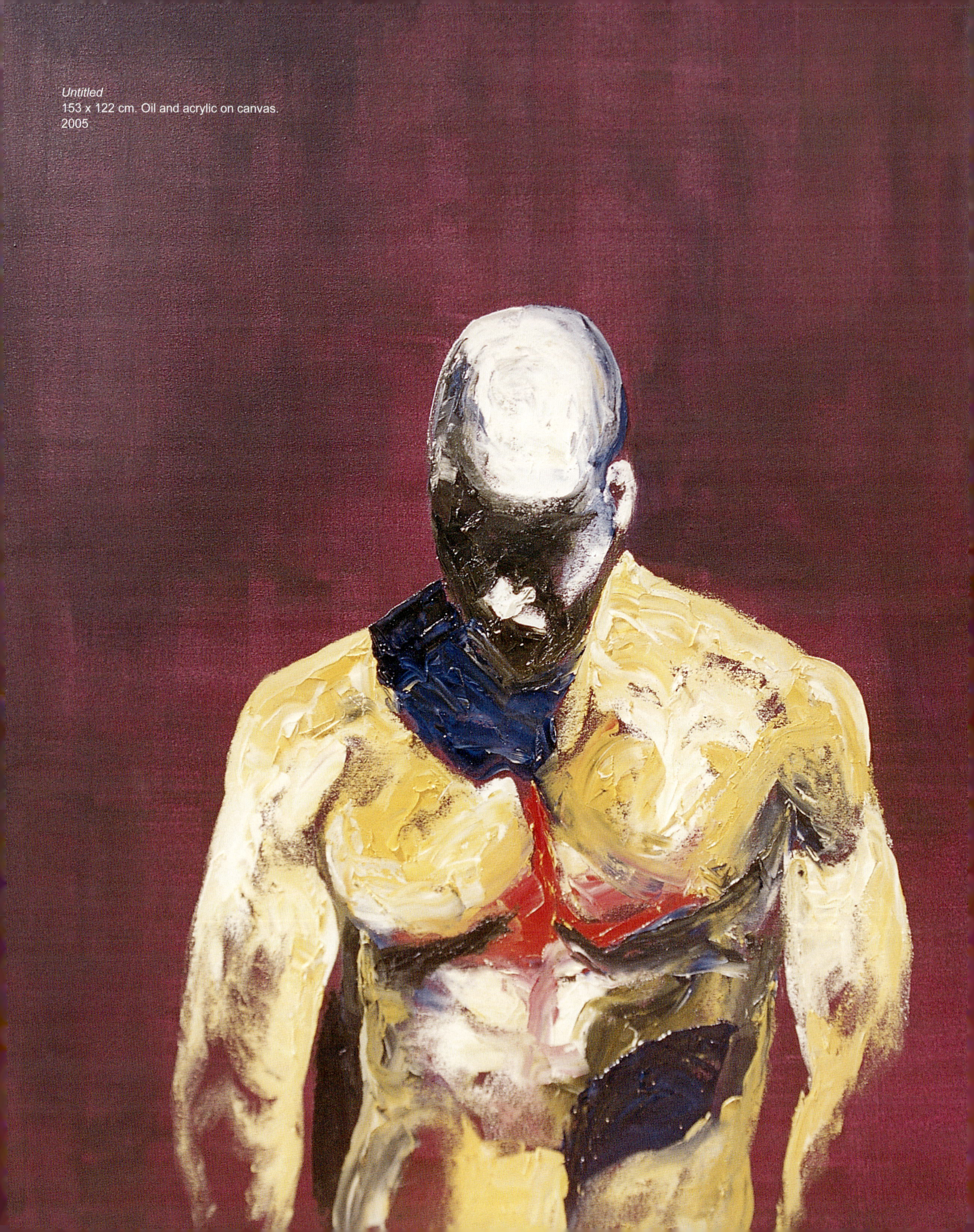

Untitled
153 x 122 cm. Oil and acrylic on canvas.
2005

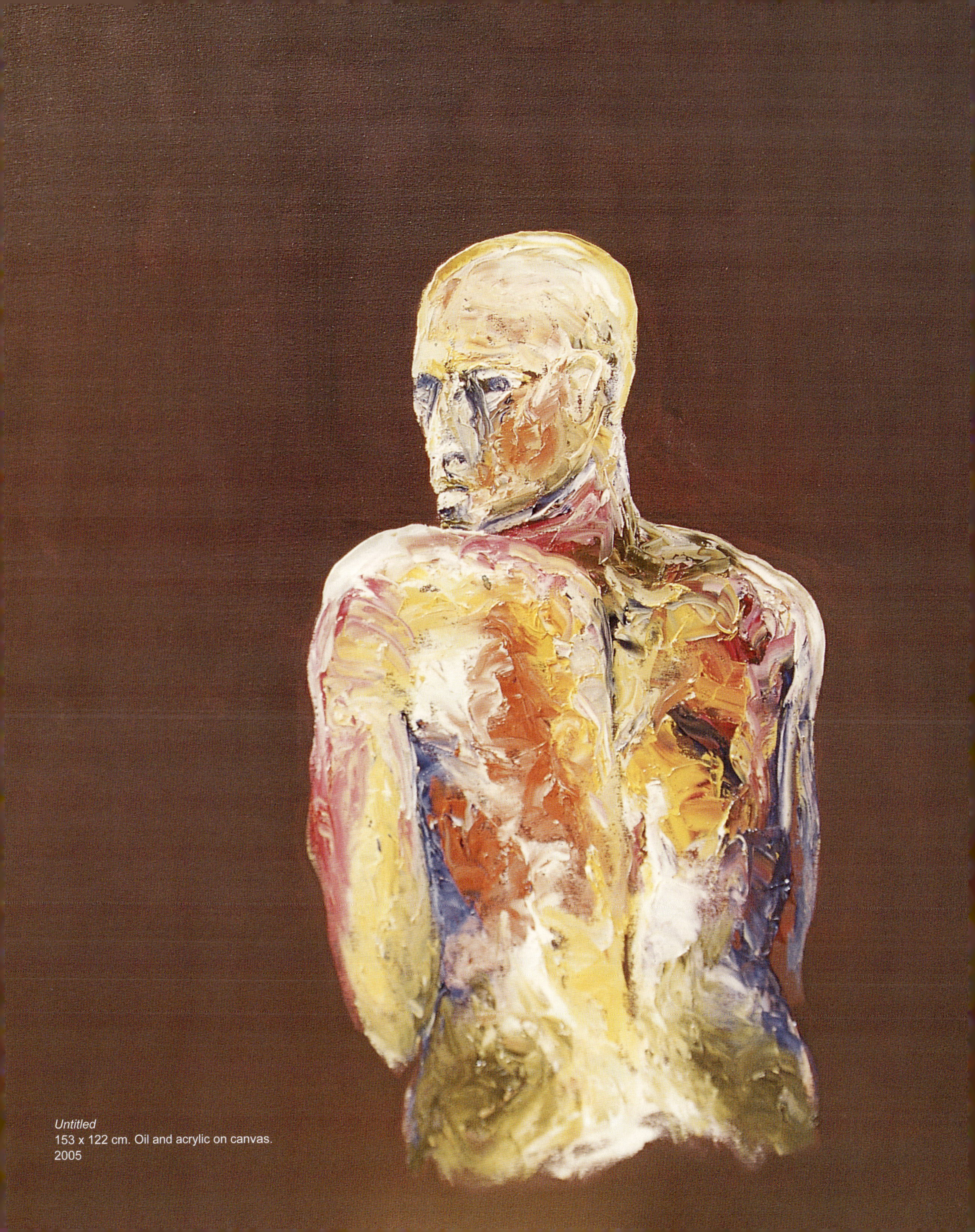

Untitled
153 x 122 cm. Oil and acrylic on canvas.
2005

Untitled
153 x 122 cm. Oil and acrylic on canvas.
2005

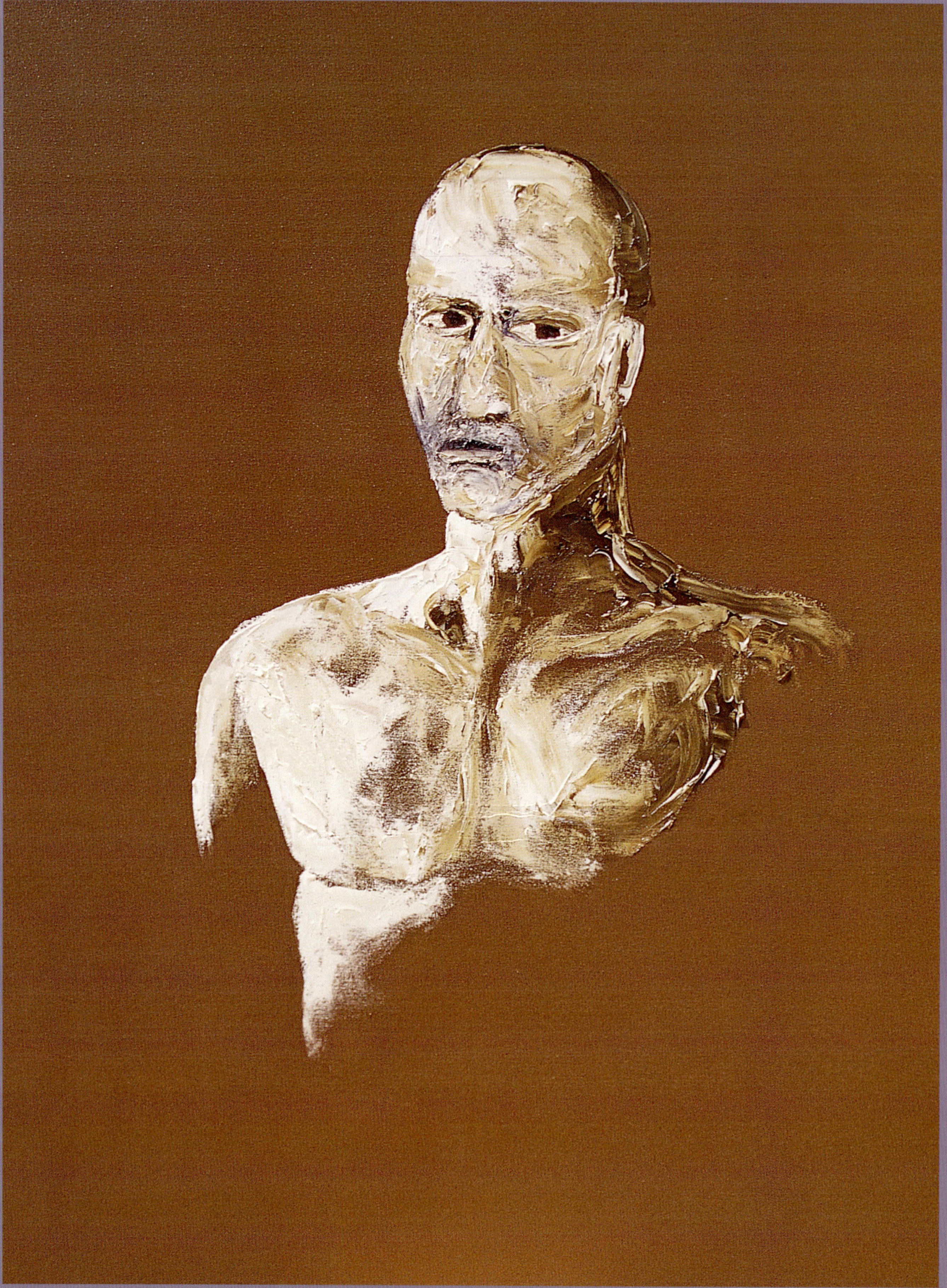

Untitled
122 x 92 cm. Oil and acrylic on canvas.
2005

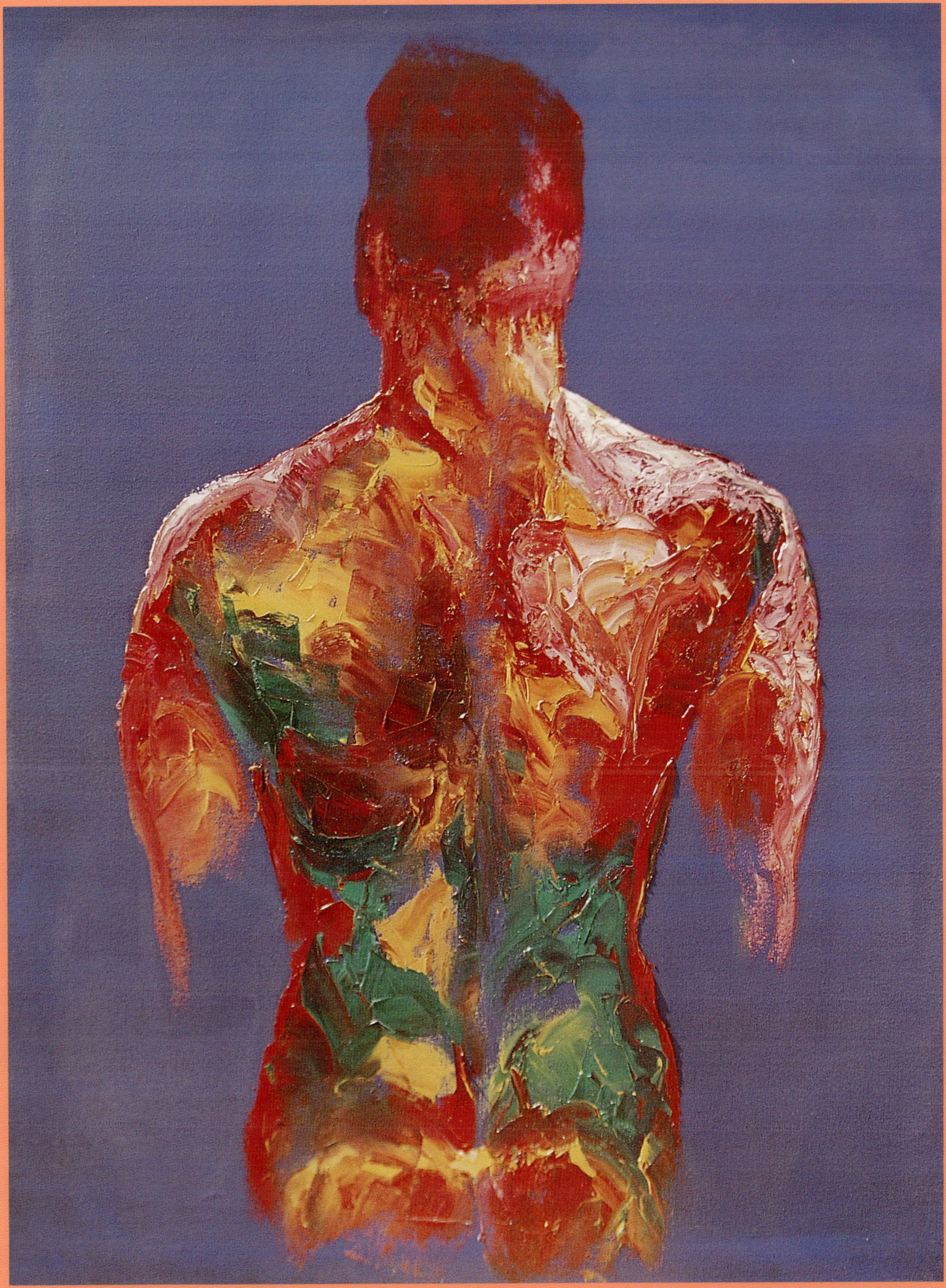

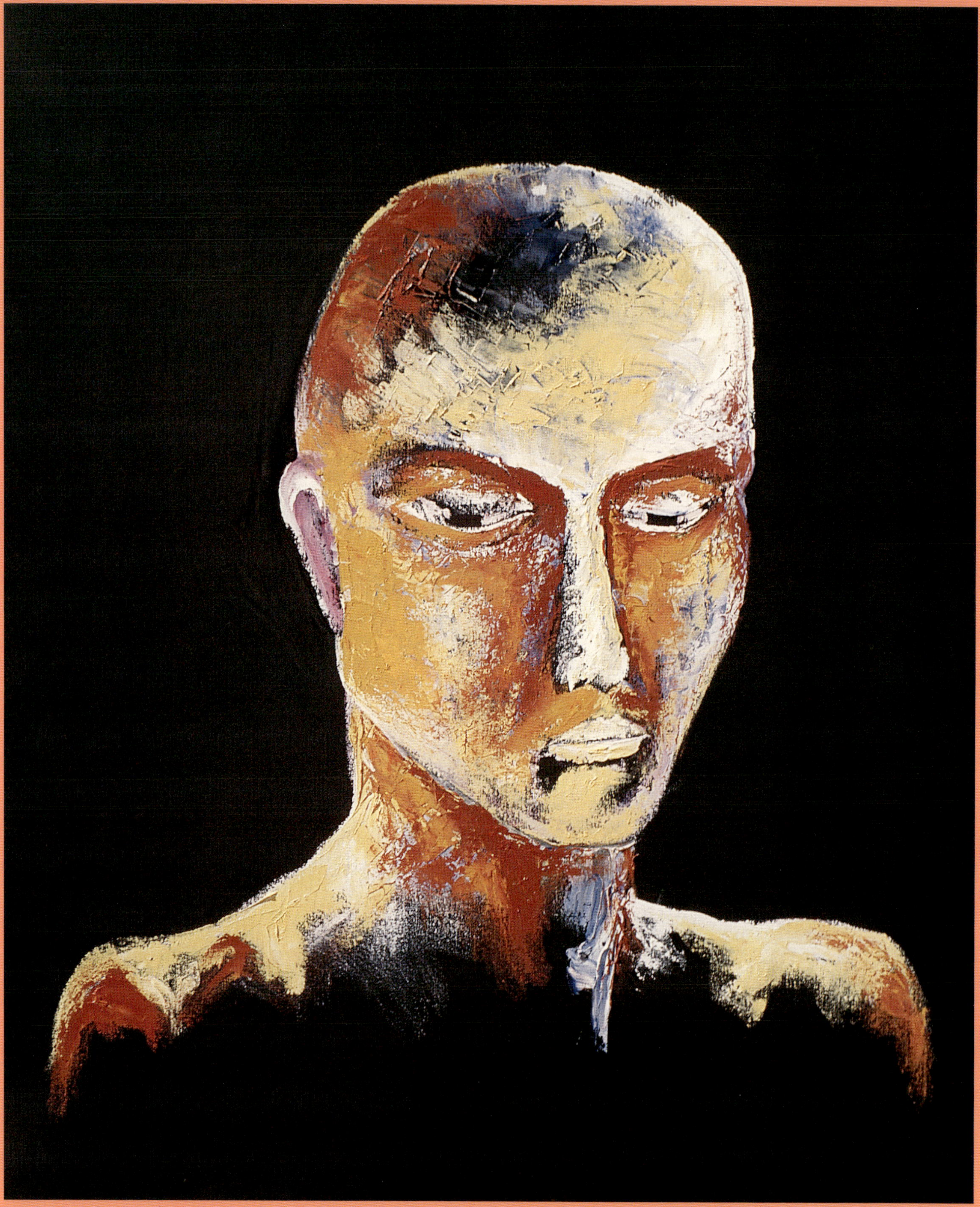

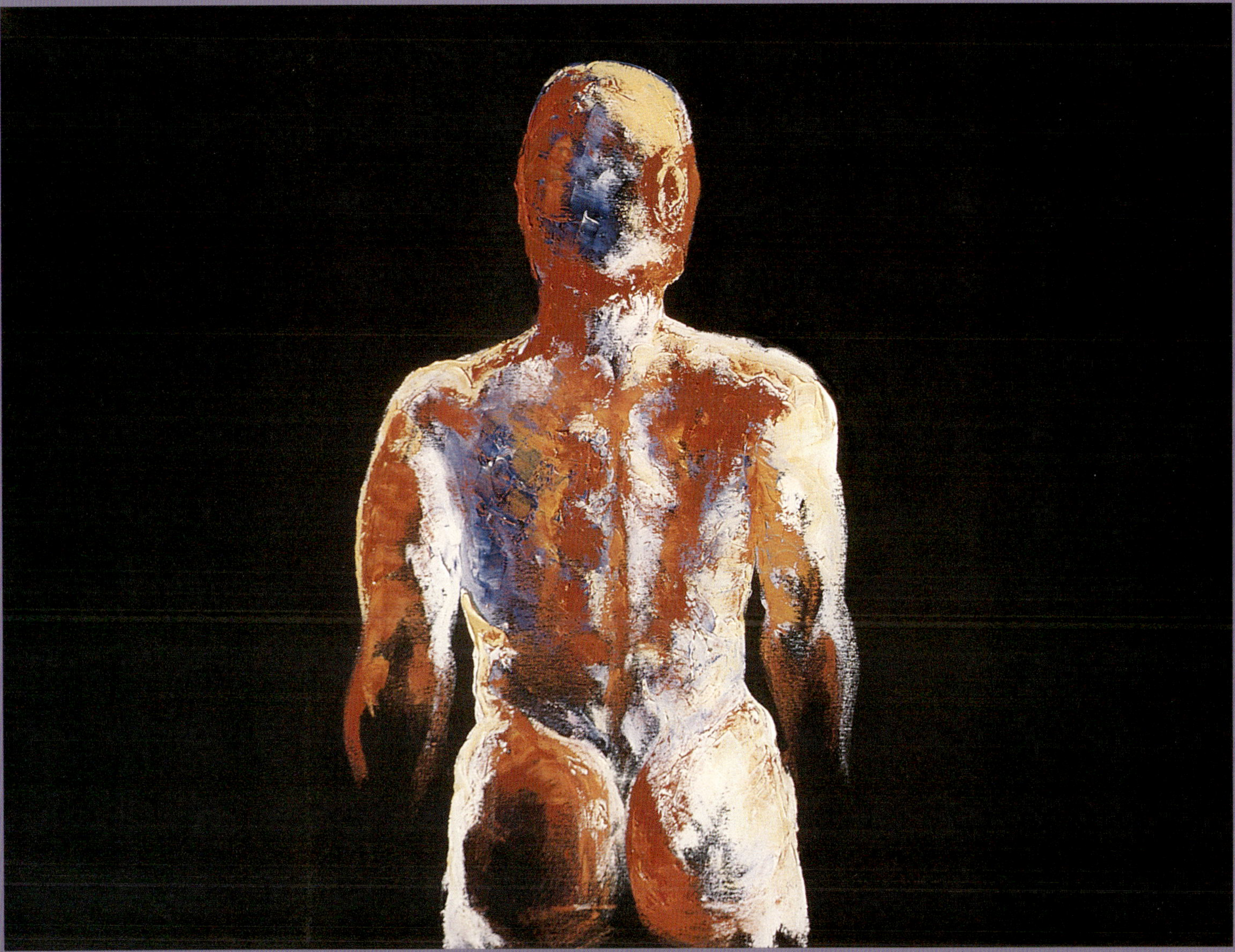

Above:
Untitled
122 x 92 cm. Oil and acrylic on canvas.
2005

Facing Page:
Untitled
122 x 92 cm. Oil and acrylic on canvas.
2005

Bombay
183 x 122 cm. Oil on canvas.
1995

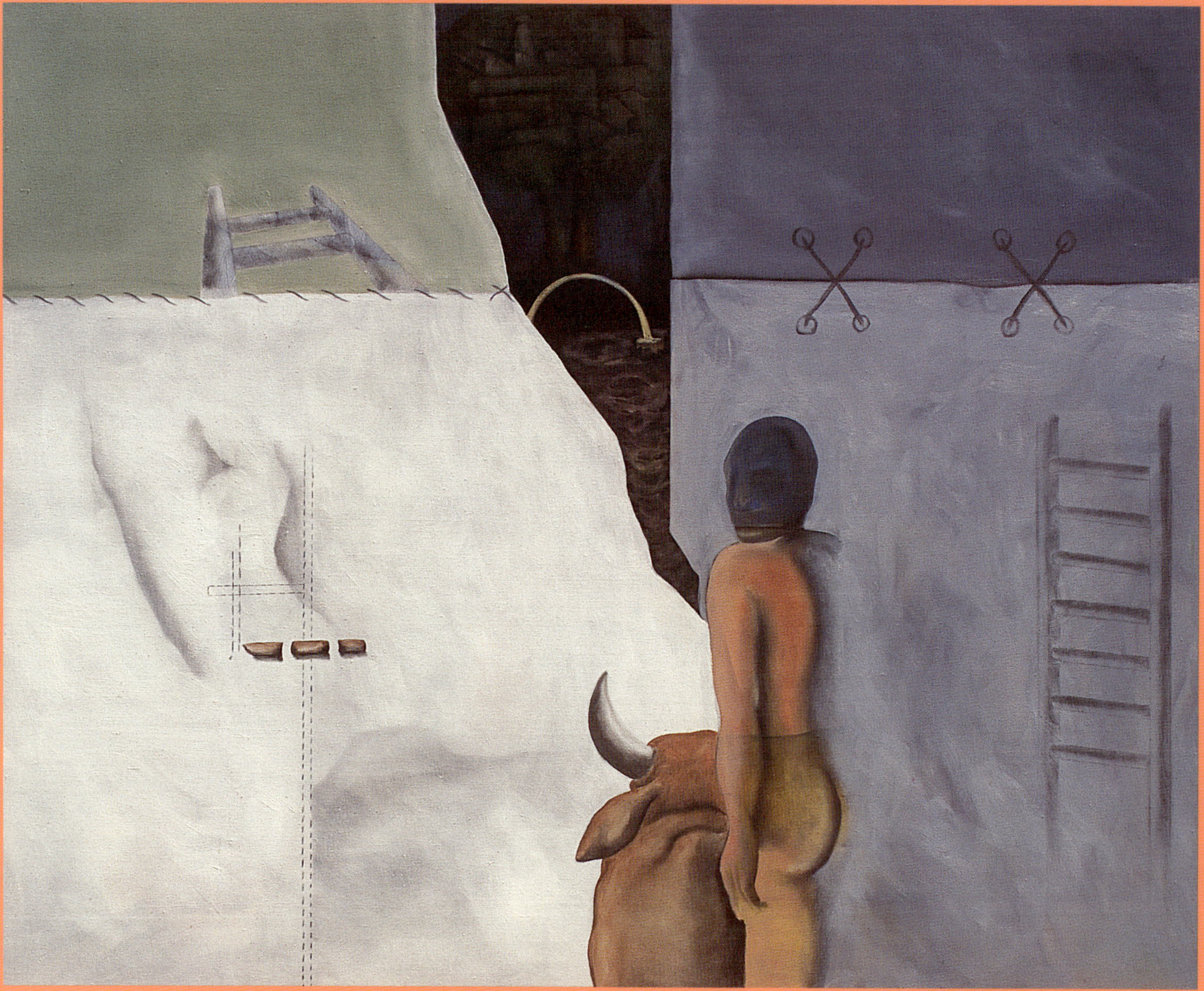

FATHER
54 x 38 cm. Oil and acrylic on canvas.
1994

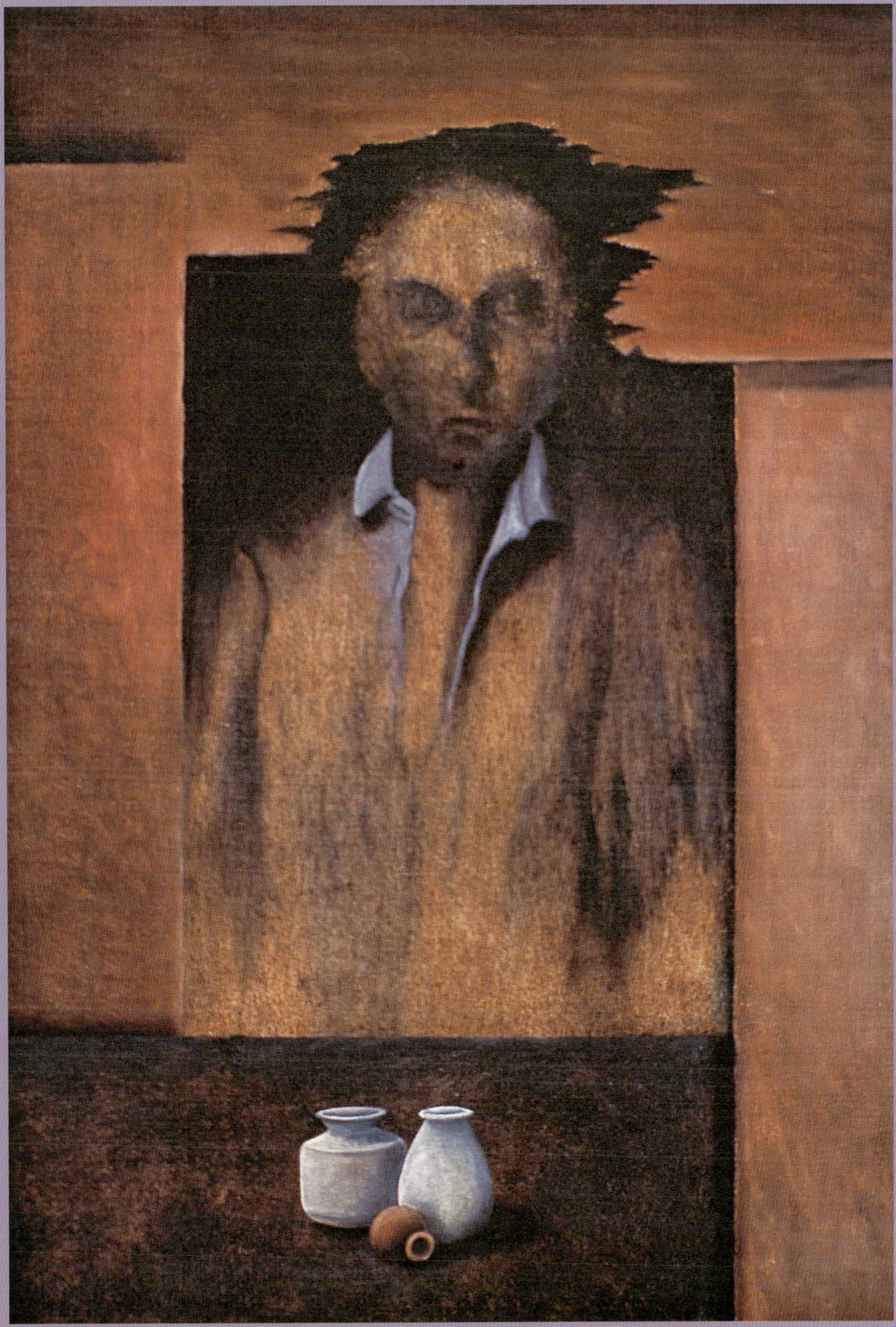

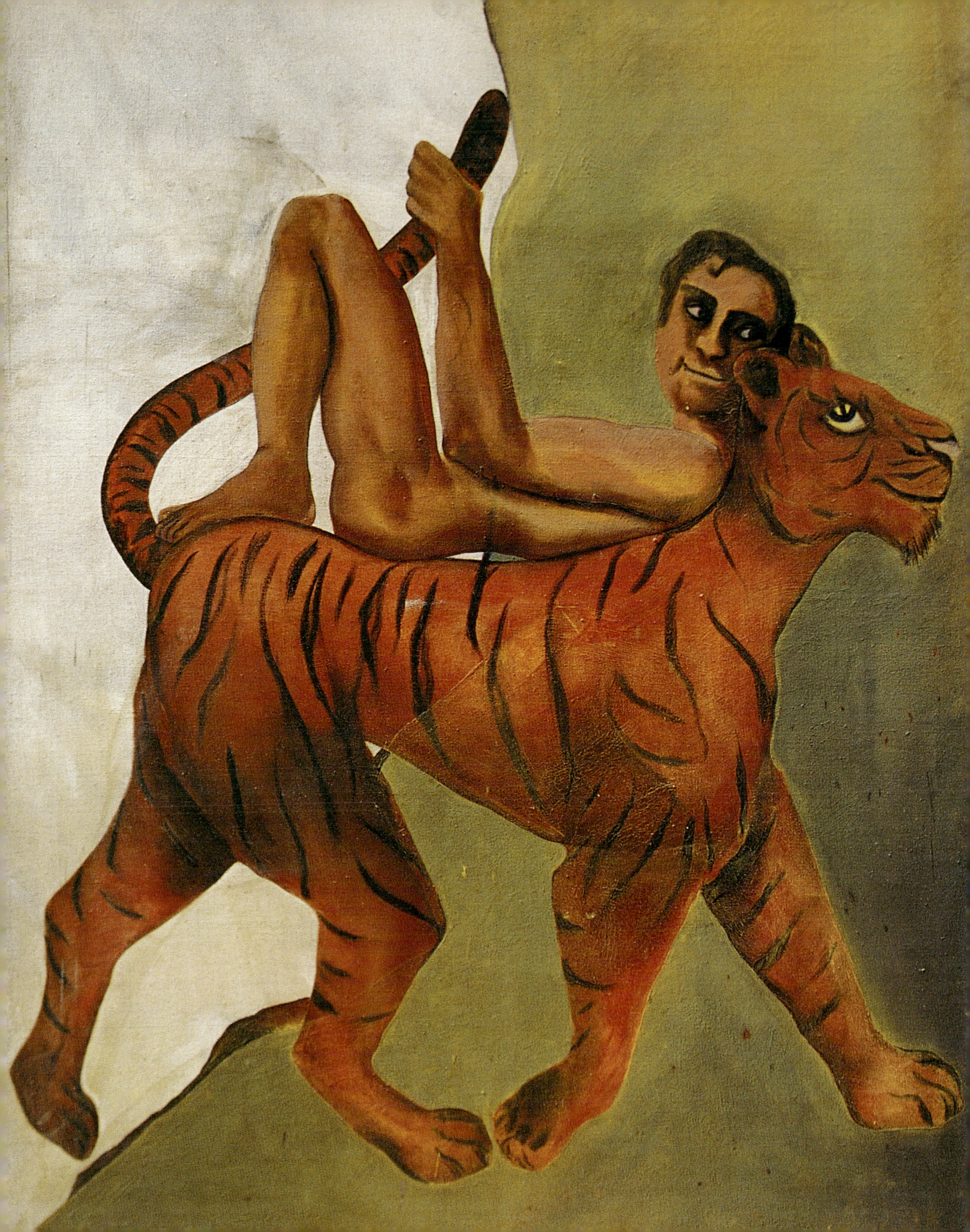

Previous Page:
Bombayite on Bombay
122 x 92 cm. Oil on canvas.
1995

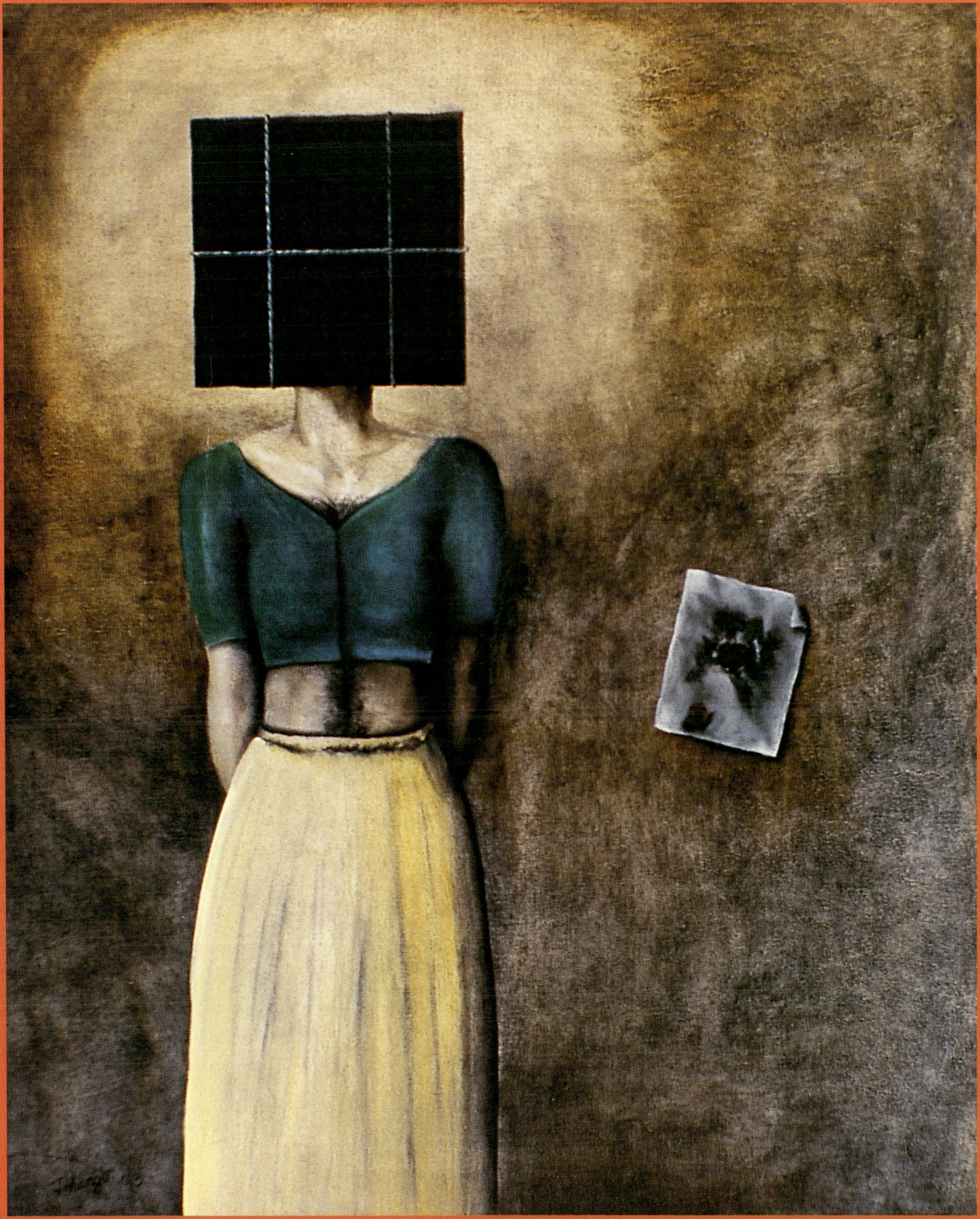

Above:
Myth II
122 x 92 cm. Oil on canvas.
1994

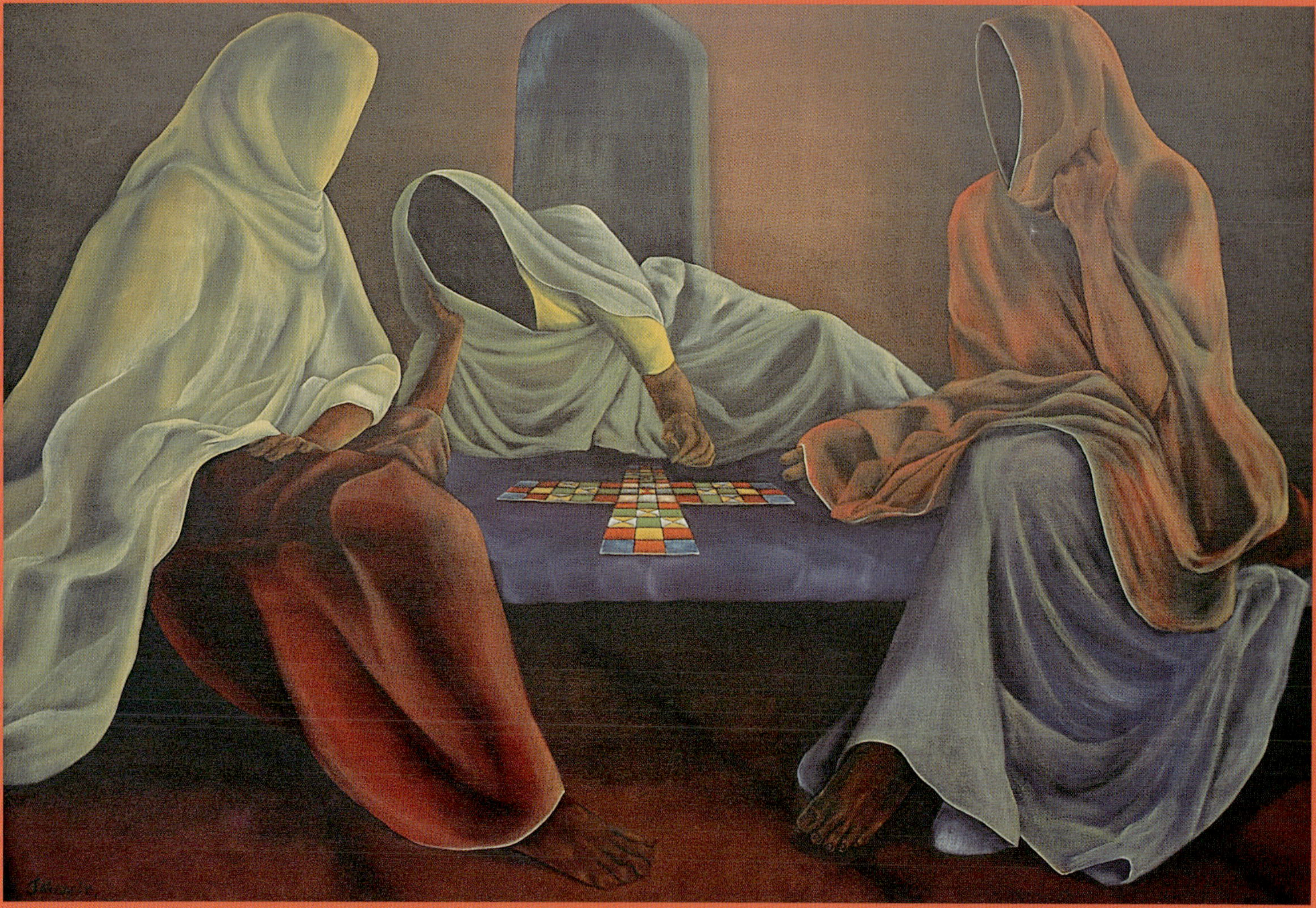

Untitled
122 x 183 cm. Oil on canvas.
1991

PAINTING THE MOMENT

Deeptha Achar

From the vantage point of 2005, two of Jehangir Jani's untitled works of 1992, rather large, in oil, carry a particularly sharp if tangential commentary on those times. The Muslim women, heads covered, faces darkened, are arranged seated indoors, three of them playing *chaupar* in one instance, and two juxtaposed curiously with a book, in another. Voluminous drapery obscures their form; we have here no titillating glimpse of breast or hip that escapes clothing. Instead, the viewer is confronted with an unremittingly political rendition of Muslim women.

From the 1986 Shah Bano case onward, when the Government overturned the Supreme Court's decision to award the deserted Muslim woman maintenance, the Muslim woman has been produced as the privileged site of reform. The move, which ignored reformist liberal Muslim opinion, smacked of political expediency. More importantly, it allowed the Hindu Right to recast itself as the champion of 'backward' Muslim women, who needed to be protected, indeed, rescued from their medieval religion and their bigoted men.

JJ bypasses this opposition between helpless women and demonic men quite simply by staging a space inhabited by women only, the men in margins existing outside the frame. These paintings appear to go along with the Hindu Right's almost exclusive focus on Muslim women, yet they do so ironically, picking up and subverting nearly all the tropes that are usually invoked to characterise women.

Quite clearly, JJ's women are a part of the upper class: belonging to a specific time and place, they resist homogenisation under the rubric 'Muslim'. At the same time, the accumulation of details that turn these figures Muslim, most particularly in the details of clothing and architecture, work against any attempt to read them as essentially women. With the interior occupied only by women, the scene invokes the *zenana*, that symbol of Muslim oppression and reformist zeal. Yet, the commonly held ideas of the closed and claustrophobic *zenana* space are gently mocked by the manner in which doors, which lead in or out, which let in light and air, are structural to the painting. Nor are the women suffering and vulnerable: portrayed in leisure, engaged in a life of the mind, their postures bespeak ease, their actions are self-directed, self-composed, unhurried, deliberate, not anxious. Indeed, they are 'modern' women, literate, versed in strategy, playing a tactical game, reading hard-cover books that surely came with colonialism.

The gaze gets arrested at their faces: these dark faces admit no feature, no expression. Yet, these figures are not merely faceless. Their very opacity denies any attempt to look for meanings hidden within, rather they gesture relentlessly at their own status as signs that cannot be tied to any simple production of meaning or truth. To that extent, these figures circumvent agendas that seek to rescue, to protect.

Baroda, September 2005

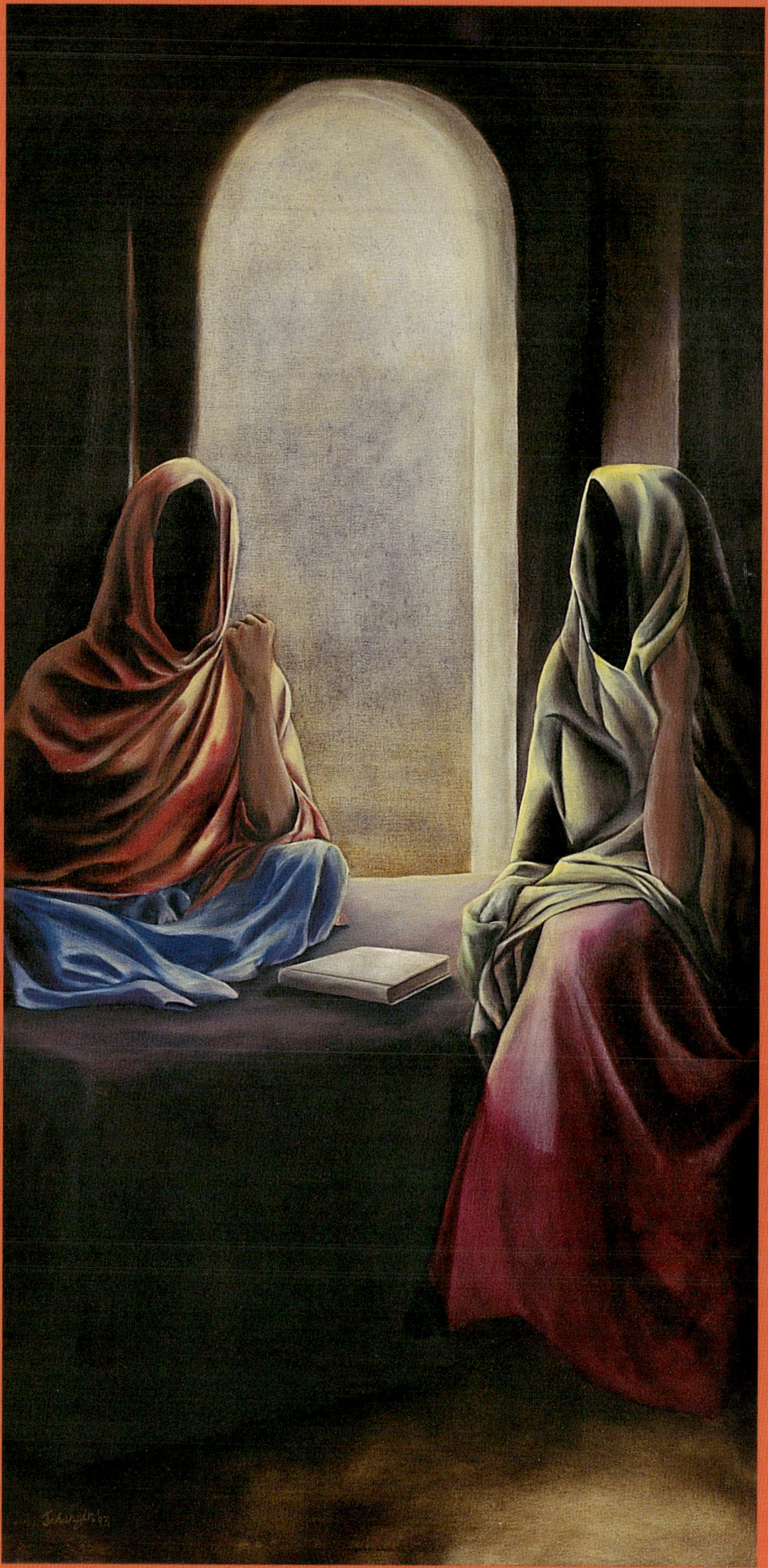

Untitled
183 x 92 cm. Oil on canvas.
1992

WATERCOLOURS

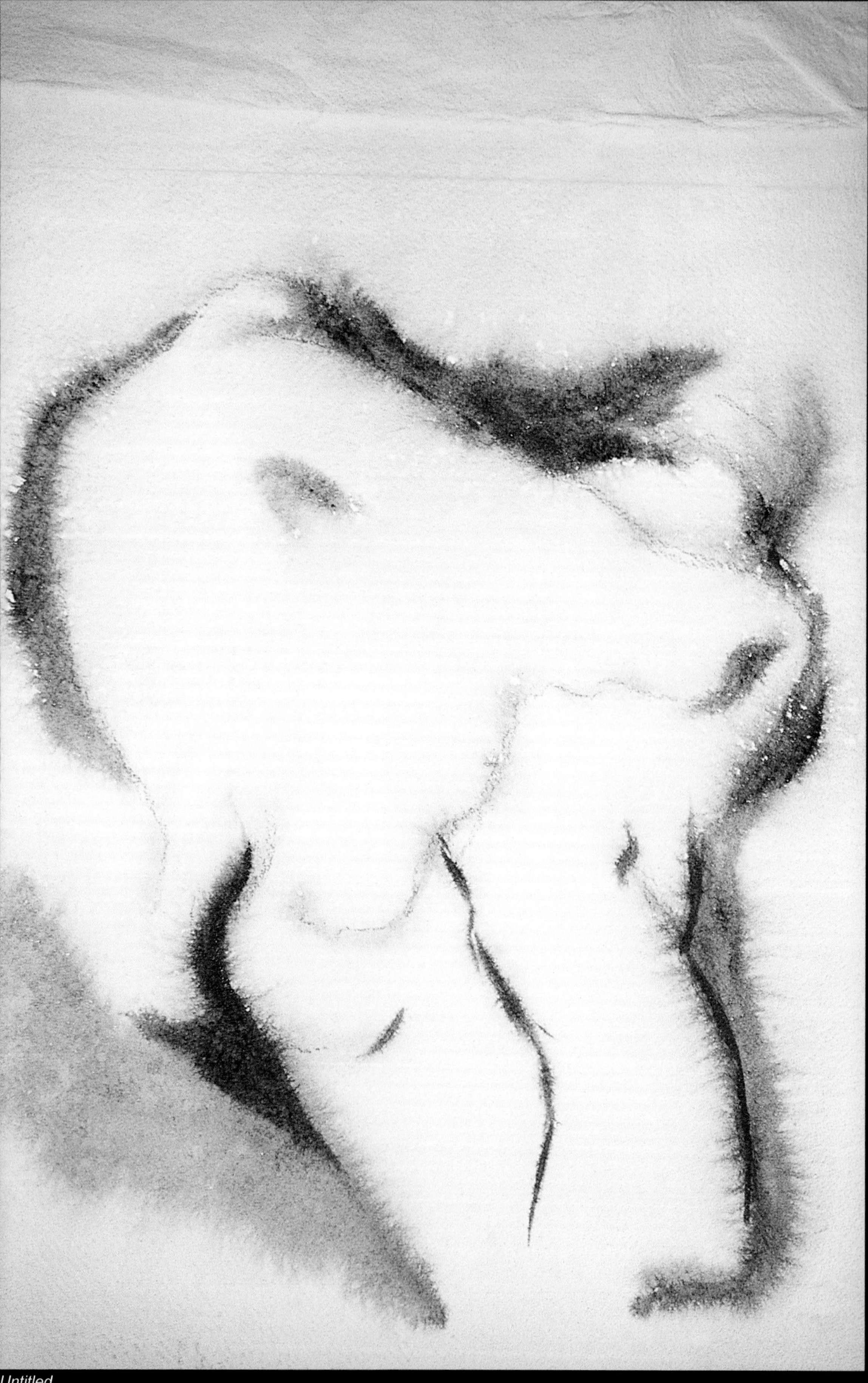

Untitled
22 x 28 cm. Charcoal and ink on paper.
1995

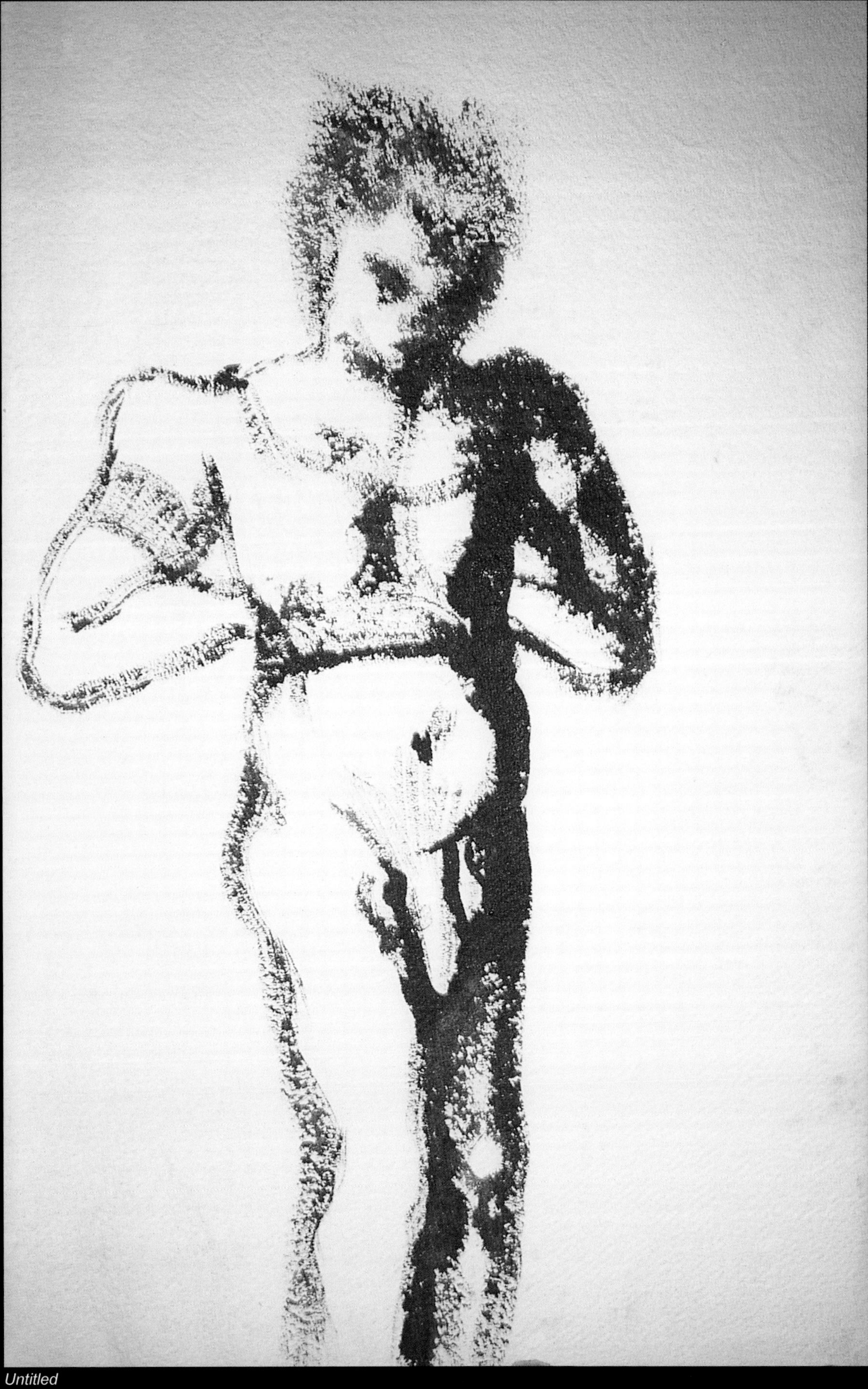

Untitled
22 x 28 cm. Ink on paper.
1995

Bharat/Bharati
29 x 22 cm. Watercolour and colour xerox.
1997

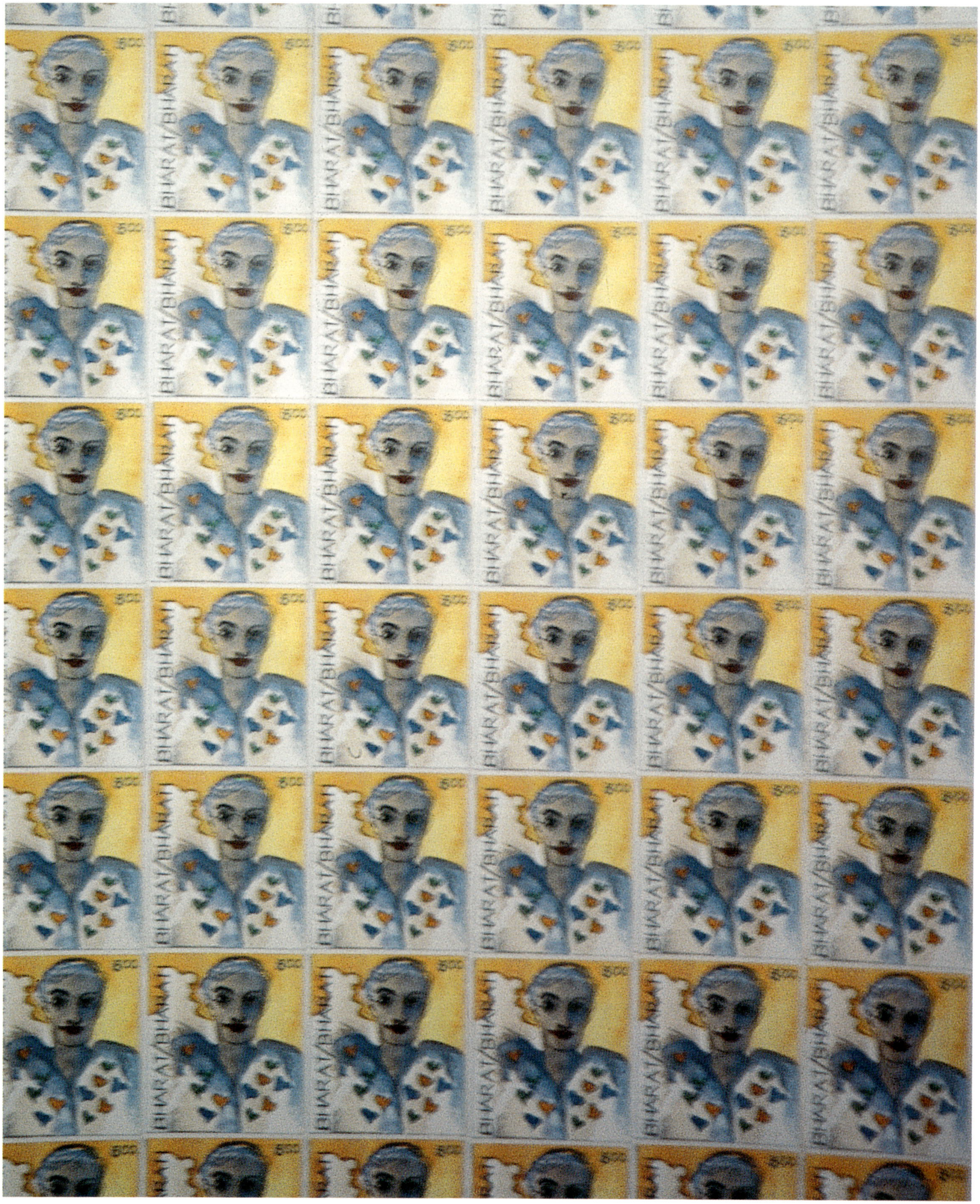

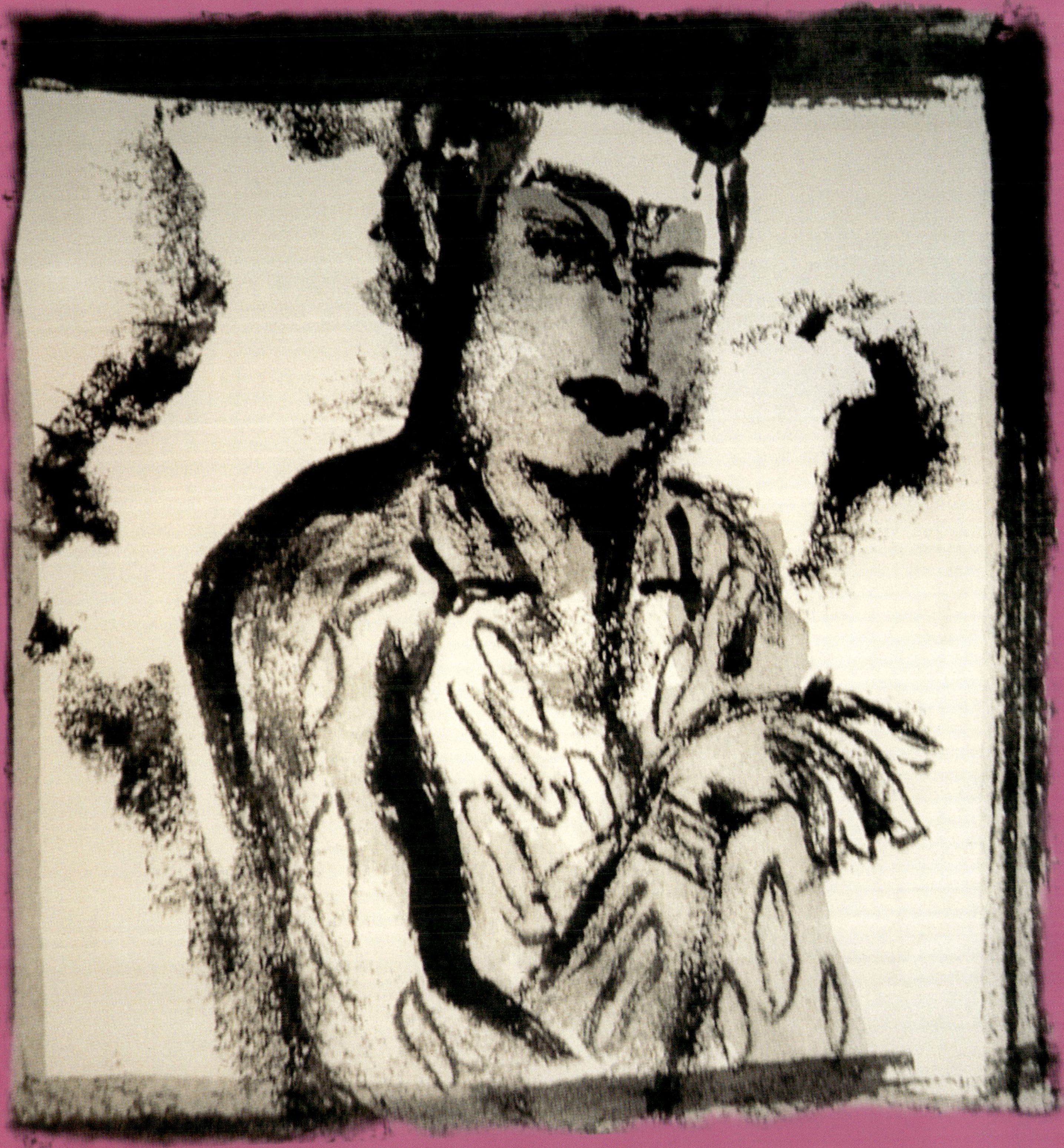

India Map I
6 x 6 cm. Ink on paper.
1997

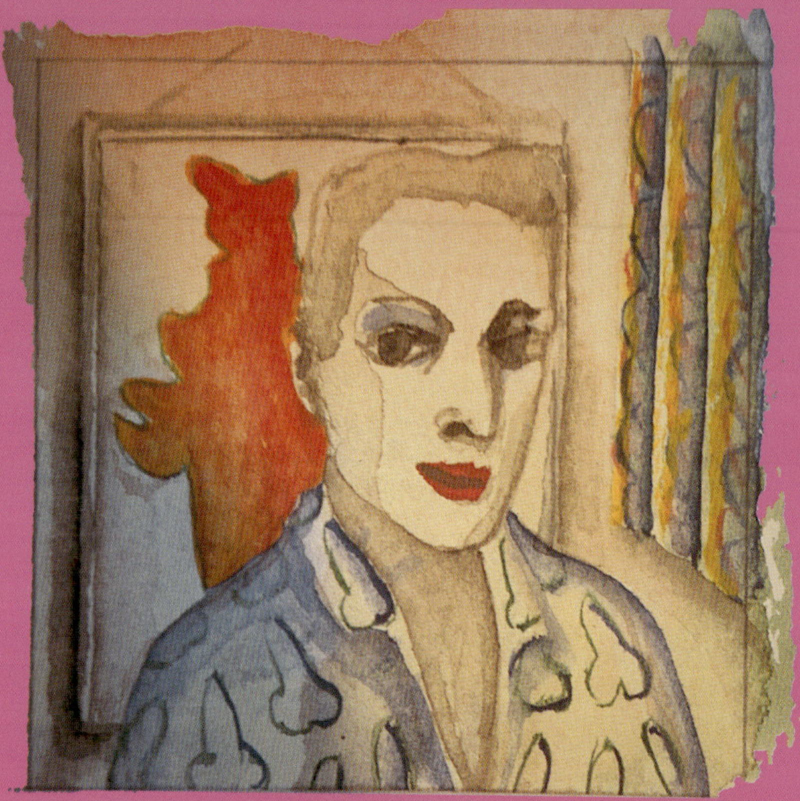

India Map II
6 x 6 cm. Watercolour on paper.
1997

Olympus
38 x 56 cm. Watercolour on cloth.
1997

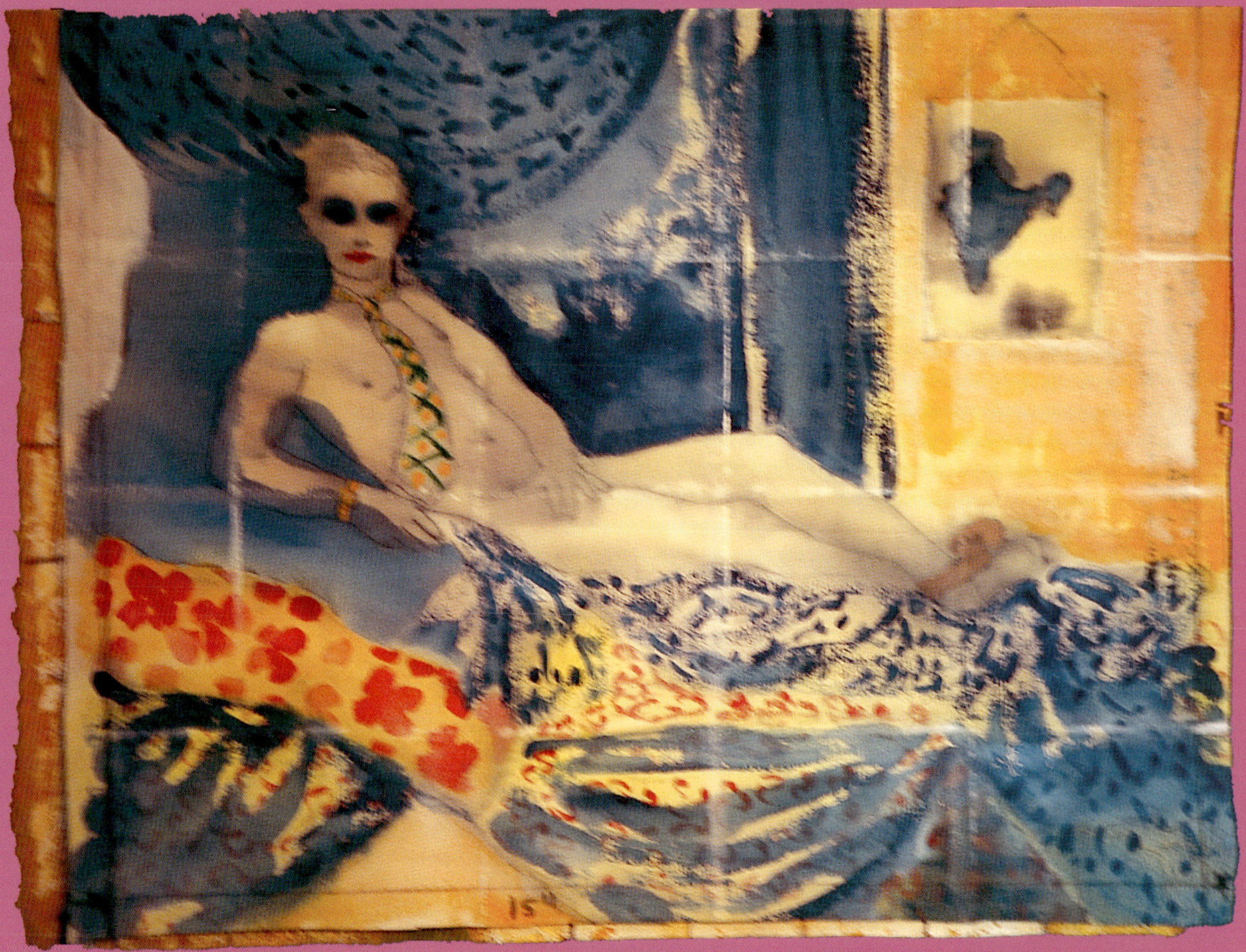

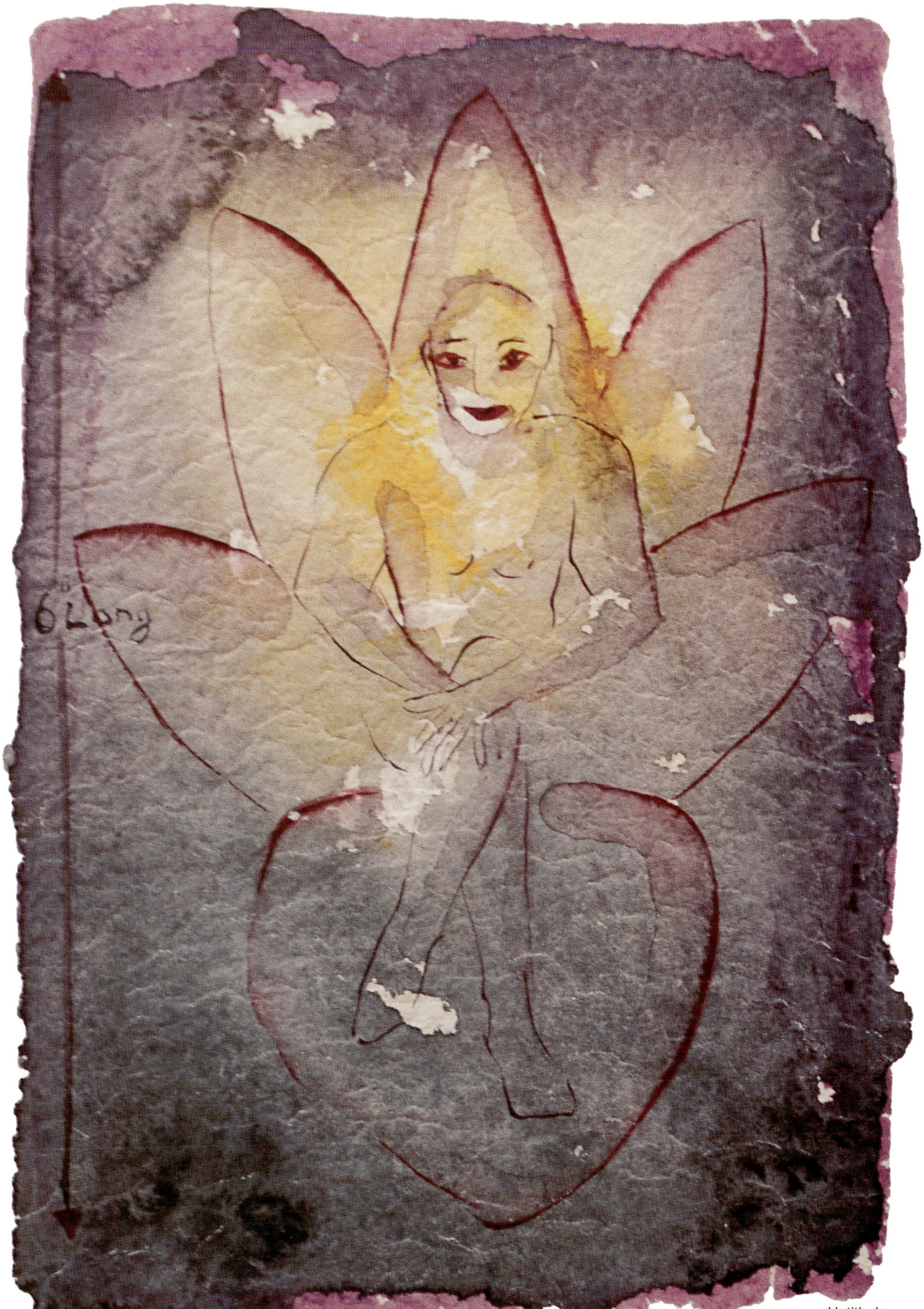

Untitled
21 x 15 cm. Watercolour on paper.
1998

Untitled
21 x 15 cm. Watercolour on paper.
1998

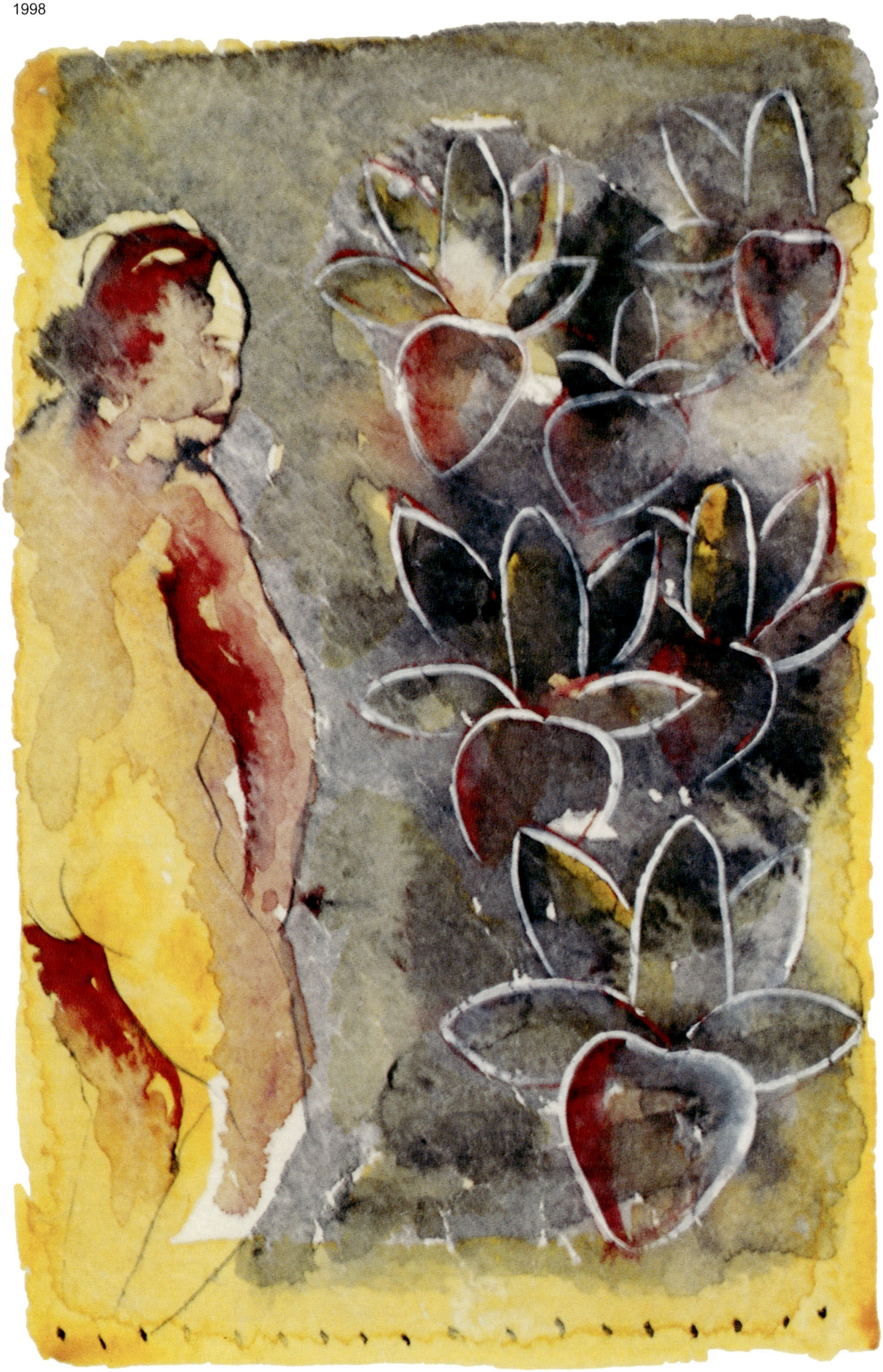

Untitled
72 x 56 cm. Watercolour on paper.
1999

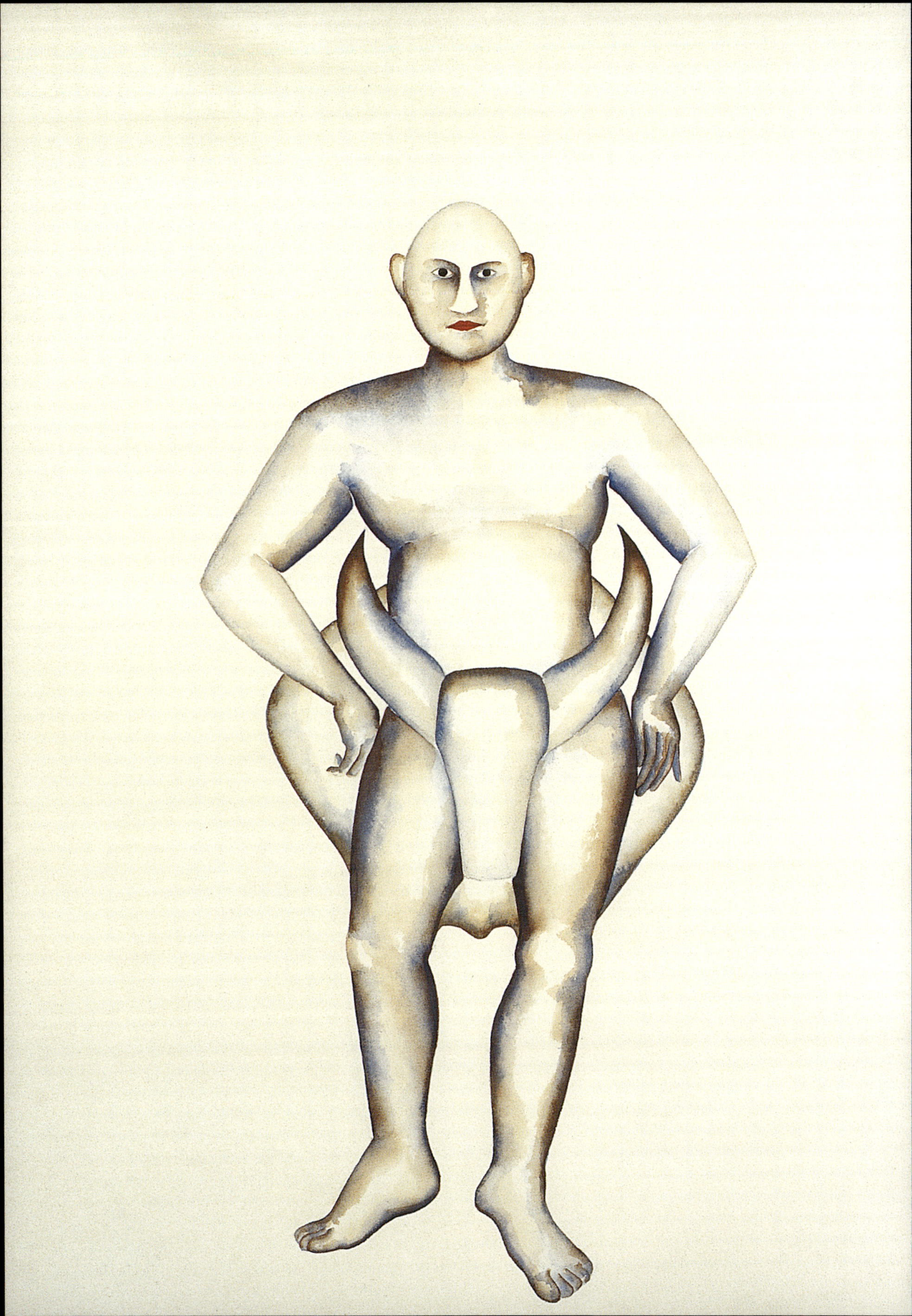

Untitled
38 x 28 cm. Watercolour on paper.
2001

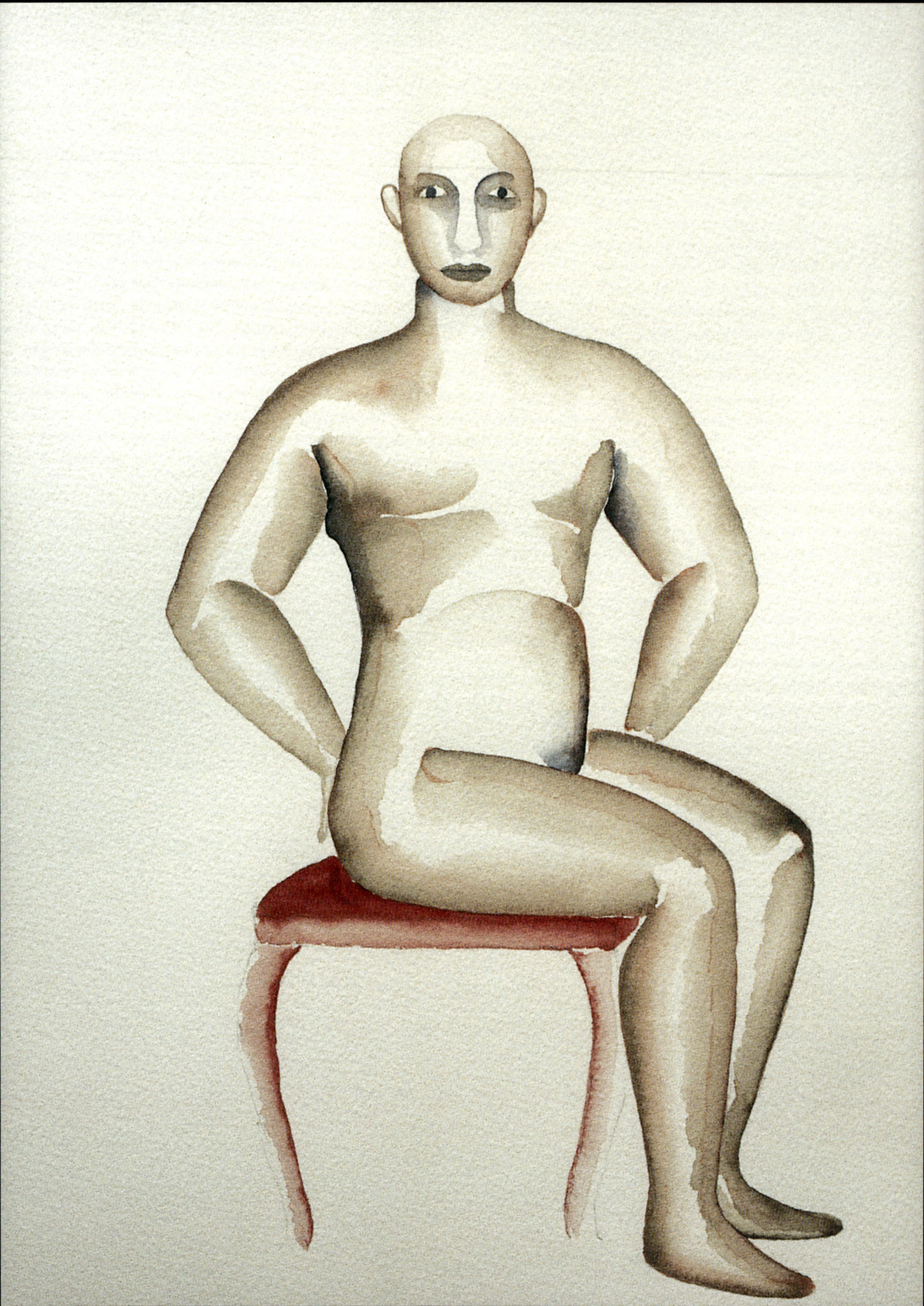

38 x 28 cm. Watercolour on paper.
2000

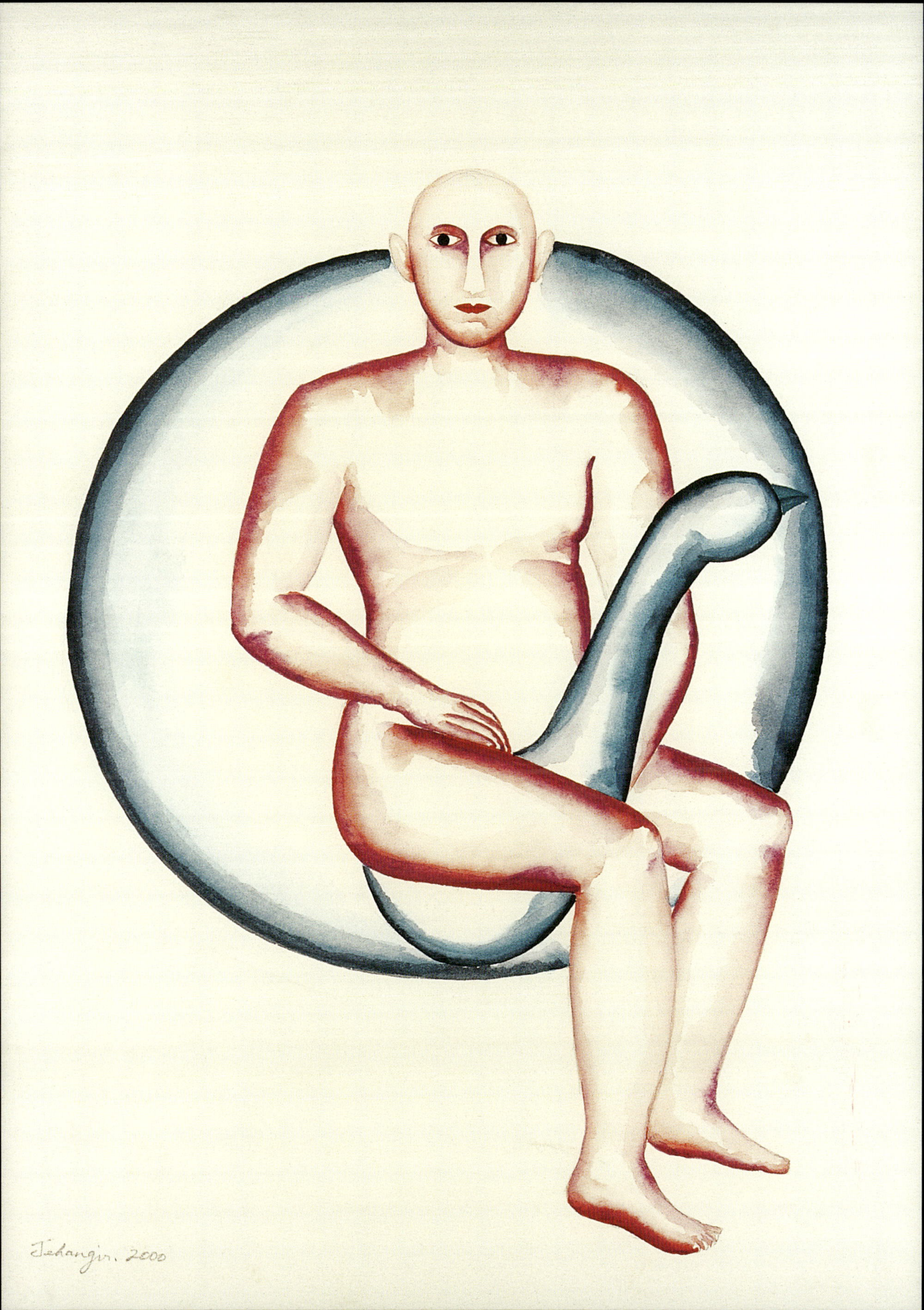

38 x 28 cm. Watercolour on paper.
1999

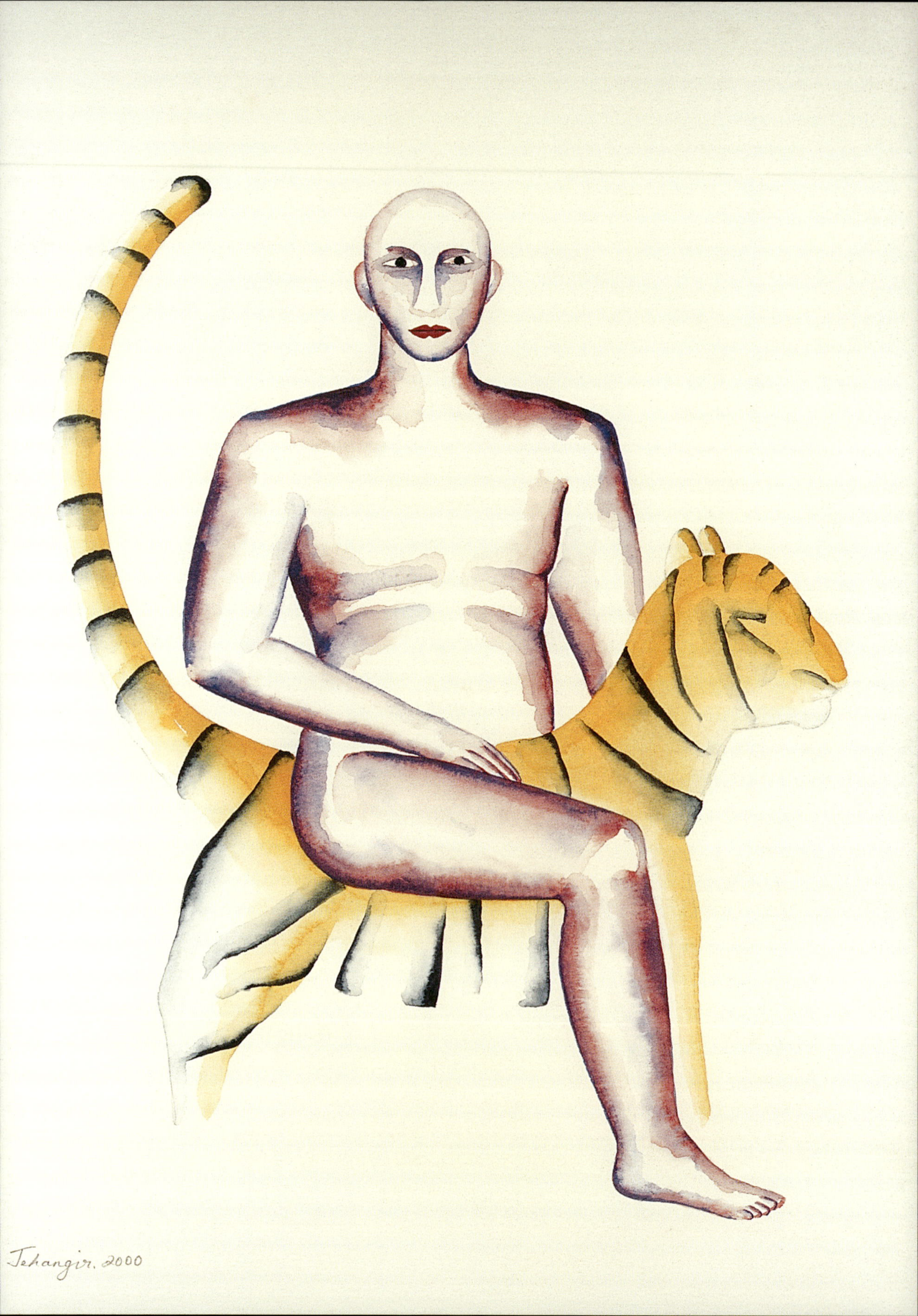

Untitled
38 x 28 cm. Watercolour on paper.
2001

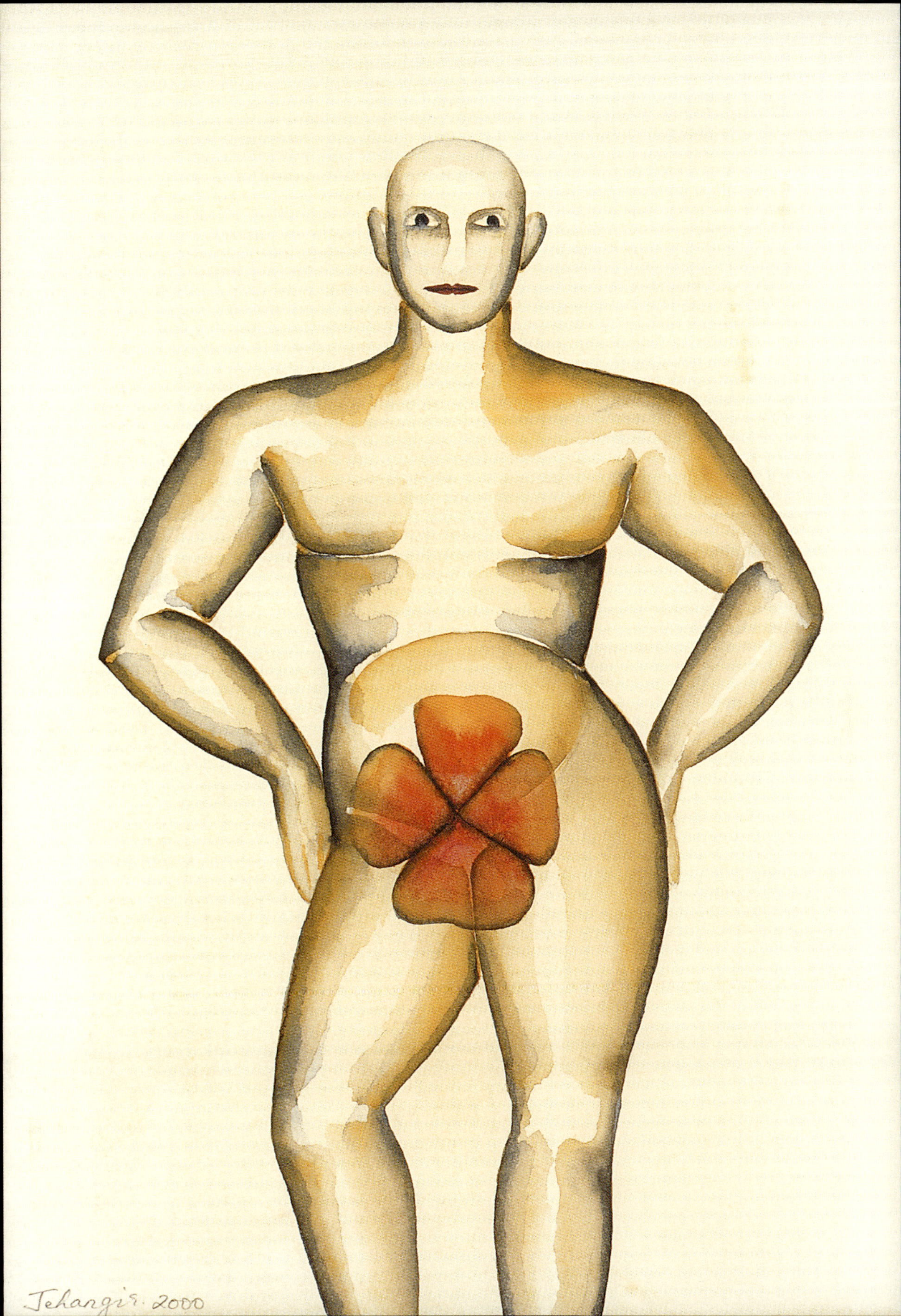

Untitled
38 x 28 cm. Watercolour on paper.
2001

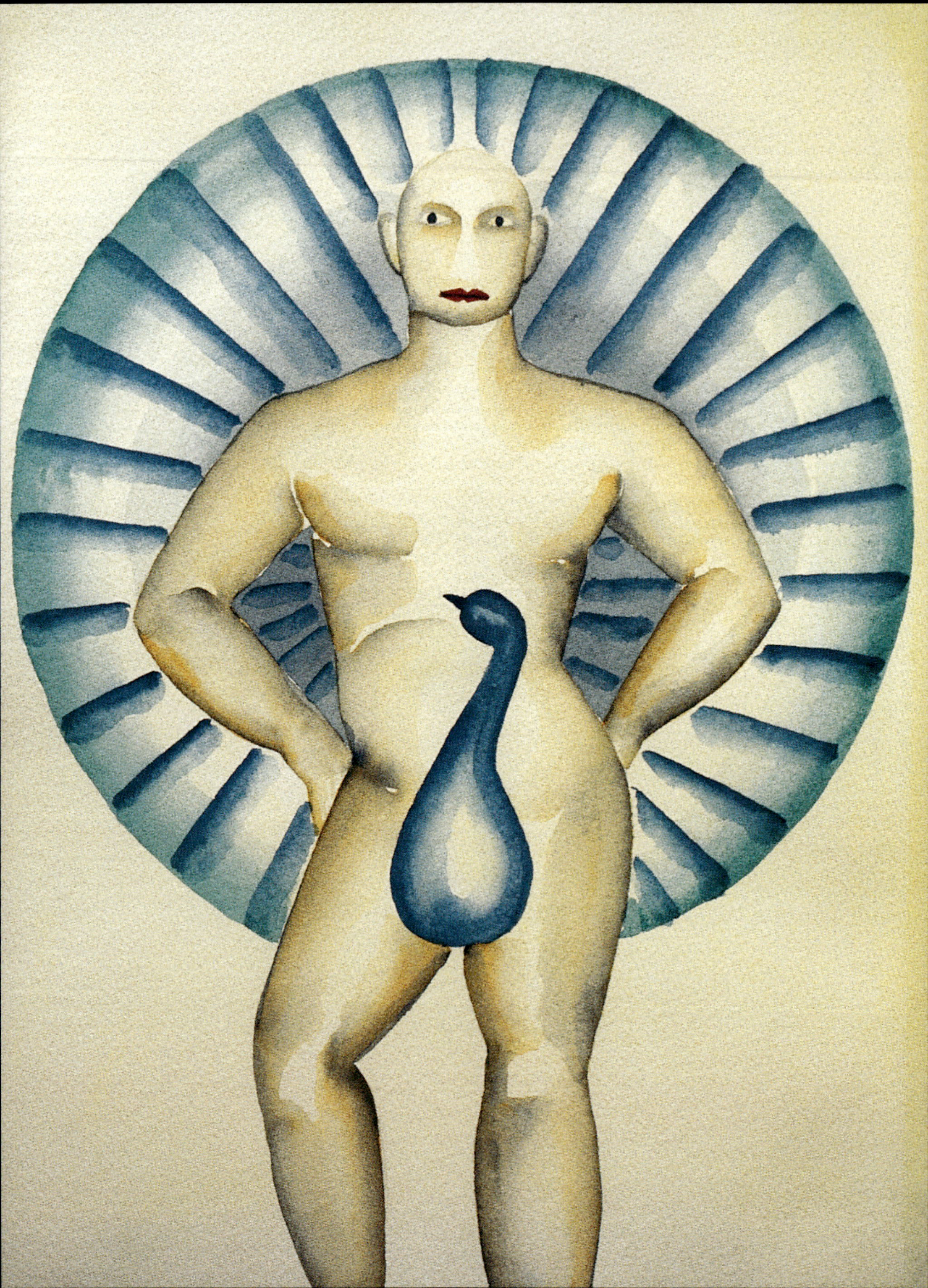

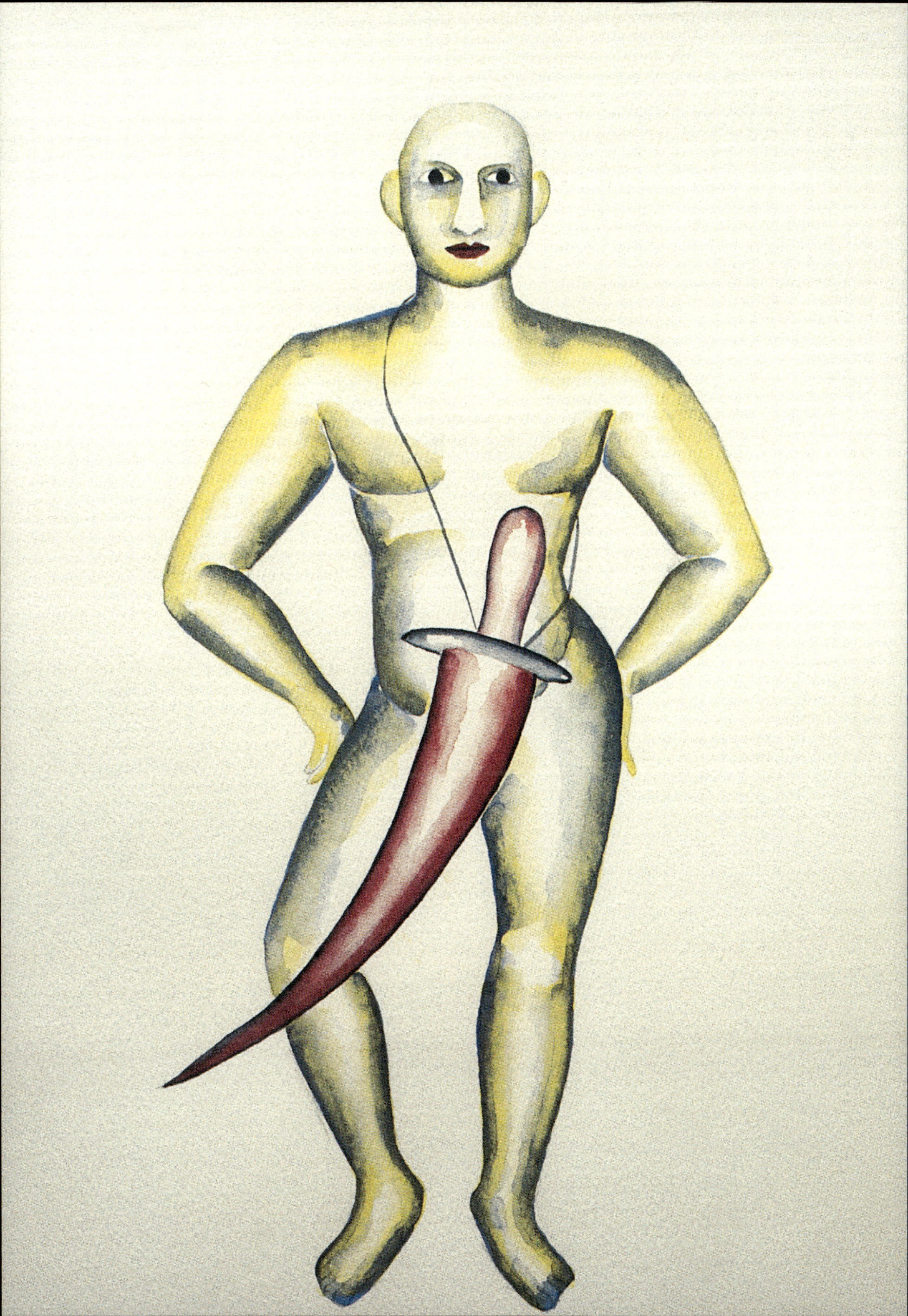

Untitled
38 x 28 cm. Watercolour on paper.
2001

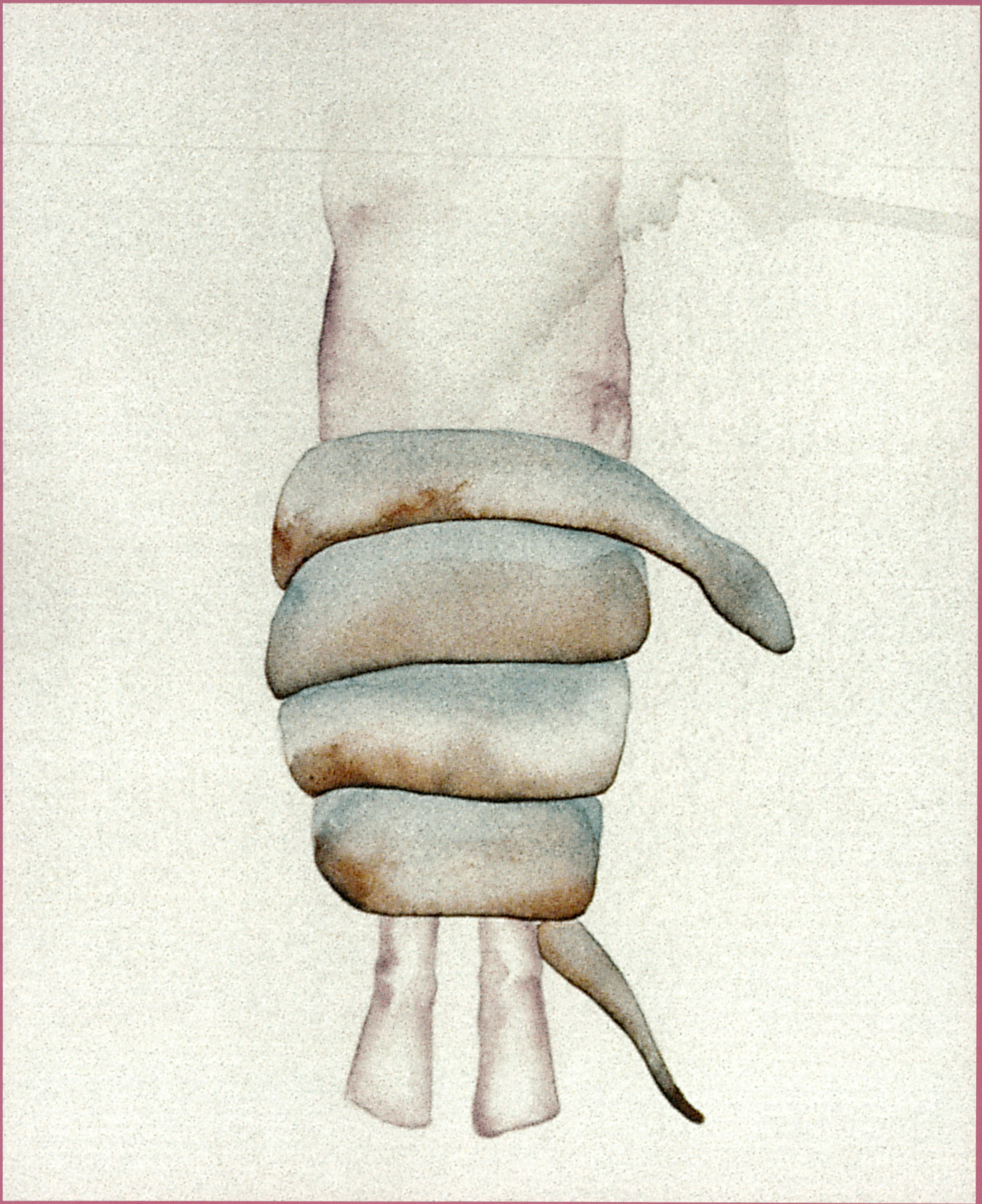

Untitled
Detail, 77 x 56 cm. Watercolour on paper.
2005

SCULPTED WATERMARKS: AN ALTERNATE LYRICISM

Anupa Mehta

Jehangir Jani's primary concern is with the beauty and aesthetics of his medium, and with form – in this case, the spare, monochromatic male figure. Its pristine nude beauty is seen juxtaposed against equally spare animal forms, rendered with delicate precision and brought to life in imploding bursts of water and restrained colour.

The artist uses these minute painterly expositions to articulate his assertions – a set of searing truths arrived at through a re-visitation of "myths, alleged historical events and dogmas. Particularly those used to perpetrate acts of othering." It is this 'othering', the "making invisible or silent,"[1] which surfaces once more in his discourse, investing his watercolours with silent, understated, but intentionally provocative, even perverse, edginess.

At a purely aesthetic level, these watercolours are lyrical and contained. At once sculptural – they emerge as though in relief from a tablet of grey paint set against a backdrop of white Arches paper – and ephemeral, they exhibit a finely controlled use of tonalities. Viridian, amber, and aqua foreground, sienna and charcoal, as white hollows outward to facilitate the impression of volume.

A well-rounded anatomy harks to JJ's facility with and preference for the sculpted image. Paradoxical as it may seem, this modeling of small and seemingly fragile bodies imbues them with a strange monumentality. The non-overt frontal or side stance, the absence of defined facial features, and rigid, delineated contours of body shape, result in figuration that is palpably vulnerable.

If in earlier suites the artist had appeared in iconic and ironical vein, as an epic figure, as "...man-god or hero, a naked figure cast in conjunction with animals that resemble totems, but in fact symbolise the often-suppressed instinctive nature,"[2] the artist now appears in a form that is 'naked', so to speak.

The symbolism of the bodied self continues in similar vein, although it is more generalised, harking to inherent animal instincts. The earlier "snake of passion, the peacock of exhibitionism,"[3] the unbridled horse of machismo, the bear

At a purely aesthetic level, these water-colours are lyrical and contained. At once sculptural – they emerge as though in relief from a tablet of grey paint set against a backdrop of white...

1. Jehangir Jani, 2002.
2, 3. Ranjit Hoskote, catalogue text, *The Bodied Self*, 2001.

JJ now speaks in a voice that is more poignant, even as he retains his perch on the soapbox of the alternate to contest "the propaganda of authority".

of engulfing desire, and the elephant of strength…JJ hones threads of earlier trains of thought to offer the pulse of a vein that is understated, even poetic.

Certainly the positioning is no longer cocky or mocking. Empathy has entered the frame: the affectionate rendering of the male figure, also "an oblique form of portraiture,"[4] yields an acute insight into the nuances of desire, 'troubled' or 'deviant' sexual preferences, and underlying or attendant pain – the sort of pain that accompanies the shrapnel of inquiry into 'identities', and a driving self-urge to negotiate positions for the minority/self within shifting social hierarchies and arenas of power.

JJ now speaks in a voice that is more poignant, even as he retains his perch on the soapbox of the alternate to contest "the propaganda of authority". This results in his work itself becoming both propaganda and weapon. Only now the hue is subtler, the statement less strident.

Aesthetic concerns continue to take precedence. The exaggerated or effeminate gesture and inflection, indeed the whole put-on persona, the inversion used to buoy a particular brand of self-deprecatory irony, has made way for introspection. The quest is for a more resolved sexuality and an artistic and social identity shorn of the burden of stereotypical expectations and observations regarding the 'effeminate' or gay male figure.

And so, while the sexuality remains unaltered, his figures are reined in. This 'containing' is heightened by a palette that is more muted and mature. Desire is now viewed through the filter of tenderness. Self-portrayal and self-exposure recede to become background devices. The burden of fantasy, if any, rests only on the viewer.

Coming full circle, Jehangir Jani's imagery makes nudity a pleasure. This suite could also be read as an elegiac lament for outcasts, the sexually humiliated – possibly the artist's life experiences lead him to bleed in a comment on the passive role thrust on to an underclass of males, 'rent boys', (often heterosexual male prostitutes or bisexuals, *transvestites* or *transgender*), despised for their submissive sexual role, but admired for their skills, even as they find themselves lost… and through them, the ever morphing self.

The artist arrives at his truths, occasional epiphanies, visible as painterly marks, in a series of delicate chiaroscuros, and the contained sweep of water and brush.

It is a process of revelation worth revelling in.

Ahmedabad, September 2005

4. Ranjit Hoskote, catalogue text, *The Bodied Self*, 2001.

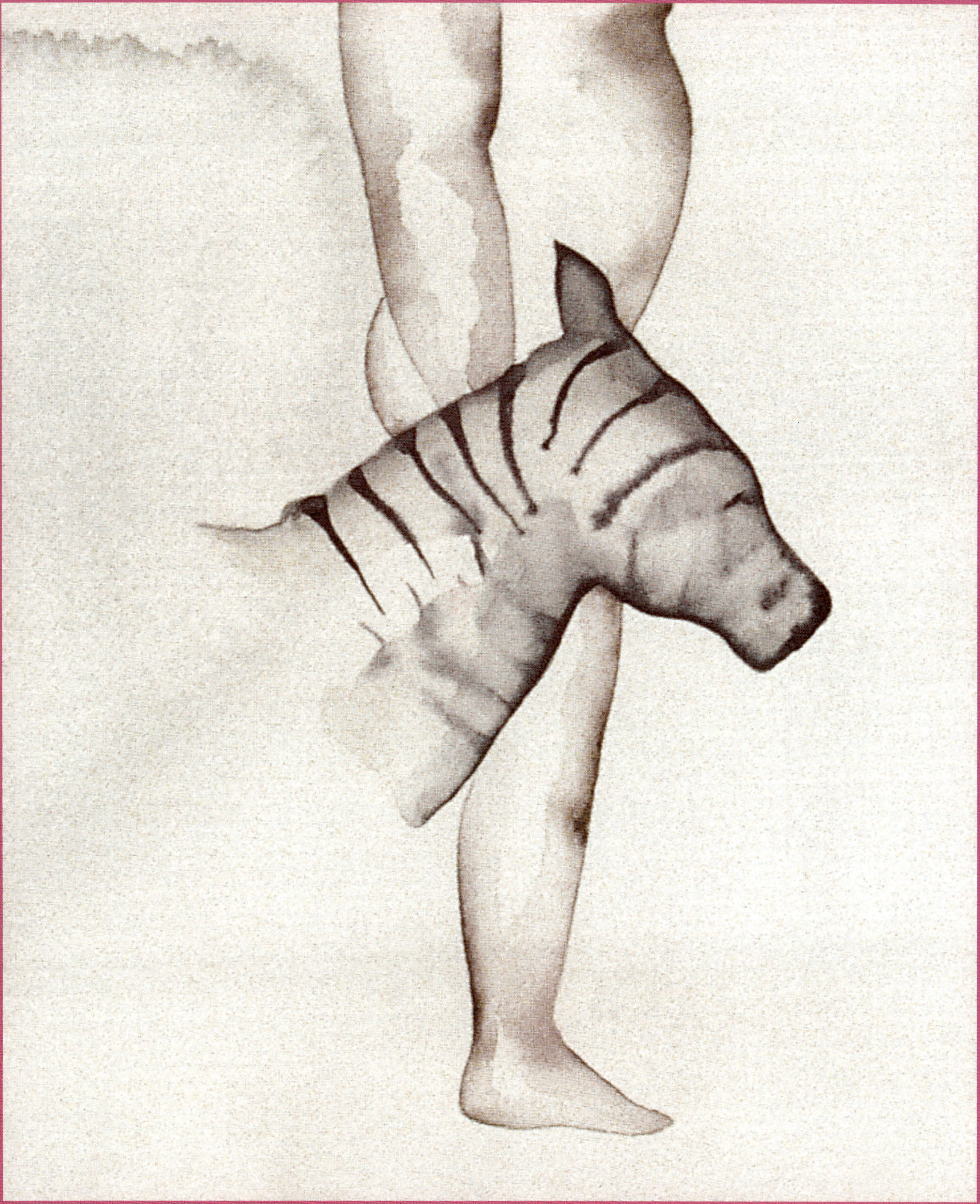

Untitled
Detail, Watercolour on paper.
2005

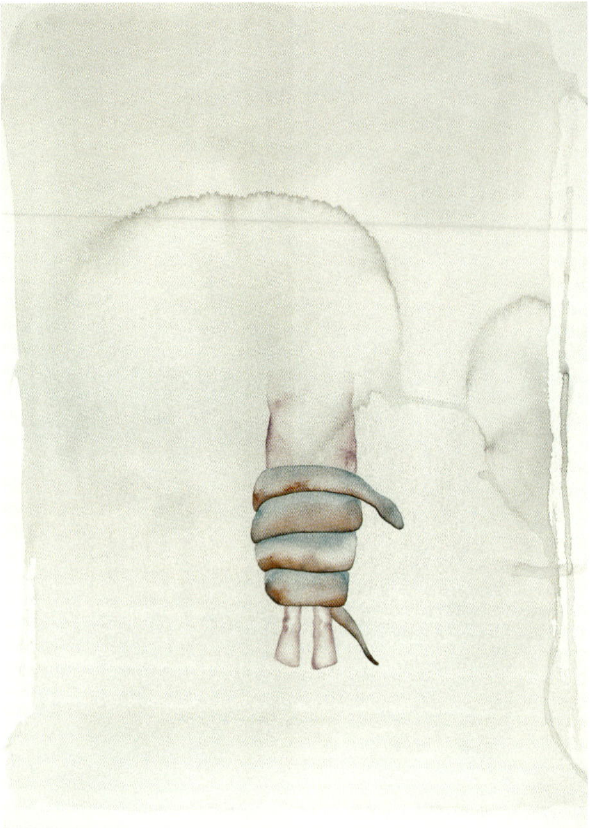

Untitled
77 x 56 cm. Watercolour on paper.
2005

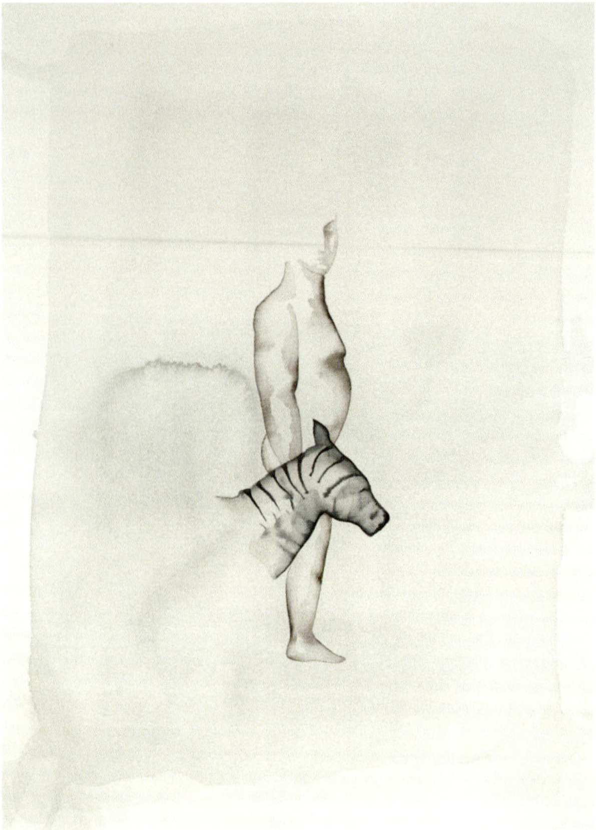

Untitled
77 x 56 cm. Watercolour on paper.
2005

Untitled
77 x 56 cm. Watercolour on paper.
2005

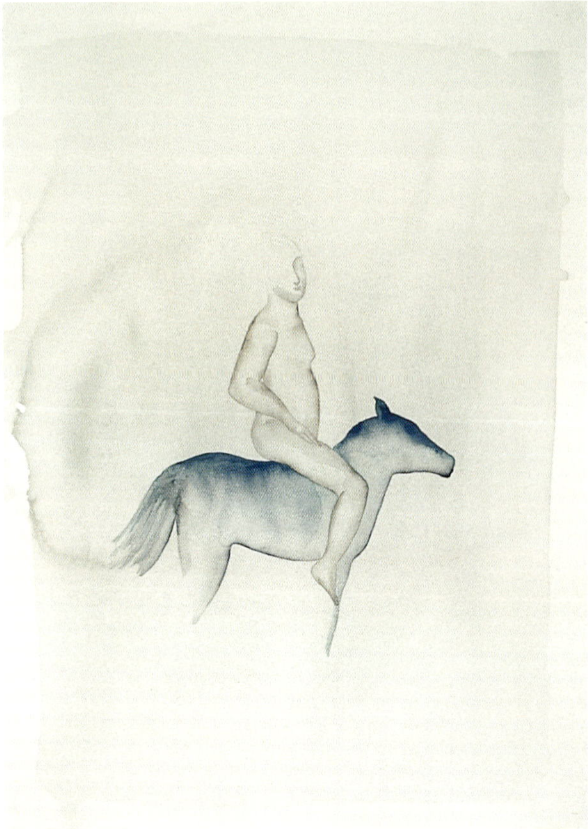

Untitled
77 x 56 cm. Watercolour on paper.
2005

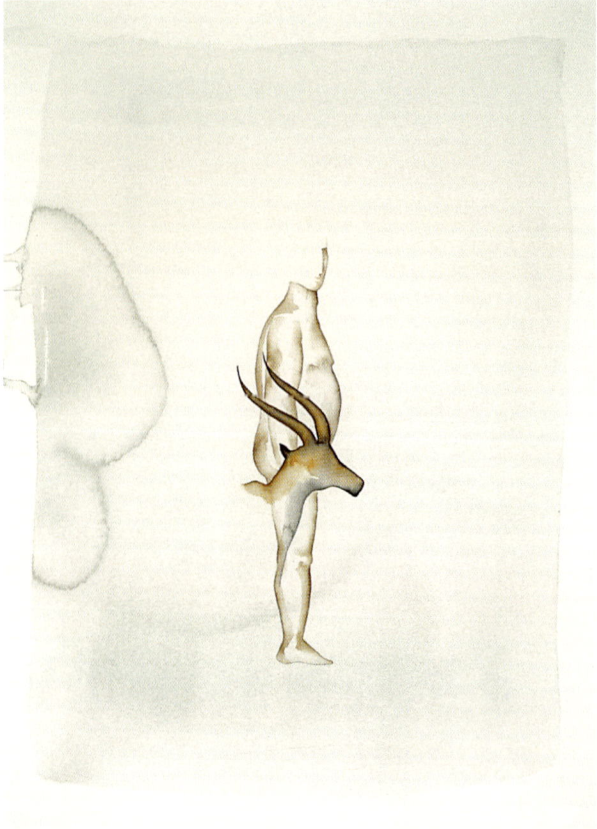

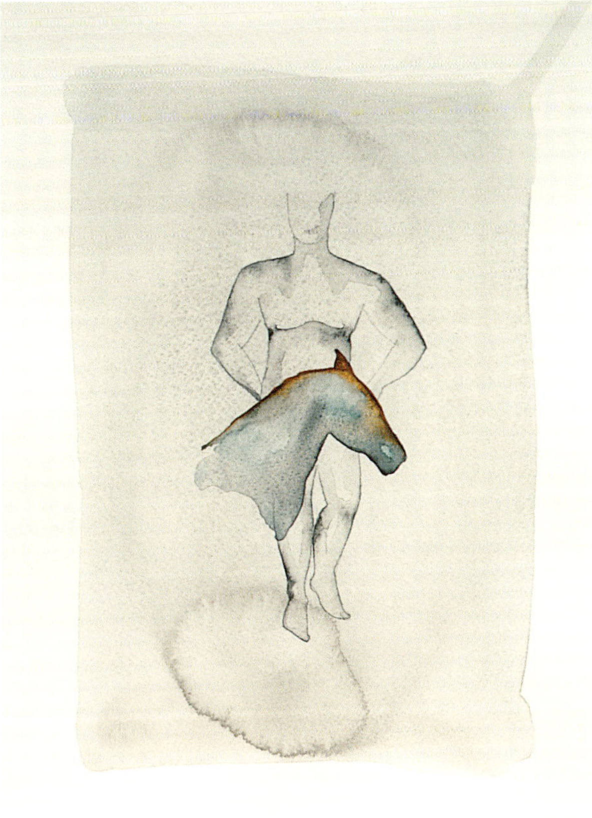

Untitled
35 x 25 cm. Watercolour on paper.
2005

Untitled
35 x 25 cm. Watercolour on paper.
2005

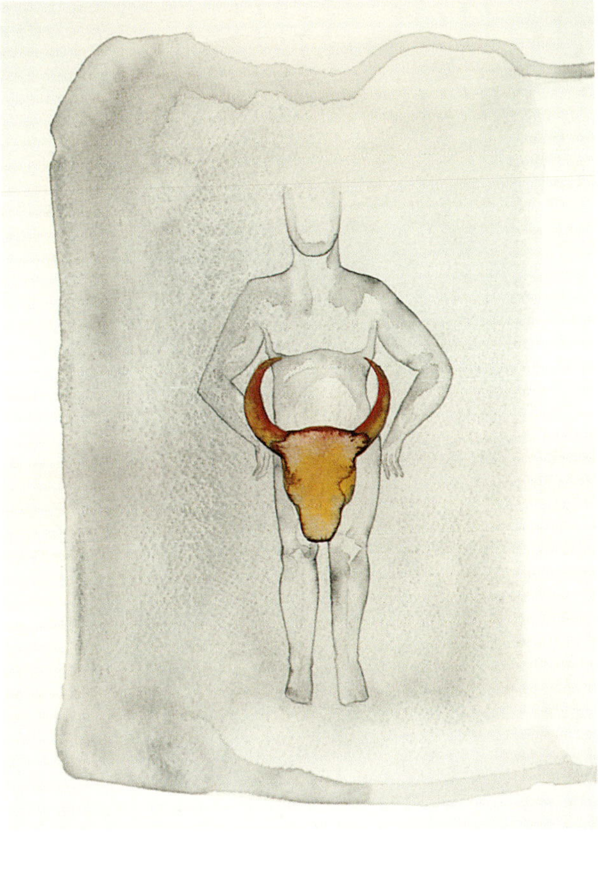

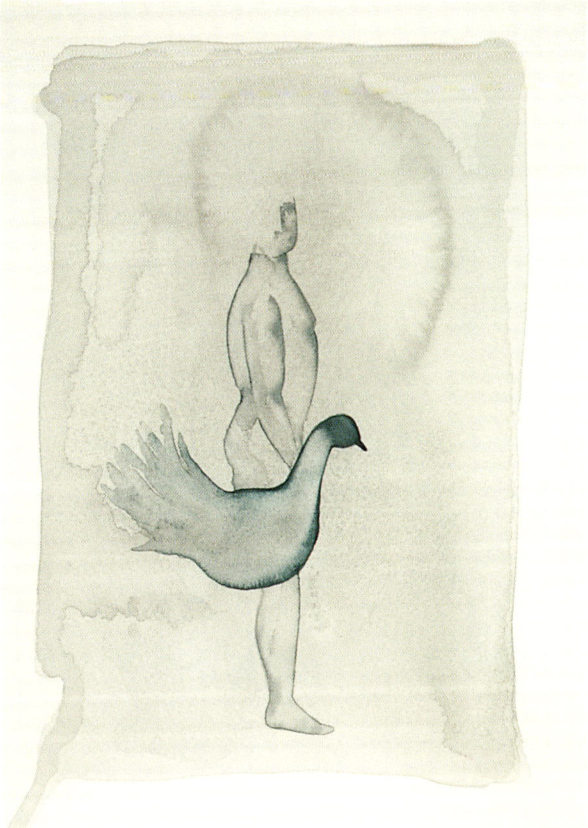

Untitled
35 x 25 cm. Watercolour on paper.
2005

Untitled
77 x 56 cm. Watercolour on paper.
2005

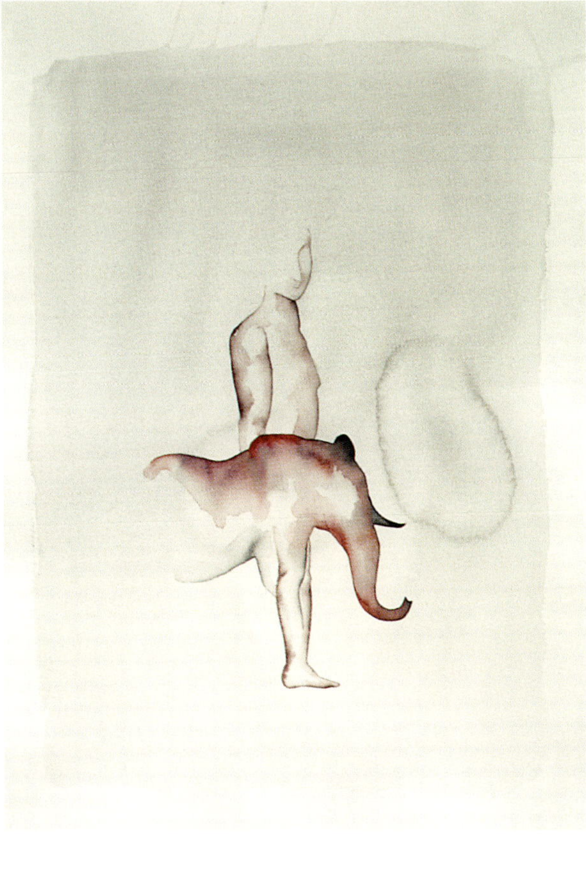

Untitled
28 x 19 cm. Watercolour on paper.
2004

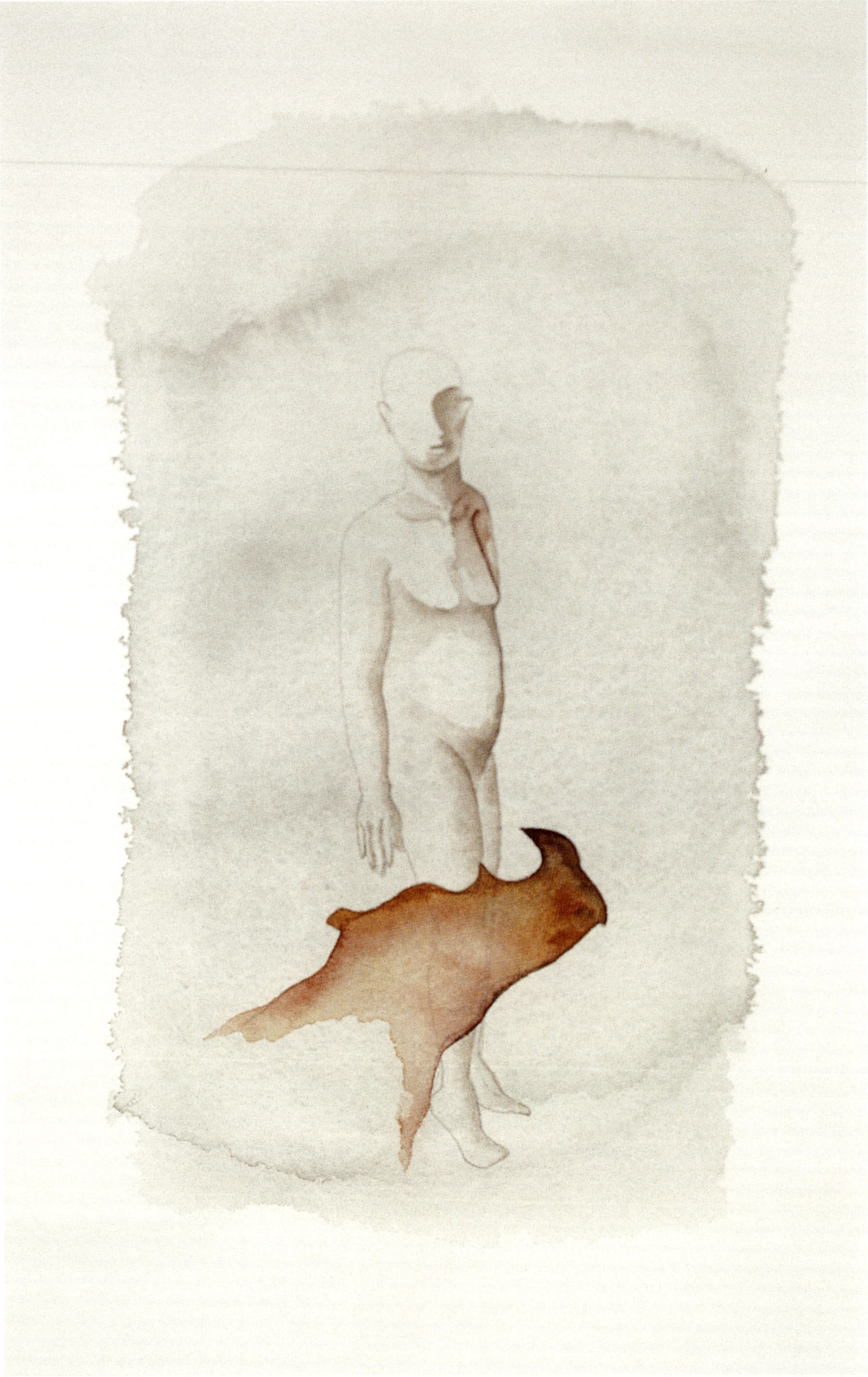

Untitled
28 x 19 cm. Watercolour on paper.
2004

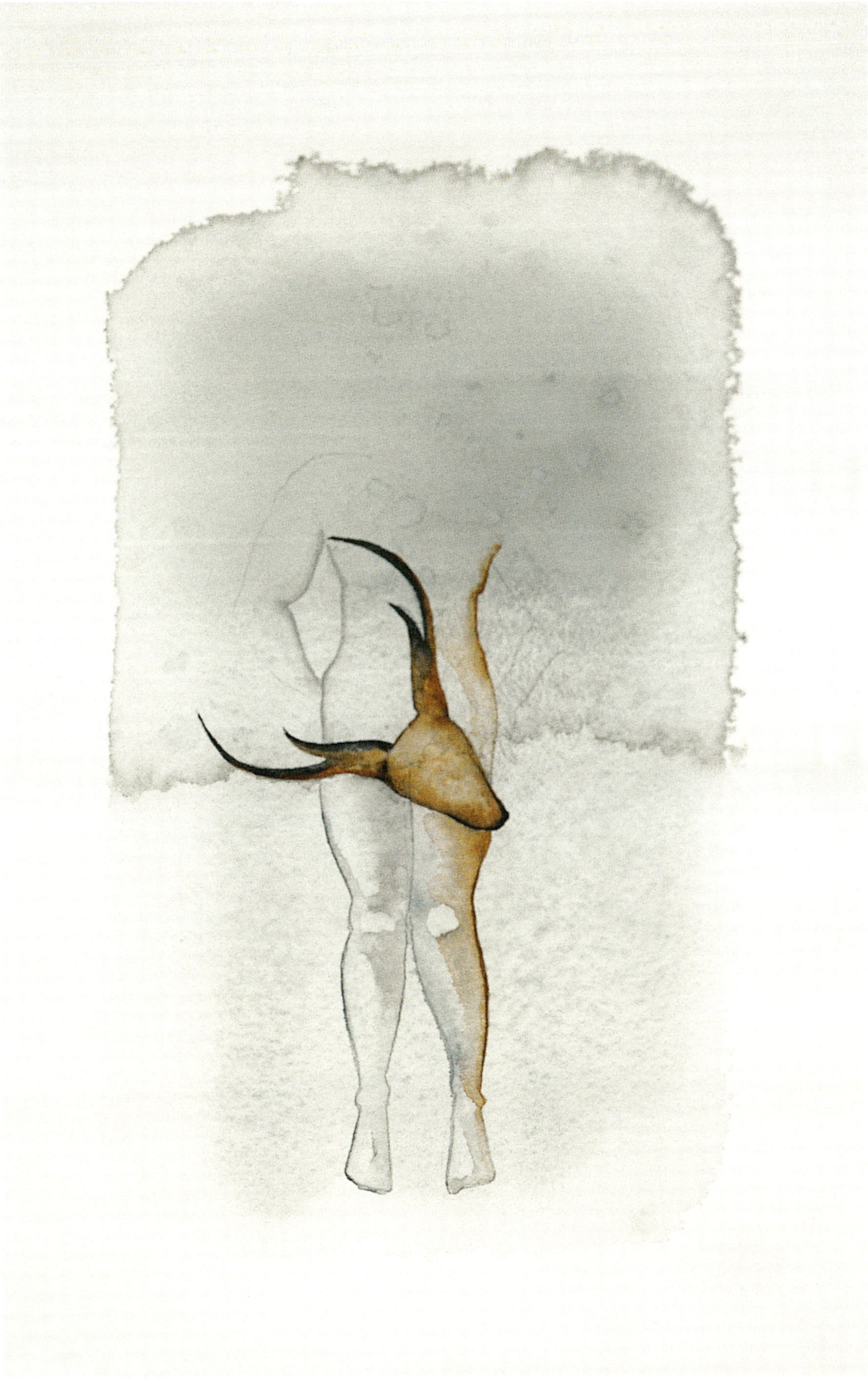

Untitled
28 x 19 cm. Watercolour on paper.
2004

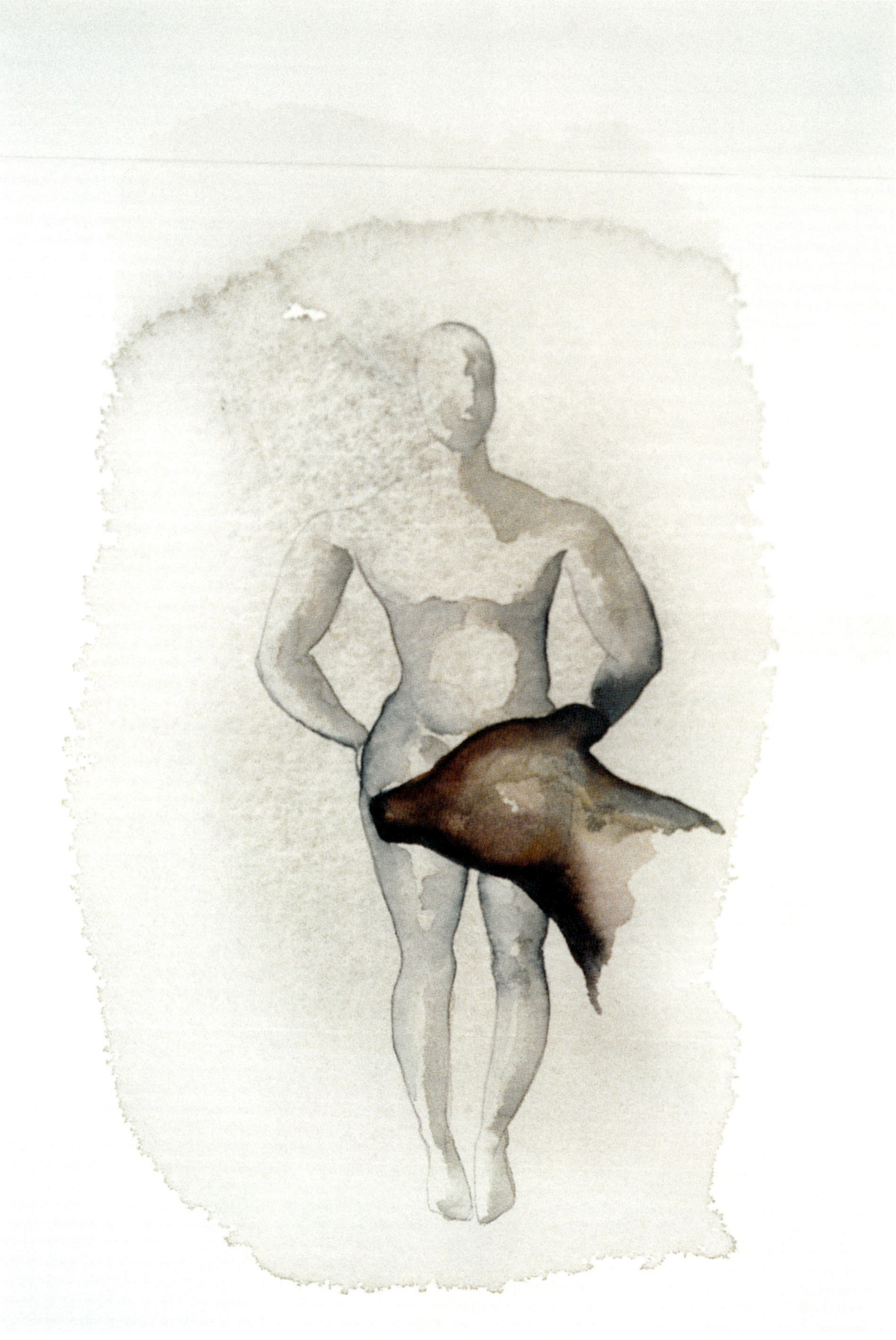

Untitled
Detail, Watercolour on paper.
2004

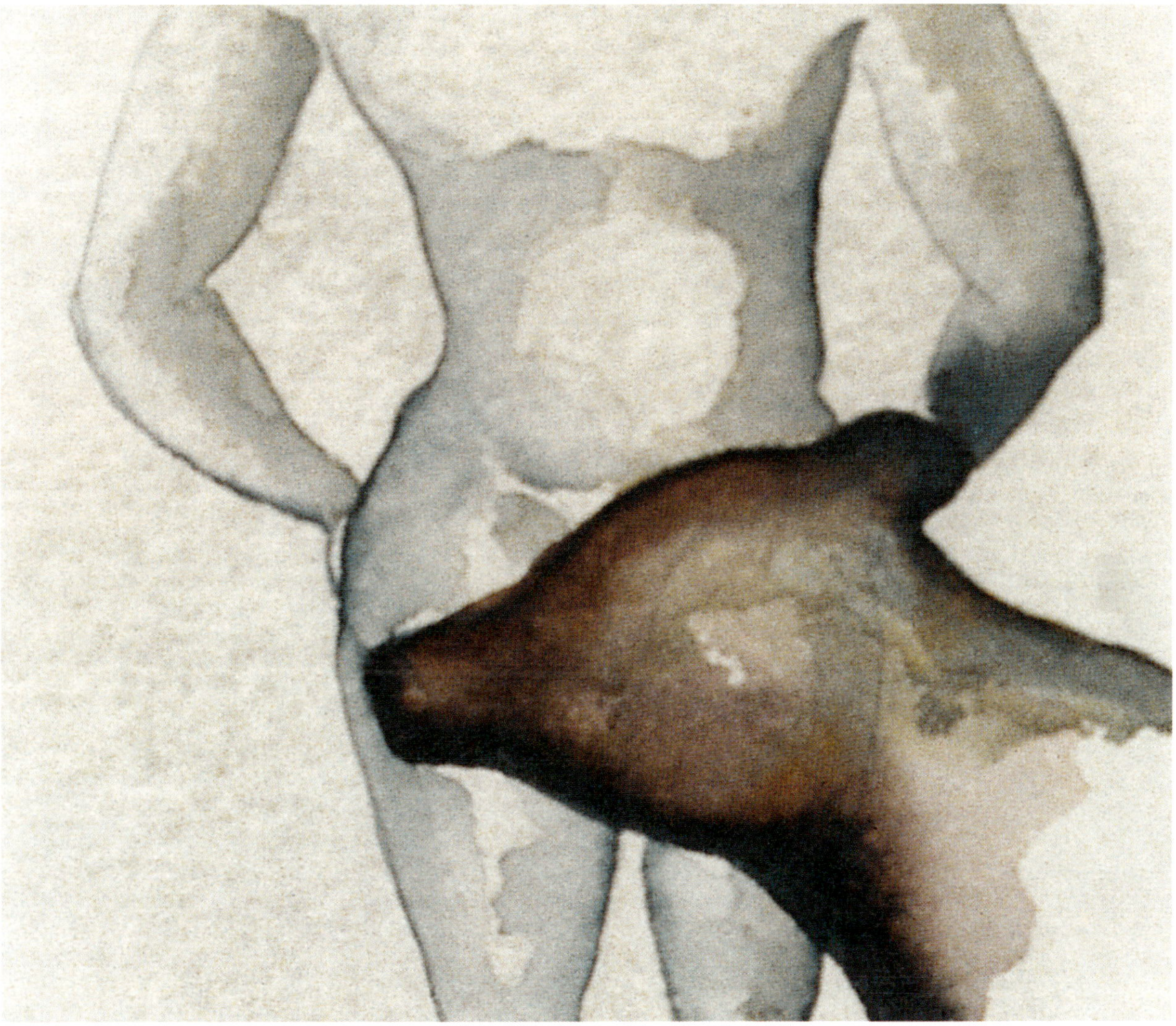

Untitled
77 x 56 cm. Watercolour on paper.
2005

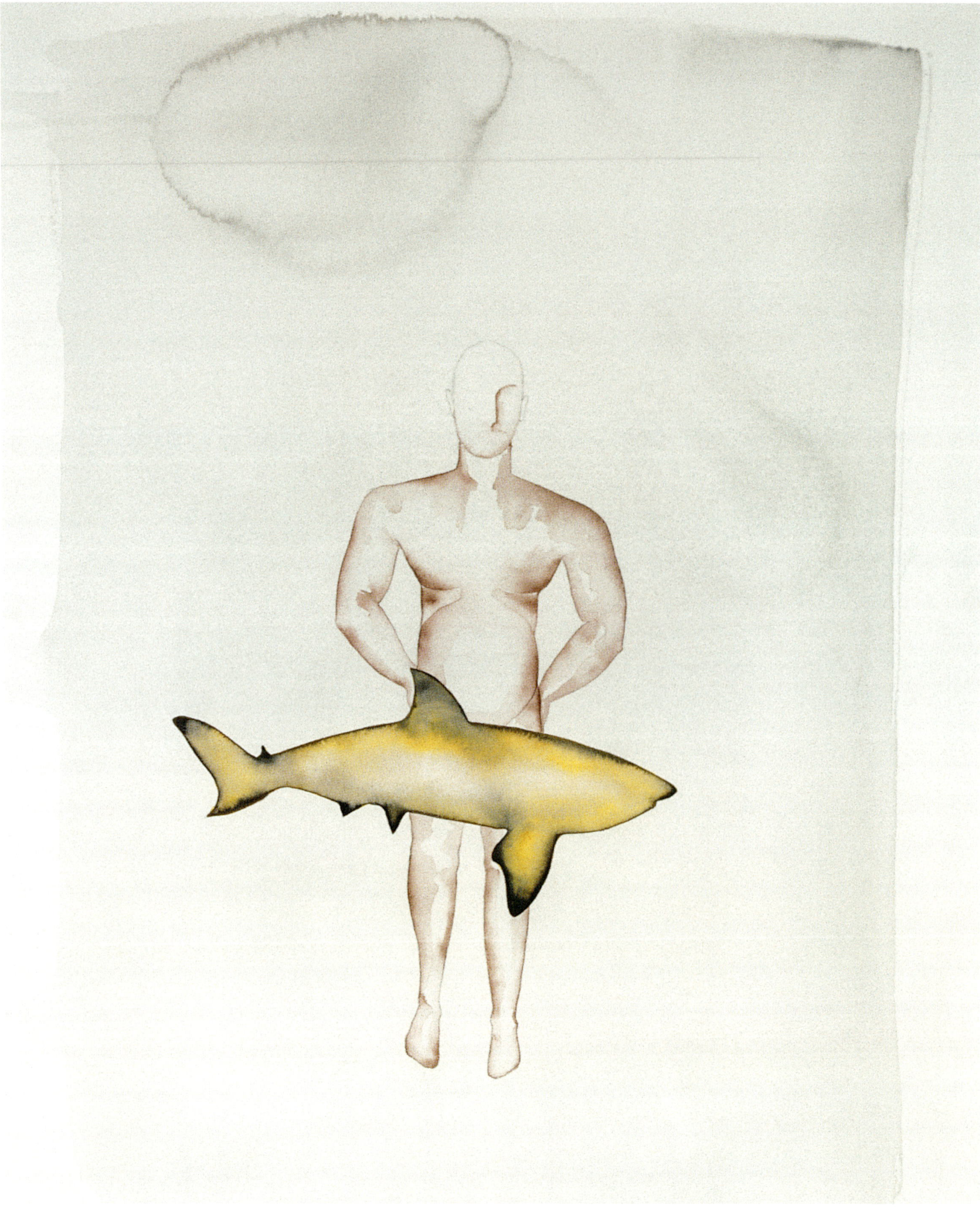

Untitled
77 x 56 cm. Watercolour on paper.
2005

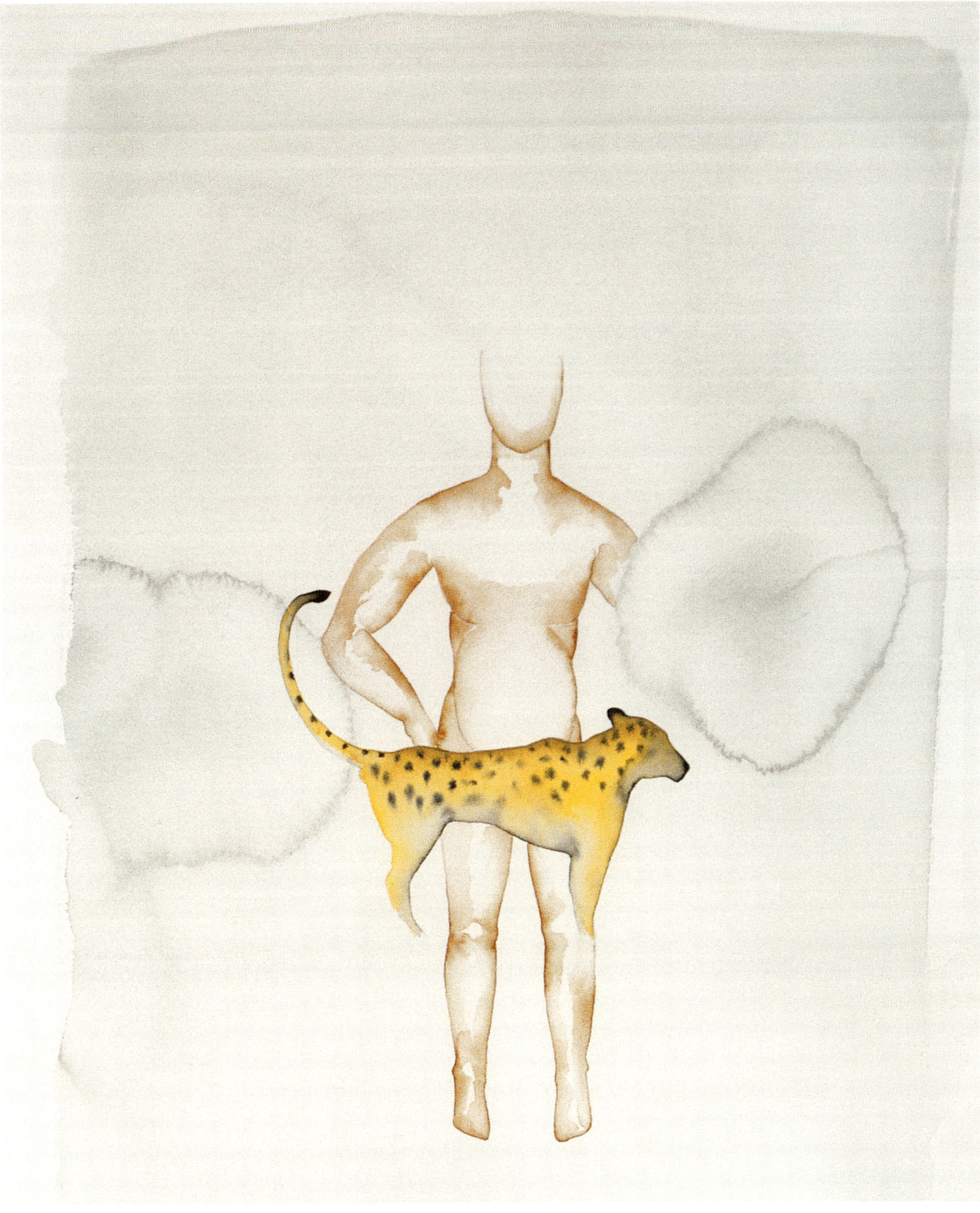

JJ IN CONVERSATION

Ratnottama Sengupta

"Like a child in a candy shop, I get excited when I see a material with some possibility."

RS: Shivaji Panikkar writes how your male nudes "displace the habitual mainstream expectations about human figuration." Your "tortured, oddly displaced images" reclaim "a humiliated hinterland's margin," he writes. Elsewhere he uses the words "sexual and communitarian minorities." Is this the conscious starting point of your art? Or is it something that is embedded deep within you and comes out unconsciously?
JJ: In other words, is art an aesthetic compulsion, or a mode of sexual/cultural activism? For me, it is both. There is a choice I make in my figuration, which is how I see the human condition of someone imbued with an inner strength, and negotiating life with dignity. The sexual/cultural part is actually my subjectivity that may be called activism. It is not my intention to propagate my politics as an activist.

RS: Yours is figurative art that is forbidden by the religion you are born into. How did you get interested in it? Was art already there in your family? Or was it an act of rebellion? (Chatterjee writes that much of your sculpture and installation is "confrontational".)
JJ: From an early age I was very good at image making. That's why I found art a befitting area for expressing my truths and giving visibility to my concerns. Where earlier I would have liked my message to be read above the aesthetics of the work, today my position is the opposite.

There is no other artist in my family, but it may have something to do with parental genes, as my brother is India's leading fashion designer. There is a radical streak in all of us, which makes the mundane intolerable. I suppose you can call that rebellion.

The sexual/cultural part is actually my subjectivity that may be called activism. It is not my intention to propagate my politics as an activist.

By education I am a Bachelor of Commerce, but I have lived a varied life. If you care to know, I started my working life in 1977, as a receptionist at the Oberoi Towers, in Mumbai. From 1978 to 1980 I worked in Muscat, as an accountant and manager with a furniture showroom. Then, till 1982, I was unemployed and did itinerant things. In 1982 I joined the Tata Electric Companies in Mumbai as an accountant. Since 1990 I have been a freelance artist.

RS: When did you decide to make this your vocation? And how did you go about it?
JJ: As said earlier.

RS: I mean, how did you train yourself? Your works are so evolved that I am curious to know. Did some incident prove a turning point in your career? Did an art event, or any sales, spur you to make it your calling? Often the term 'self taught' masks the arrogance of one who has no use for the 'discipline' involved in any discipline. Did you observe any master at work? Or see paintings in the museums of the world? Did you pour over 'learn drawing' books? Were you ever a studio assistant? Or did you simply pick up a brush, and that was that?
JJ: Well, then, let me answer your questions in detail. Since I did not have the luxury of affording canvas, I used to paint on the back of discarded picture frames that I bought in Mumbai's Chor Bazaar. At that time I never imagined that I would become an artist! One day, after a fashion show, my brother Abu brought home a large canvas – and I painted it. I gifted him that work for his studio. A client of his saw it and pushed me to do a body of work that she exhibited in her gallery in Mumbai. This was in 1990. That gallery has closed down since. But that is when I experienced the thrill of expressing myself through painting, and resolved to make art my vocation. I drove into the field vertically. I had a common man's understanding of art, and I was anti 'modern painting' at the time. I deliberately chose the realistic/ surrealistic mode of working. This, I now realize, was due to my inclination towards the three-dimensional. But I stopped working for three years, between 1995 and 1998 — excepting an odd group-show here and there – as I wanted to resolve my crisis vis a vis sculpture and painting.

I stayed in Delhi and went through the entire Lalit Kala library, including all the issues of *Marg*, and came to understand Indian modern and contemporary art. I also got a good knowledge of classical art and the history of art. I read in the libraries of Baroda and Mumbai – I maintained a low profile, since access was not always easy. I bought catalogues from galleries (some, like Sakshi, would not give them to me free) and rummaged second hand bookshops as well.

Since I did not have the luxury of affording canvas, I used to paint on the back of discarded picture frames that I bought in Mumbai's Chor Bazaar. At that time I never imagined that I would become an artist!

Basically I had a hunger to understand and know the field I was working in. So you can say that I have educated myself. As a result of this self education, I now have an incisive opinion of contemporary art. I think Arpita Singh and Jayshree Chakravorty are two of our finest painters. Arpita grows on you: the more you look at her work, the more you find rich areas of experience, but one of our popular senior painters remains only at the surface in terms of gesture and colour and line. These are my personal views after my BFA and MFA on my own.

Arpita grows on you: the more you look at her work, the more you find rich areas of experience, but one of our popular senior painters remains only at the surface in terms of gesture and colour and line.

RS: Your watercolours show a deep impression on your imagination of Bhupen Khakkar. How did that come about? Who are the other masters or contemporaries to have impressed you?
JJ: The artist I have closely looked at is Akbar Padamsee. He handles the medium beautifully. I don't agree with you that my work is Bhupen referential. While I admire his work, he has never inspired me.

RS: Sculpture, though it has a strong tradition in India, finds fewer takers (read 'buyers') today than painting. This didn't hinder your shift to the genre from oil painting. Why did you feel compelled to sculpt?
JJ: I was searching for the three-dimensional in my earlier paintings, in the sense of heavy modeling and dense coloration. This need brought me to sculpture as a logical step. This move has freed my approach to the other mediums, oil and watercolours.

RS: You have worked with a wide range of materials, from metal and fiberglass to latex and steel, from ceramics to cement and carpet… How did you equip yourself for these shifts in medium?
JJ: I see my journey as an artist as that of a child in a candy shop. I get excited by a material the moment I see some possibility in it. I have learnt to handle these mediums with my own research and experimentation, and therefore I see new possibilities. In a way it is fortunate that I have not been to any art school, as I feel that would have made me a single-faculty or single-medium centric.

I don't agree with you that my work is Bhupen referential. While I admire his work, he has never inspired me.

RS: But surely you have a favourite among these mediums (or genres, if you prefer)?
JJ: All the three mediums excite me, sculpture and oil for the act of making and gesture, and watercolour for its sheer beauty. I have no favourites and work in them as and when I feel like.

RS: In your installation, *The Dancer in the Tomb*, you chose to write the invocation to God in Gujarati rather than Arabic calligraphy. What determined your choice of language?
JJ: Born a Muslim, and taught to read parts of the Koran translated from Arabic into Gujarati, I have understood my religion, like so many others from my community, in a script and language different from the original. I thought it apt to use this method, especially after the riots in Gujarat, to emphasise my claim of belonging to the land.

RS: *The Peers* series, named after Muslim saints, is perhaps your boldest attack on social taboos. Do you anticipate any repercussion to the work?
JJ: I have no clue. I have never thought of these things.

RS: Over the last decade or so, your art seems to have transformed – from gay activism *(CHakka CHakka....)* to communitarian reforms (*Painting the Moment*). What does the future hold? Is your art likely to move to purely artistic, or aesthetic, concerns?
JJ: I moved from communitarian reforms advocacy, to gay activism, to the search of beauty, mostly in the rejects of life and the mainstream. This is the order in which I have travelled.

I moved from communitarian reforms advocacy, to gay activism, to the search of beauty, mostly in the rejects of life and the mainstream.

NOTES ON CONTRIBUTORS

Shivaji K Panikkar teaches at the Department of Art History and Aesthetics, M.S. University of Baroda in Gujarat. Professor and presently Head of the Department, his research and publications are in the areas of pre-modern and modern Indian art. His published works include *Saptamatrka Worship and Sculpture: An Iconological Interpretation of Conflicts and Resolution in the 'Storied' Brahmanical Icons* and the exhibition catalogue *Creative Process: Tangible Realities, Concrete Myths* for the Guild Gallery in Mumbai, among others. He has edited *Twentieth Century Indian Sculpture: Last Two Decades* and co-edited *Towards A New Art History: Studies in Indian Art* and *Art of Ancient India: Contextualizing Social Relations*. Currently he is engaged in editing the books *Art and Activism in India, Art of Medieval India: Contextualizing Social Relations* and *'Elite' and 'Popular' Interface: India's Art History*.

Mortimer Chatterjee is an art dealer with several years of auction house experience both in India and in the UK. He received his MA in the History of Indian Art and Architecture from the School of Oriental and African Studies, University of London. Mortimer, along with his wife, Tara, set up Chatterjee & Lal based in Mumbai, in 2003, in order to promote experimental Indian art. He lives in Mumbai.

Ranjit Hoskote is a cultural theorist, art critic, poet, and independent curator. He is the author of eight books; most recently, of *The Complicit Observer: Reflections on the Art of Sudhir Patwardhan* and *The Crucible of Painting: The Art of Jehangir Sabavala*. Hoskote has contributed to various anthologies, such as *Private Mythology: Contemporary Art from India* (Tokyo, 1998), and *Kapital und Karma: Aktuelle Positionen Indischer Kunst* (Vienna, 2002). He has curated exhibitions of Indian and Asian art since 1993, including a mid-career retrospective of Atul Dodiya (Japan Foundation, Tokyo, 2001). Hoskote also co-curated the trans-Asian exhibition *Under Construction* (2002–2003).

Nancy Adajania is a cultural theorist, art critic, and independent curator. She was editor of *Art India* and has written and lectured extensively on the arts in relation to post-colonial politics, the cultural effects of globalization, and the emergence of new-media forms. Adajania has lectured on Indian new-media art and its socio-political contexts at prestigious international venues, including Documenta 11 (Kassel, 2002), ZKM (Zentrum fur Kunst und Medien; Karlsruhe, 2002), Transmediale (Berlin, 2002), the Danish Contemporary Art Foundation (Copenhagen, 2003), and the Neuer Berliner Kunstverein (Berlin, 2003). Adajania was co-curator of the exhibition *Zoom: Contemporary Art in India* (Lisbon, 2004).

Girish Shahane is a freelance writer based in Mumbai. He has been editor and, later, consulting editor of *Art India*. He currently writes an opinion column for *Time Out*, Mumbai.

Anupa Mehta is a writer, freelance editor, curator, columnist, and arts manager. Founder editor, *Art India*, she was contributing editor, *Asian Art News* and *World Sculpture News*, Hong Kong. She lives and works out of Ahmedabad and Mumbai.

Deeptha Achar is Reader at the Department of English, M.S. University of Baroda.

Ratnottama Sengupta is a writer with an expansive interest in arts and culture. She has been writing for newspapers and journals since 1978; participating in discussions on the electronic media; teaching mass communication students, and curating art exhibitions. She has authored *Krishna's Cosmos*, on the pioneer printmaker Krishna Reddy; written on Indian films for the *Encyclopaedia Britannica*; edited volumes on cinema and art; served on the National Awards jury, and won a national award for writings on cinema. She is currently editing an Encyclopaedia of Culture.